D1480516

SECRET HISTORY OF CONFEDERATE DIPLOMACY ABROAD

SECRET HISTORY OF CONFEDERATE DIPLOMACY ABROAD

EDWIN DE LEON
Late Confidential Agent
of the Confederate Department of State in Europe

EDITED BY WILLIAM C. DAVIS

UNIVERSITY PRESS OF KANSAS

© 2005 by the University Press of Kansas

Published by the University Press of Kansas (Lawrence,
Kansas 66045), which was organized by the Kansas Board of
Regents and is operated and funded by Emporia State
University, Fort Hays State University, Kansas State
University, Pittsburg State University, the University of
Kansas, and Wichita State University

Frontispiece from T. C. De Leon,
Belles, Beaux and Brains of the '60s, 1907.

Library of Congress Cataloging-in-Publication Data
De Leon, Edwin, 1818–1891.
Secret history of Confederate diplomacy abroad /
Edwin De Leon ; edited by William C. Davis.
p. cm.
Includes bibliographical references and index.
ISBN 0-7006-1411-7 (cloth : alk. paper)
1. Confederate States of America—Foreign relations.
2. United States—Foreign relations—1861–1865. 3. De Leon,
Edwin, 1818–1891. I. Davis, William C., 1946– II. Title.
E488.D45 2005
973.7'21—dc22 2005020931

British Library Cataloguing in Publication Data is available.

Printed in the United States of America

10 9 8 7 6 5 4 3 2 1

The paper used in this publication meets the minimum
requirements of the American National Standard for
Permanence of Paper for Printed Library Materials Z39.48-1984.

CONTENTS

———•◆•———

Chapter 17

Chapter 18

Chapter 19

Chapter 20

Chapter 21

Appendix 1

Appendix 2

Appendix 3

Index

ACKNOWLEDGMENTS

Several friends and colleagues have been most helpful in the preparation of this edition of the "Secret History" and the appended documents. Sara Eye prepared the basic transcript of the text from the pages of the New York *Citizen* and did an excellent job, helping further with research in the De Leon Papers in Columbia. One problem from the time the series was discovered several years ago in the file of the newspaper at the Library of Congress was the omission of the issue containing chapter 20. With incredible improbability, every other extant run of the paper located from New York to San Diego also lacked exactly that same issue. Old friends Harold Holzer of New York's Metropolitan Museum of Art and Pamela Keyes of Miami, Oklahoma, lent a hand in the effort to track down the elusive issue. Finally through the efforts of Jared Peatman, a graduate student at Virginia Tech, a copy was found at the Newberry Library in Chicago on almost the same day that Sara Eye turned up one in De Leon's scrapbook. Thus thanks to the efforts of all of them, the text of what was originally published is here complete. Deborah Petite ran down De Leon's dispatches to Richmond in the Library of Congress, and Lynda Crist of the Jefferson Davis Papers project at Houston's Rice University graciously provided references to some De Leon–Davis correspondence. Robert Rosen, historian of Confederate Jewry, provided some helpful background on De Leon's family, and Christina Vella of Tulane University, as so often before, was a lifesaver with translating some of the occasional expressions in French that De Leon rather ostentatiously liked to insert in his text. Jocelyn Couture Nowak of Virginia Tech did a complete translation of *The Truth about the Confederate States of America* included here as appendix 3. Most sincere thanks are due to all of them for their unselfish assistance.

De Leon wrote well, as would be expected of a professional propagandist. Thus, obvious typographical errors by his editor have been corrected without mention, since such misspellings would not have been his intent. However, some words had acceptable, even customary, spellings in his day that would be incorrect today. His spelling has not been modernized.

INTRODUCTION

The term "propaganda" has such strong connotations of World War II and the Cold War for Americans of the twentieth and twenty-first centuries that it comes as a surprise to many that the word, and the concept it defines, have been around quite a long time. It would especially surprise many Americans North and South to learn that propaganda was a serious and substantial part of the war effort of both the Union and the Confederacy during the Civil War. Yet such is the case. In a conflict in which issues and values were so inextricably involved, the war was as much one for opinion and sympathy as for territory. That was especially the case far from the battlefields, on the other side of an ocean, where both contestants believed it possible that England and continental Europe might hold the key to victory. Should foreign powers, especially Britain and France, choose to grant diplomatic recognition to the Confederacy and follow that with treaties and alliances resulting in military intervention, the Union would almost certainly be doomed. If those powers took sides with the North, or simply chose to stay out of the fray and let the Americans settle their differences themselves, then Abraham Lincoln's prospects of putting down the rebellion and reuniting his country stood dramatically improved. Consequently, the Union government early on sent diplomats abroad to represent its aims and viewpoint to curious and uncertain European heads of state. At the same time, unofficial agents crossed the ocean to infiltrate the press and even the pulpit to work on the sentiments of the people at large. The new Confederacy also sent diplomats to London and Paris, hampered though they were by the limited powers given them by President Jefferson Davis, and even more by the fact that, as representatives of an unrecognized state, they could not gain access to the highest chambers of government to make their case. Not long afterward the South, too, recognized the need for a multifront assault on foreign opinion and undertook to win public sympathy to its cause. First through the agency of amateurs and men who simply happened to be overseas already, the Confederate message began to find its way into foreign print. But by 1862 something more concerted and systematic had to be implemented, and thus Jefferson Davis sought a "propagandist" to serve the cause.

Edwin De Leon was born in Columbia, South Carolina, on May 4, 1818, the son of Dr. Mordecai Hendricks De Leon and Rebecca Lopez, Sephardic Jews who originated in Leon, Spain, from which they took their name. Mordecai De Leon had been mayor of Columbia and was a close friend and associate of the distinguished educator and political theorist Dr. Thomas Cooper, for whom he named another of his sons, Thomas Cooper De Leon, the noted Confederate memoirist and author of *Four Years in Rebel Capitals* and *Belles, Beaux and Brains of the 60's*. A third De Leon brother, David, became the first surgeon general of the Confederacy.[1]

Edwin attended the South Carolina College—later the University of South Carolina—where he edited the college literary journal, and then read law and was admitted to the bar in 1840. The literary bent that ran through the De Leon genes manifested itself early, however, with Edwin producing lectures before the college's literary societies such as one on "The Position and Duties of 'Young America'" in December 1845, showing his interest both in oratory and in Democratic politics. Within a year publishing lured him from the bar to become coeditor of the Savannah (Georgia) *Republican*. He and the newspaper prospered, but in 1847 friends in Columbia persuaded "Ned" De Leon to return to his birthplace to assume editorship of the new Columbia *Telegraph*, and there he remained until 1850. His editorials in support of Southern rights attracted the attention of Southern delegates in Washington, and in 1850, during the heated debate over the bills constituting the Compromise of 1850, when Southern hard-liners led by Robert Barnwell Rhett of South Carolina raised money to start what would be in all but name a pro-secession newspaper in the capital, they asked De Leon to assume the coeditorship.[2] Living in a city boardinghouse, he worked until 1854 with Ellwood Fisher to produce the Washington *Southern Press*.[3] For reasons that are unclear but probably had much to do with removing an incendiary voice from a city that he hoped to calm, President Franklin Pierce in 1854 appointed De Leon to his first and only foreign service post, consul general and diplomatic agent to Egypt. De Leon held the position until he resigned in 1861 to begin his Confederate career, and during that time was twice thanked by resolu-

---

1. Robert N. Rosen, *The Jewish Confederates* (Columbia, SC, 2000), p. 17.

2. William C. Davis, *Rhett: The Turbulent Life and Times of a Fire-Eater* (Columbia, SC, 2001), p. 272.

3. U.S. Census, 1850, District of Columbia, Ward 4, p. 216.

tion of Congress: first for helping to save Greeks in Alexandria, Egypt, from massacre by the *pasha;* and again for successfully demanded reparation for the murder of American missionaries in Jaffa.[4]

De Leon speaks for himself on the Confederate years that followed in his "Secret History of Confederate Diplomacy Abroad," published here in book form for the first time, and for the first time in any format since 1867–1868. An excellent sketch of those years, unfortunately written without access to the "Secret History," appeared in Charles P. Cullop's article "Edwin De Leon, Jefferson Davis' Propagandist," in the December 1962 issue of *Civil War History.*[5] Using the best sources then available, Cullop drew a fine portrait of the proud, conceited, yet undeniably intelligent man who would be a diplomatic king, yet who in the end lost his position in some disgrace. Finding himself in Europe when secession and Civil War came, De Leon hoped at first to come back to the South and obtain a position in the army from his Washington friend Jefferson Davis. Before he could reach the Confederacy in early 1862, however, De Leon was already drawn into the intrigues and confused whirl of European diplomacy as an unofficial confidant of the inept first Confederate commission sent abroad in 1861.

De Leon reached Paris in May 1861, and London soon thereafter. In France he wrote letters to the press attempting to sway public opinion and counteract similar efforts by the Yankees. When he sent a letter to the *Times* of London in response to published statements of Cassius M. Clay, the Union's minister to Russia then on his way to St. Petersburg, De Leon found himself a marked man and feared he might be arrested. The Confederate commissioner in London, William L. Yancey, asked De Leon to write for the friendly press there and in Paris, and the South Carolinian agreed. Typical of his self-importance, by October 1861 De Leon believed he had taken care of British public opinion and was ready to go to Paris to do the same there, including circulating copies of an engraved portrait of Jefferson Davis that he presumed would impress Europeans with the Mississippian's statesmanlike visage. De Leon informed President Davis that England and France had an agreement to act together on the American question—which they did not— with only the Union war fleet, British leaders, and the uncertain military

---

4. Except where otherwise cited, this brief sketch is drawn chiefly from Thomas Cooper De Leon's sketch of his brother in Rossiter Johnson, ed., *The Twentieth Century Biographical Dictionary of Notable Americans* (Boston, 1904), vol. 3, p. 206.

5. Volume 8, pp. 386–400. This article later appeared verbatim as a chapter in Cullop's *Confederate Propaganda in Europe, 1861–1865* (Miami, FL, 1969).

situation in Virginia preventing Napoleon III from acting unilaterally in the Confederacy's behalf, a gross misjudgment by De Leon, and not his last.

He also visited Ireland and concluded that the South was riding high in European opinion, so much so that he could do no more there and wanted to come home, feeling left out of the war. "I cannot undergo the Martyrdom much longer and therefore propose returning soon," he wrote to Davis in October. "My hair is turning gray under the fret & fever of my exile." The reason for De Leon's anxiety was a common one to Southern hotbloods in the fall of 1861. They feared the war would be over in a matter of weeks before they got a chance at glory. "The cause is won—and unless some signal disaster befals your army, a very short time indeed will elapse, er'e Europe will recognise the South—and break the blockade," he told Davis.[6]

De Leon was still abroad when the second Confederate commission, that led by James M. Mason and John Slidell, was dispatched, only to be taken forcibly from the British mail steamer *Trent* by an overzealous Union naval commander, thus sparking an international incident between the United States and Britain that some expected to produce war and a British alliance with the Confederacy. Certainly De Leon held such hopes and worked his pen in the foreign press toward that end. Only after the crisis waned did he finally leave for the Confederacy in January 1862. He reached Richmond in late February, to find that Davis had no interest in turning a potentially valuable publicist into just another soldier. There would be no commission in the military for De Leon. Rather, after discussions in which De Leon told Davis his impressions of the Confederacy's needs and potential in Europe, the president concluded that the South Carolinian's experience as a propagandist for Southern rights before the war made him a natural choice to continue in that role. This was especially important since the Union already had a number of men abroad actively pursuing public opinion. De Leon could do good work to counter them by representing the new Confederacy to the governments in France and England, whose good favor Davis wanted, and whose diplomatic recognition and possible foreign armed intervention could mean the difference of life or death for the Confederacy.

Davis vouchsafed this opinion to his new secretary of state, Judah P. Benjamin, for on April 12, 1862, Benjamin wrote a dispatch to Mason in London in which he observed that "Mr. De Leon possesses to a high degree the con-

---

6. Edwin De Leon to Jefferson Davis, October 24, 1861, Lynda Lasswell Crist and Mary Seaton Dix, eds., *The Papers of Jefferson Davis*, vol. 7, *1861* (Baton Rouge, LA, 1992), pp. 374–376.

fidence of the President as a man of discretion, ability, and thorough devotion to our cause."[7] It was on that same day that Davis gave De Leon an *ex officio* appointment to oversee Confederate propaganda efforts in England and France. The position came with $25,000 to begin to carry out the program of getting favorable print for the South, but with no salary for De Leon, which he seemed happy to waive. Perhaps it was because he did not expect to be overseas for long, so great was his confidence in his abilities as a publicist and his conviction of overwhelming sympathy for the Confederacy abroad. On his way to Wilmington, North Carolina, to the blockade runner that would take him to sea, he wrote to the daughter of Christopher Memminger, the Confederate secretary of the treasury: "If only we can hold on till July!" Writing with the news of the fall of New Orleans fresh in the papers, and with a Union army then on the peninsula between the James and York Rivers a mere fifty miles from Richmond, De Leon presumably meant that if the capital could just hold out until the summer, the Yankees would have to turn back. Memminger, however, perhaps after discussions with the agent before he left Richmond, already perceived that De Leon's concept of his mission was considerably more exalted than what Davis or Benjamin conceived it to be, and that his conceit in the importance of his commission was so great that he really meant the Confederacy need only hold out "till he gets to England."[8]

De Leon left Richmond with dispatches for Mason and Slidell that contained within them the germ of his own downfall eighteen months in the future. Benjamin had originally put Slidell in charge of propaganda in Europe, and so said one of the dispatches carried by De Leon. But then Davis informed Benjamin of De Leon's new mission. Instead of redrafting the dispatch to Slidell to remove news of his own appointment, Benjamin simply added a postscript with word of the change. Worse, De Leon apparently got bored at sea, despite having his wife, Ellen, and his daughters with him, or

7. Judah P. Benjamin to James M. Mason, April 12, 1862, U.S. Navy Department, *Official Records of the Union and Confederate Navies in the War of the Rebellion* (Washington, DC, 1894–1922), Series 2, vol. 3, pp. 385, 390. This volume, containing the diplomatic correspondence of the Confederacy, will hereinafter be cited simply as *ORN*. Charles P. Cullop, "Edwin De Leon, Jefferson Davis' Propagandist," *Civil War History* 7 (December 1962), pp. 389–390, suggests that Benjamin was not happy about De Leon's appointment and felt jealous of De Leon's close friendship with Davis, making him a potential rival for influence with the president. Cullop cites no evidence for this inference, which seems groundless at this point, though soon enough Benjamin would have misgivings about the propagandist.

8. C. Vann Woodward, ed., *Mary Chesnut's Civil War* (New Haven, CT, 1981), June 2, 1862, p. 355.

more likely he just could not contain his curiosity. In a severe breach of diplomatic etiquette, he opened and read Benjamin's dispatches to Mason and Slidell.[9] Thus he discovered that Slidell had been the first choice for the post he now held. De Leon seems to have had little love for Slidell already, but seeing this surely did not endear the commissioner to him. Moreover, De Leon clearly thought he was himself the better choice not just as propagandist, but as commissioner to France. Slidell had little experience of the country, and what De Leon had seen of Slidell's efforts in the short time he had been in Paris did not impress the South Carolinian.

Indeed, when De Leon reached Europe, he made no secret among Confederate sympathizers there of his wish to have a proper ministerial position, nor of his lack of regard for Slidell. Paul Pecquet du Bellet, with whom De Leon soon became rather intimate, believed that De Leon came from Richmond with *"no very good feelings* towards Mr. Slidell," and expected that he would before long be asked to replace him.[10] For his part, as soon as he saw that his dispatches from Benjamin had been opened, Slidell formed an immediate distrust and resentment of De Leon, the more so after seeing his own control over propaganda taken from him in the same letter that gave him the task in the first place. Slidell said nothing to Benjamin about the opened dispatches for the moment, but thereafter he and De Leon lost no opportunity to make subtle points against one another in their letters to Richmond, nor to display otherwise what du Bellet thought was "open contempt for each other."[11]

De Leon reached London on June 29 to find public opinion for the Confederacy somewhat declining thanks to defeats at Forts Henry and Donelson in February, and Shiloh, Fort Pulaski, and New Orleans in April. He met with the prime minister, Lord Palmerston, in a nonofficial interview and tried to represent the South's claims to independence, but the Englishman effectively dodged all efforts at persuasion. De Leon secured introductions to other influential British statesmen and met for the first time with Henry Hotze, who had just commenced publication of the new pro-Southern propaganda newspaper *The Index*. De Leon may not even have known of Hotze's activities, for communication was so poor that Benjamin himself scarcely

9. Slidell to Benjamin, December 6, 1863, Records of the Confederate States of America, 1854–1889, Consular and Other Missions, 1861–1865, Library of Congress, Washington, DC.

10. William Stanley Hoole, ed., *The Diplomacy of the Confederate Cabinet of Richmond and Its Agents Abroad* (Tuscaloosa, AL, 1963), pp. 68, 69.

11. Ibid., pp. 70–71.

knew of them. Certainly he did not approve of *The Index*, not from animosity to Hotze, but because, as he later said in the "Secret History," he thought the fact of its being openly published by the Confederacy destroyed any impression of its objectivity and limited its influence to men already in sympathy with the South.[12] Still, before leaving London De Leon gave Hotze half a year's salary from his funds, but only a smattering of sums followed thereafter as De Leon consistently opposed the continuation of the sheet, preferring to save his money for his own efforts.[13]

In August De Leon went on to Paris and there he began to establish himself with newspaper publishers and influential men friendly to the Southern cause, especially in engaging a friendly and venal press in publishing pro-Confederate propaganda as described in the "Secret History." Before long, thanks to influence and bribes, hundreds of French newspapers carried articles friendly to the South, and De Leon used some of his gold to persuade the editor of the Parisian journal *Patrie* to make it virtually a French counterpart to Hotze's *Index*. If he did not entirely counteract Union influence on public opinion in France, at least the Confederacy, too, now had a voice in the debate.

De Leon himself wrote avidly, and often anonymously. Seeing the string of Confederate defeats that spring and summer depressing French opinion, he published a pamphlet in August, which he titled *La Vérité sur les États Confédérés* (*The Truth about the Confederate States of America* [see appendix 3]). In it he emphasized the ineffectiveness of the Union naval blockade of the South, the determination of the Confederate people to win their independence, and most of all the benign nature of slavery. He had seen very quickly that slavery posed a major obstacle in the competition for the sympathies of the French people, regardless of whether or not it mattered to the Emperor Napoleon, and thus De Leon exaggerated familiar themes of the loyalty of the slaves to their masters and the benefits the labor system brought to the South and the world by way of its cotton. He believed, and boasted, that the pamphlet put the Union propagandists on the defensive at a single stroke.

12. Cullop, "De Leon," p. 391, maintains that De Leon was jealous of the fact that Hotze already had a working propaganda effort going in London when De Leon arrived, and feeling threatened, decided thereafter to concentrate on France as his own sphere. Again, Cullop's sources do not support this conclusion, but the inference of pique at finding someone else on turf he may have thought would be exclusively his own is not unreasonable and is in keeping with De Leon's later demonstrated resentment of Hotze and others with whom he felt himself in competition.

13. Hotze to Benjamin, August 4, 1862, *ORN*, p. 505; December 20, 1862, p. 633.

He also made efforts to meet with Napoleon to represent Confederate views and claims, something just as inappropriate in his position as his previous meeting with Palmerston.

De Leon soon came to believe that the cause could be served by promoting the statesmanlike qualities of President Davis himself, thus utilizing the propagandist's old trick of exemplifying a cause in the person of its leader. It was a sensible course, especially since the marginally aristocratic Davis could be contrasted with the humbly born Lincoln to good effect in the minds of upper-class men of influence in England and France. Thus De Leon played on the prevalent myth in the South that Southerners descended from the aristocratic Norman stock who kept civilization alive in Europe for centuries, while the Yankees' Saxon and Celtic ancestors still wore animal skins and painted their faces blue. Through Davis the Confederacy could be associated with socially, politically, and even genetically elevated stock, while Lincoln exemplified the mean log cabin roots of poor whites and European refugees. De Leon placed great import in circulating an engraving of Davis and used it as frontispiece to *La Vérité.*

That fall he authored an essay on Davis for London's *Blackwood's Magazine,* a piece that helped to prompt Union propagandists to react with Robert J. Walker's subsequent suggestions that Davis had supported Mississippi's repudiation of bond debts in the 1840s, costing English investors alone some $10 million, and would do the same with any European loans made to the Confederacy after the war. The attack was false, but just then the Confederacy was starting to realize substantial funds from a bond loan handled by the French firm of Erlanger and Company, and Unionists hoped the Walker attack could blunt the effectiveness of the loan. De Leon responded in 1863 with a pamphlet that he published in London under the pseudonym Jonathan Slingsby, titled *A Familiar Epistle to Robert J. Walker, Formerly of Pennsylvania, Later of Mississippi, More Recently of Washington, and Last Heard of in Mr. Coxwell's Balloon, from an Old Acquaintance, to Which Is Prefixed a Biographical Sketch.* De Leon took the battle to Walker, linking him with repudiation himself, and not failing to point out that as a slave-owner, Walker made a questionable champion of the Union. De Leon later claimed that the pamphlet and follow-up editorials by Hotze drove Walker from the fray, and perhaps they did. Nevertheless, Confederate defeats at Gettysburg and Vicksburg that summer cripplingly undermined the Erlanger loan all the same, and De Leon would not be reticent in reporting to Richmond that he had never approved of the loan in the first place, placing the blame for it squarely with Slidell, whose daughter just happened to be married to Emile Erlanger's son.

De Leon also entered British journals with an account of how easily he had penetrated the blockade, to emphasize the points on its ineffectiveness made in France in *La Vérité*. In short, despite Hotze being in London to coordinate propaganda efforts in England, De Leon largely ignored him and conducted his own campaign independently as it suited him, though he did cooperate with Hotze occasionally. Still the two did not agree on much. Hotze wanted *The Index* to be entirely English in approach and format, thinking that the best way to influence British minds. De Leon thought the paper a waste of money and advised Hotze to close it down in October 1862, saying the cost of it could be spent more productively elsewhere. In January 1863, when De Leon published a response to a thundering anti-Confederate speech in Parliament by John Bright, he declined to have it appear in *The Index* and instead paid from his own funds to print and distribute 10,000 copies in major cities. He told Benjamin that if he had given it to Hotze to print, he feared that the editor would have bowdlerized or even suppressed it entirely.[14] De Leon's complaints of other Confederate agents abroad extended also to its purchasing officers. When he was involved in aiding the purchase of pistols for the Confederate navy and army, he complained to Richmond that purchasing agent Caleb Huse was not cooperating with him, thus costing time and money.[15] As he repeatedly hinted in his reports to Richmond, no one, it seemed, was doing proper work overseas but Edwin De Leon.

Such claims often characterized De Leon's monthly dispatches to Benjamin in Richmond, all more or less on the same theme: in De Leon, Benjamin had a hardworking agent in Paris, and sooner or later his efforts would almost single-handedly bring about French intervention for the Confederacy. The accredited diplomat John Slidell would be mentioned only in passing, and often just to point out his failure to achieve something that De Leon himself managed to accomplish through his superior contacts. De Leon also wrote almost constantly, letters to editors, editorials, pamphlets, magazine articles—whatever he could get into print to support Southern claims to independence. Much of it was published anonymously, some under pseudonyms, and some rehashed out of shape by journalists. The important thing to

14. De Leon to Benjamin, January 28, 1863, Records of the Confederate States of America.

15. De Leon to Benjamin, September 30, 1862, U.S. War Department, *War of the Rebellion: Official Records of the Union and Confederate Armies* (Washington, 1880–1901), Series 4, vol. 2, p. 105 (hereinafter cited as *OR*).

De Leon was to spill as much ink as possible. And all the while he tried to impress Benjamin with the extensiveness of his efforts, the secret networks of operatives he established, and the inactivity of Slidell and Huse.[16]

Benjamin would have been naive indeed not to anticipate that in employing a propagandist abroad for the Confederacy, such an agent would use his literary skills to promote his own importance to his employers. Meanwhile, in his dispatches De Leon increasingly crossed the line between reporting his activities as an agent and attempting to suggest diplomatic policy to the state department, something as much outside his brief as his visit to Palmerston. By early 1863 De Leon's original optimism was giving way to a feeling that England and France would adhere to a policy of staying out of American affairs and leaving North and South to settle the issue on their own, and in the ensuing months that conviction led to a cynicism about French intentions that would end in causing him considerable embarrassment.[17] At the same time, De Leon became increasingly convinced that the only thing that might move France to act would be a voluntary emancipation in the Confederacy, something that Richmond was not yet prepared to entertain.

Knowing that, and being himself opposed to any thought of forfeiting slavery, De Leon began to recommend to Benjamin that the secretary of state recall all diplomatic operatives in Europe and cease efforts to bring about recognition, thus saving money and self-respect at the same time. He also noted that important as Southern cotton was to manufacturers in England and France, the looms were still operating and sources were being found elsewhere, thus blunting what some had hoped to be the South's sharpest weapon.[18] He complained of the lack of coordination of Confederate financial affairs abroad and the "want of a proper business head to control them," another dig at Huse and at new financial agent Colin J. McRae. As for Confederate efforts to secure financing abroad, he repeatedly harped on his lack of enthusiasm for the Erlanger loan negotiated at considerable benefit to everyone but the Confederacy by Slidell and others in 1862, a theme he would expand upon shortly in his "Secret History."[19]

However much De Leon's dispatches back to Benjamin lauded his own efforts, others saw him in rather a different light. Thirty years later De Leon

16. De Leon details some of his writing in his dispatches to Benjamin dated January 28, February 23, March 31, June 14, and August 3, 1863, Records of the Confederate States of America.

17. De Leon to Benjamin, February 23, 1863, Records of the Confederate States of America.

18. Ibid., June 14, 1863.

19. Ibid., August 3, 1863.

would speak of du Bellet as "a short, enormously stout, and heavy-looking man," but one with "a warm heart and a noble soul; and an intelligence as quick and alert as its outward case was unwieldy." Even then De Leon did not mention him by name in his 1890 memoirs and did not refer to him at all in the 1867–1868 memoir presented here.[20] De Leon's reticence may have stemmed from the fact that du Bellet's contemporary appraisal of De Leon was not reciprocally flattering. Du Bellet, whose opinion of Confederate agents abroad was no more flattering than De Leon's, thought him pompous and impractical and liked to tell of a supposed occasion when De Leon gained an interview with a member of Napoleon III's cabinet, said that the lives of 8 million Confederates depended on his mission, and then gave the official a portrait of Jefferson Davis as if that somehow would win French aid.[21]

Du Bellet's opinion was no doubt influenced by his own wounded pride. Shortly after the two first met in August 1862, du Bellet introduced De Leon into the world of the French press and got him access to the "correspondences" that put Confederate sentiments into some 200 or more newspapers (see chapter 17). Du Bellet later took credit for this "without egotism," he said, but De Leon gave him little credit or none at the time, and then suspended the use of the "correspondences" after a couple of months when he concluded that French intervention would not be forthcoming immediately, whereas du Bellet thought they would have been useful much longer.[22] That failure to give credit to others is evidence that De Leon did not restrict his jealousy to Slidell. He seemed to resent anyone else meddling in French affairs on behalf of the Confederacy. When du Bellet published his own commentary on affairs in the Union, De Leon became visibly upset.[23] In August 1862 when De Leon published his pamphlet *La Vérité sur les États Confédérés*, du Bellet mocked the work, saying that though it was "beautifully conceived and does great credit to the intelligence of the author," it was something De Leon "threw out" and came too late to be of use. Worse, De Leon did not consult du Bellet before publishing it, since du Bellet had been in Paris much longer and thought he knew sentiment there much better. Consequently, said du Bellet, the Paris press all but ignored De Leon's work.[24] The caustic

---

20. Edwin De Leon, *Thirty Years of My Life on Three Continents* (London, 1890), vol. 2, pp. 50–51.
21. Hoole, *Diplomacy*, p. 68.
22. Ibid., pp. 66–67.
23. Ibid., pp. 72–73.
24. Ibid., pp. 65–66.

du Bellet also charged De Leon with employing an English assistant who proved to be something of a fool, and who insulted some of the French press. Du Bellet even managed to find something critical to say in the matter of a white Arabian horse that De Leon brought for Davis when he sailed for the South in early 1862.[25]

Finally the combination of De Leon's frustration at Napoleon's inaction on intervention, his jealousy of Slidell's more exalted position, his pique that Slidell did not confer with him, and Benjamin's failure to take his unsolicited advice on matters outside his mandate all combined to cost the propagandist his job. On September 30, 1863, he wrote a dispatch to Benjamin, and the next day penned a private letter to Davis, and the sentiments contained in the two were anything but diplomatic. He called the French "a far more mercenary race than the English" and declared that the only way to win French opinion was to buy it. "France wants money," he said, the possible suggestion being that the nation was either bankrupt or else ready to be bribed. Neither was flattering. Nor were the opinions he expressed about Slidell's handling of his portfolio and his complaints that Slidell did not share information with him, which in fact De Leon had no right to expect. De Leon entrusted the letters to the blockade runner *Ceres*, which had the misfortune to be captured by Union naval forces. On November 16 the two letters appeared in the *New York Daily Tribune*, and by the end of the month copies passed across the battle lines to reach Richmond.[26]

To say that Davis and Benjamin were surprised and chagrined would be an understatement. Benjamin had been increasingly irritated with De Leon for some time, first for his slights at Slidell, then for his failure to send adequate receipts for his expenditures of Confederate funds, and throughout for his habit of entrusting his dispatches to the state department to private individuals to deliver through the blockade rather than through the British mail to Bermuda, a safer and faster route.[27] De Leon's failure to follow Benjamin's instructions finally resulted in the capture of these dispatches and their subsequent embarrassing revelations. The insult to France would only make Slidell's task the more difficult, while the insult to Slidell risked compromising any efforts he made, as it revealed the lack of accord within the Confederate diplomatic community.

25. Ibid., pp. 65, 67–68.

26. Cullop, "Edwin De Leon," p. 398.

27. Benjamin to De Leon, August 17, 1863, Records of the Confederate States of America.

Davis and Benjamin did not react immediately, but in their discussion of the incident it was quickly apparent that the public interest demanded that De Leon no longer be allowed to speak for the Confederacy.[28] On December 9 Benjamin wrote a cold and pointed letter to the propagandist informing him that his correspondence had reached the enemy press, and thereby the world. "Their contents have been read with painful surprise and are such as not only to destroy your own usefulness in the special service entrusted to you, but to render your continuance in your present position incompatible with the retention in the public service of our commissioner to Paris." In short, De Leon had to go if Slidell was to stay, and to punctuate that, Benjamin went on to assert Davis's undiminished confidence in Slidell and his services and his repudiation of the sentiments expressed by De Leon as to both that gentleman and the French people at large. That said, Benjamin ordered De Leon to turn over any government funds remaining in his care to the Confederate agent in Paris, Colin McRae.[29]

Benjamin wrote to Slidell on the same day to affirm to him that De Leon's mission had "not the least diplomatic character" and that there was no way in which it should have interfered with Slidell. "The President has been much mortified by this very extraordinary conduct of Mr. de Leon," said the secretary of state. Benjamin observed that he had sensed from De Leon's earlier correspondence with the department that De Leon felt irritated that Slidell did not take him into his confidence, but nothing in those earlier letters "displayed the existence of such feelings as are prominent in this published correspondence."[30] Benjamin could not forbear from chiding Slidell, too, for not informing him right away when Slidell discovered that De Leon had opened and read Benjamin's confidential dispatches to him the year before. That alone would have warranted dismissing the agent at the time, and thus the state department might have been spared the embarrassment it now suffered.[31] That mild scolding only added to the glee Slidell felt at De Leon's disgrace. In response he told Benjamin of De Leon's opening of the dispatches, then argued that De Leon had accomplished nothing at all of consequence for the Confederacy abroad.[32] When he learned of his rival's dismissal, Slidell called immediately on the French minister of the interior,

---

28. Benjamin to Slidell, December 9, 1863, *ORN*, p. 973.
29. Benjamin to De Leon, December 9, 1863, copy in Henry Hotze Papers, Library of Congress.
30. Benjamin to Slidell, December 9, 1863, ibid.
31. Benjamin to Slidell, January 28, 1864, *ORN*, p. 1013.
32. Slidell to Benjamin, December 6, 1863, Records of the Confederate States of America.

showed him the letter recalling De Leon, and asked the minister to have it published in the *Constitutionnel* in order to publicize Richmond's repudiation of the man.[33]

The minister declined to publish the recall letter, but the affair did not remain a secret. Indeed, the publication of De Leon's captured correspondence in Northern newspapers was a great embarrassment to the Confederates in France. Confederate agent Rose O'Neal Greenhow, then abroad to publish and promote her memoirs of imprisonment by the Yankees as a spy, wrote to President Davis on January 2, 1864, advising him that De Leon's captured dispatch gave "a most correct summary of things here—altho it has excited a great deal of ire against him."[34] Du Bellet felt greatly dismayed at the sensation produced in Paris. He later asserted disbelief that an agent would send such a condemnation of Confederate officials in a letter to its president unless the writer's relations with Davis made him feel authorized to do so, which was in fact what De Leon would claim. Du Bellet even suspected that Davis wanted such a frank appraisal from De Leon and told him to author one by prior instruction, then had to discountenance it and De Leon when it became public.[35]

De Leon did not receive Benjamin's note of recall until the beginning of February 1864, and before then had himself dismissed the captured and published correspondence as a matter of only passing insignificance. "But one Journal in France has made mention of my intercepted dispatches in an unfavorable sense, and that one struck them with a feather," De Leon wrote Benjamin on December 23 in a letter that was at sea the same time as Benjamin's letter of dismissal. For a change, De Leon closed this letter optimistically, for he thought he sensed a shift in British public opinion. "We may yet get aid where you least hope for it," he concluded in his last cordial words to the secretary of state.[36] When Benjamin's letter arrived, however, De Leon reacted with a degree of petulance typical of a prideful man and responded with equal candor and characteristic intemperance. Smugly he an-

33. Hoole, *Diplomacy*, pp. 70–71.

34. Lynda Lasswell Crist, Kenneth H. Williams, and Peggy L. Dillard, *The Papers of Jefferson Davis*, vol. 10, *October 1863–August 1864* (Baton Rouge, LA, 1999), p. 143. Greenhow and De Leon met, as he referred to her and her book in his December 23, 1863, dispatch to Benjamin cited below. On January 16, 1864, De Leon bought several copies of her book to circulate in England. Receipt, January 16, 1864, Edwin De Leon Papers, South Caroliniana Library, University of South Carolina, Columbia.

35. Hoole, *Diplomacy*, p. 69.

36. De Leon to Benjamin, December 23, 1863, Records of the Confederate States of America.

nounced that he cheerfully shed himself of "a commission I have never exhibited, of a title I have never used, and of a salary which I have never accepted." He even refused Benjamin's offer of expenses for his return to the Confederacy. Then De Leon went on to assert that his public dispatches to Benjamin contained no words to justify his dismissal, and neither did anything he wrote in private letters to Davis, "with the latter of which you have no concern, as a public man," he added haughtily. Not content with that, he went on to say that "if there be any person who should not feel flattered by my 'estimate' of his 'conduct & capacity'—the 'galled jade' is not Mr Slidell, but one of the *men who surround the President* at home." There was no missing the meaning of that. De Leon was insulting Benjamin himself.

Warming to the theme, De Leon went on to say he was happy to leave Benjamin's service, for now he could follow his own inclination in furthering the Confederate cause, "a cause, to which the better part of my life has been devoted; commencing some years before you took an active interest in the Southern Question, or had espoused the doctrine of Secession." In other words, Benjamin was a Johnny-come-lately to the cause of Southern independence, just as Slidell was a dilettante at diplomacy. As for De Leon's sentiments about the French, he accused earlier published remarks of Benjamin's captured with Mason and Slidell of being far more damaging to Confederate interests abroad, "and yet, you did not consider that publication as impairing your usefulness, or requiring even your voluntary resignation." Indeed, De Leon maintained that he had spent the intervening months trying to counteract the ill effects of Benjamin's own expressions. In a final explosion of pure petulance, he told Benjamin that he would take his case directly to his old friend the president. "I shall appeal to him, as our common superior, to judge between us," he declared, and implied that he would come to Richmond to do so in person, expecting Davis to side with him.[37] It was something of a declaration of war with Benjamin.

De Leon did not stop at expressions of pique. In a last shot at his rival Hotze, when he left his field of endeavor De Leon apparently told his contacts in France that he had no replacement to take over, when in fact both he and Hotze had been informed that Hotze was to do it.[38] Soon thereafter Hotze, in fact, extended his control of propaganda efforts over virtually all of Europe where Confederate efforts were to be made. De Leon did not carry

37. De Leon to Benjamin, February 3, 1864, ibid.

38. Hotze to Felix Aucaigne, January 29, 1864, *ORN*, p. 1027; Benjamin to Hotze, January 9, 1864, *ORN*, p. 995.

through his threat to go to Richmond, however, and if he wrote any appeals to Davis, they have not survived. In fact, De Leon would never go on record with his side of the episode of his dismissal, though his brother Thomas Cooper De Leon would take several pages in his 1890 *Four Years in Rebel Capitals* to vindicate his brother indirectly by questioning Benjamin's wisdom in office.[39] Indeed, Edwin De Leon did not return to the Confederacy at all during its remaining fifteen months of life.[40]

In the end, De Leon's mission had been largely a failure thanks to his own personality, the alienation of Benjamin, Slidell, and Hotze, and to a lesser extent Huse and other agents. All he had succeeded in doing was highlighting the need for a strong and coordinated propaganda effort abroad, but thereafter he repeatedly demonstrated that he was not the man for the job. He did not set foot on American soil again until 1867, when he came home in part to use his pen to aid the campaign to end Reconstruction and defeat the forthcoming presidential candidacy of General Ulysses S. Grant. That effort failed, of course, and De Leon and his family returned to Egypt, not to come back home again until 1879 when he became involved with Alexander Graham Bell and two years later helped to introduce the telephone to Cairo.

De Leon lived out his days in Constantinople, in Greece, and finally in London, supporting himself largely by writing extensively for the monthly literary journals in America. He produced a number of travel books and novels, including *Askaros Kassis the Copt* in 1870, *The Khedive's Egypt or the Old House of Bondage under New Masters* in 1878, and *Under the Stars and under the Crescent* in 1887. He formed close friendships with fellow writers, including William Makepeace Thackeray; Charles Dickens; Alfred, Lord Tennyson; and Nathaniel Hawthorne. He also befriended such noted public men as the soldier and adventurer Charles "Chinese" Gordon, the engineer Ferdinand de Lesseps—who had helped him with Confederate propaganda—King Otho of Greece, and others. In November 1891 he returned to the United States a final time to arrange a series of lectures, but no sooner did he arrive than his health collapsed and he died in New York City on December 1.[41]

In 1890, a quarter century after the death of the Confederacy, De Leon published his last book, his two-volume memoir, *Thirty Years of My Life on*

---

39. Pp. 274–277.

40. De Leon's whereabouts are not known after June 1864, when he was certainly in Europe at the time of the sinking of the CSS *Alabama* by the USS *Kearsarge*. In *Thirty Years* De Leon recalled his meeting with the captain of the *Alabama* shortly before the event.

41. Thomas C. De Leon sketch of De Leon, *Dictionary of Notable Americans*, vol. 3, p. 206.

Three Continents. When the time came for him to address his experiences during the Civil War, he told his readers that he would not try to recount the history of the Confederacy or its leaders because "it is too early or too late to do either impartially."[42] His text lived up—or down—to that declaration, for the 102 pages that he devoted to the Civil War in *Thirty Years* disappoint anyone looking for real meat or detail on his experiences or the events he witnessed. Rather, De Leon satisfied himself by devoting almost half of it to travel narratives of his trips through the blockade and the rest to pen portraits of a few famous men he met, including Napoleon III, Palmerston, and Thackeray. De Leon's *Thirty Years* account virtually ends with his failure to influence Napoleon at Vichy in the summer of 1862. The only subsequent content is a brief account of his hosting Captain Raphael Semmes of the Confederate commerce raider *Alabama* in his Paris home shortly before the *Alabama* was sunk by the USS *Kearsarge* off Cherbourg. He says nothing of his feud with fellow diplomat John Slidell and Confederate secretary of state Judah P. Benjamin, nor of his dismissal in December 1863, topics he also did not discuss in the published portions of his 1867–1868 memoir, though his antipathy toward Slidell and Benjamin is there quite outspoken. Not surprisingly, *Thirty Years of My Life on Three Continents* has been of little use to diplomatic historians seeking to illuminate the diplomatic history of the Confederacy.

Nevertheless, more than twenty years earlier De Leon attempted to do exactly what he eschewed doing in his memoir, when in 1867 he began writing what he styled a "Secret History of Confederate Diplomacy Abroad." De Leon was a writer by instinct, thus it was natural, probably inevitable, that he would set down his war memoirs, especially with events still fresh in his mind, while he still had his own copies of his dispatches to Richmond and other correspondence in hand, and with the wound to his pride from his dismissal still sore to give added incentive. He had scores to settle with Benjamin and Slidell that made it imperative for him to have his say. A propagandist always wants to have the last word.

De Leon began writing during his 1867 visit to the United States, and the first installment of the "Secret History" appeared on December 7 of that year. De Leon's choice of a venue was itself of interest. Rather than give it to the London press or a newspaper in the South, he published it in Charles G. Halpine's New York *Citizen.* Halpine had been a noted Northern war corre-

42. De Leon, *Thirty Years*, vol. 2, pp. 1–2.

spondent under the nom de plume Private Miles O'Reilly, and almost immediately after the war began editing the *Citizen*. It was, from the first, like
Halpine himself, an erratic yet brilliant journal. Halpine, a Democrat and an
ardent opponent of the Radical wing of the Republican Party that was standing against President Andrew Johnson's more lenient policy toward the defeated South, had already published in June 1866 his *Prison Life of Jefferson
Davis*, under the pseudonym of Dr. John Craven, Davis's actual prison doctor
at Fort Monroe, Virginia. Halpine's purpose was to highlight and exaggerate
cruelty, blaming it on the Radical Republicans. Similarly, in the pages of the
Citizen he emphasized the contrast between the Radicals and the kindliness
of the martyred Lincoln through series like the 1866 sketches provided by
William Stoddart of his life inside the Lincoln White House. Halpine may
even have been the animus that brought De Leon back to America, to cooperate in the campaign against the Radicals and Reconstruction.

Halpine also published Confederate memoirs, as yet a novelty in a Northern newspaper, starting with "Rummaging through Rebeldom," which began
to appear on April 6, 1867. Credited as the work of "Col. C. S. Armee," the
series of recollections of a minor bureaucrat in the Southern government
really came from the pen of fellow New York journalist Charles E. L. Stuart.
The *Citizen* offered to Confederate memoirists a double attraction. It was the
only Northern journal in a major city to be publishing Confederate material
so soon after the war, while at the same time it allowed those Confederates to
take shots at their own former comrades. Stuart, for instance, was very critical of Jefferson Davis and other Confederate leaders, something no current
Southern paper edited by a loyal Confederate alumnus would countenance
just yet.

After the appearance of that first installment of "Secret History," De Leon
contributed one and sometimes two chapters a week until he had turned in
twenty-one. Then something happened. As evidence of his eccentricity,
Halpine had a way of not finishing things. "Rummaging through Rebeldom"
simply came to an abrupt end when the author had scarcely taken his readers
through the summer of 1861, and Stuart would not finish it in any other
venue. Either he or Halpine apparently just lost interest. Similarly, after
chapter 21, the "Secret History" suddenly ceased to appear, leaving several
aspects of De Leon's war experiences undelineated, most important of all
the circumstances of his dismissal. By the time of that last published chapter
De Leon was increasingly relying on extended excerpts from his dispatches
to Benjamin, and Halpine may simply have decided that there was no longer

enough personal observation from the author to make it worth continuing the series. Halpine also suffered perpetual financial troubles and may not have been able to pay De Leon to continue. It is certain, however, that De Leon intended for the memoir to be finished and did indeed complete the writing of it. In his own scrapbook containing clippings of all the published chapters, he added a note after the final clipping explaining the fate of the rest of the work. "This is all that was published in the newspaper," he wrote in a note dated in London in June 1875. "Six chapters more, completing the record, exist in MSS. in the author's possession."[43] Halpine may have simply lost interest. Perhaps De Leon left to return to Europe before finishing the memoir and never got the remainder to Halpine. In any case, the "Secret History" ended in the April 4, 1868, issue. The last six manuscript chapters De Leon referred to in 1875 do not seem to have survived in his existing personal papers.

Regardless of the "Secret History's" incomplete publication, it is evident that De Leon intended to revise it either in its own shape or as part of a more extended memoir. He copyrighted the work as he wrote it and kept his copies of the articles in that scrapbook, now in the Edwin De Leon Papers, South Caroliniana Library, University of South Carolina, at Columbia. Sometime prior to 1875 he began making corrections and notes to himself in the margins of the scrapbook, indicating topics he apparently intended to expand upon at a later time. Yet it is also evident that *Thirty Years* is not the result of that earlier intent to revise and expand, for *Thirty Years* scarcely touches on most of the topics in the "Secret History," let alone expanding on them. The content of *Thirty Years* helps to explain why. After the passage of more than two decades, De Leon no longer felt the animus for revenge or self-explanation. His dislike for Benjamin and Slidell still come through, but very muted, wholly unlike the undisguised contempt expressed in the "Secret History."

It is De Leon's candor and evident personal feeling that inject much of its life into the "Secret History." At the same time, De Leon is remarkably even-handed except where Benjamin and Slidell are concerned. Indeed, De Leon is repeatedly complimentary of his Yankee counterparts in the diplomatic game, often paying tribute to the skill of William L. Dayton and Charles Francis Adams, even speaking favorably of William H. Seward, and certainly more so than for his own secretary of state. He also offers refreshingly ob-

---

43. Scrapbook, De Leon Papers, South Carolina.

jective portraits of the British and French leaders encountered, both those who shared his views and those who opposed his goal of diplomatic recognition for the Confederacy. None impressed De Leon more than Napoleon III of France, and his appraisal of the emperor is more flattering than that left by other contemporaries or by historians since. That is probably because De Leon thought the roll of France in European affairs regarding the Confederacy was much more important than in fact it was, thus by association exaggerating De Leon's own importance as an agent in France. Moreover, he believed that Napoleon had favored him with what he thought to be some significant diplomatic intimacies.

It is in the details, however, that the "Secret History" makes its major contribution, for De Leon was a keen observer and a bit of a gossip. His background on the workings of Napoleon's court, on the efforts of the Confederate commissioners to gain access to high counsels, and on the workings of friends and foes in Parliament and the Corps Legislatif offer, in many instances, our only inside look. His conversations with William L. Yancey are especially illuminating, since so little else survives to limn the Rebel diplomat's tenure. De Leon's own prejudices certainly show to a far greater extent than in *Thirty Years,* and so does the portrait of confusion and cross-purposes among the several Confederate agents abroad, some official, some quasi-official, and far too many simply self-appointed. Not surprisingly, De Leon also exaggerates the possibilities and "what if's" had Southern diplomacy been more successful—which is to say, if Benjamin had listened to De Leon. Hindsight allows historians to discern that there was probably never really a moment when diplomatic recognition and intervention on behalf of the Confederacy were a probability. It simply was not in Britain's interest to risk a war with the Union, and France was not about to take any action without Britain moving first. The rest of Europe simply did not matter in the game. But writing in 1867 to 1868, De Leon did not know that, and as yet could not, and probably would not have accepted such a conclusion in any event. His associates in France were chiefly those who favored the South and French intervention for the Confederacy, and naturally he would thus emerge from his experience believing such sentiments to be preeminent.

The "Secret History" will not so much change modern understanding of Confederate diplomacy as illuminate what we already knew, yet in a field in which first-person narratives are so few, that is indeed important. De Leon's memoir is also significant in that it is the earliest known account by any Confederate foreign agent, giving it an immediacy lacking in other published works. It is also, in its way, an extension of his wartime work, for De Leon's best efforts were in print. The number of his essays and pamphlets published in the attempt to influence European public opinion may never be known, since he issued so many anonymously or under noms de plume.

To add breadth to the "Secret History," three examples of his wartime writing are here included in appendices. The first is *Three Letters from a South Carolinian, Relating to Secession, Slavery and the Trent Case*, published in London late in 1861. Even though France was officially his "beat," De Leon had good connections with the British press, and in this compilation of three separate letters written to the *Times* of London he became the first Confederate abroad to try to set before the British public at large the background of secession, the pretensions of the Confederacy to nationhood, and the case to demand a stern response from Britain to the seizure of Confederate diplomats from a British vessel by a Union warship. As a concomitant to that framework justifying British recognition and intervention, De Leon in 1862 turned his pen to publicizing the ineffectiveness of the Union blockade by writing a memoir of his successful penetration of the cordon that spring. He published "How We Broke the Blockade" in London's *Cornhill Magazine* in October 1862. Finally, in an effort to promote his cause among the public in France, he issued *The Truth about the Confederate States of America* in Paris in August 1862. It is an able example of the use of all the weapons of diplomacy—truth, exaggeration, hyperbole, fiction, and the verisimilitude of genuine information from the war, alongside the studied untruths of the foreign propagandist. Published in French, it has not been translated into English until now.

It all demonstrates that if De Leon failed, it was not for want of trying. No Confederate agent abroad was more energetic, and few if any enjoyed better connections to people of influence. How the French and British leaders with whom he met felt about the man and his actions, none seem to have testified. His own fellow Southern diplomats were not in the main flattering, though even they gave him credit for industry. That he could hardly achieve what was probably an impossible task cannot blot his record. If his own follies ruined relations with his superiors in Richmond, there is every evidence that most members of Parliament and the press took him very seriously, indeed.

CHAPTER 1
FORESHADOWING OF THE WAR—THE TRUE POSITION
OF JEFFERSON DAVIS

————•◦•————

It was at Thebes, in Upper Egypt, in the early spring of 1861, that the first news of the formal secession of South Carolina from the American Union reached me. Sitting on a fallen column amid the ruins of the earliest recorded civilization, it was my fate to hear the first sounds of that alarm which awoke both Europe and America from the pleasant dreams of universal peace in which they had been indulging since the Italian war.[1]

On receiving the news of Mr. Lincoln's election, some time previous, I had sent in my resignation of the office which I then held, to take effect on his accession; for under the circumstances of his election, and with the principles and policy he represented, it was impossible for me to serve under his administration. Now I felt more strongly than ever the necessity of immediately returning home to share in the fortunes of my kindred and friends, and to link my destiny with that of my native State, which my education and convictions taught me had the first claim on my allegiance.

Leaving, therefore, the tranquil delights of an Eastern life and the duties of a position which habit had made almost a second nature to me, I returned to Alexandria, put my house in order, and sailed for Europe with the least possible delay. Even in remote Egypt the vibration of the earthquake shock on the other continent was felt. In my parting interview with the Viceroy we conversed on the topic, and he manifested much interest on the subject.

The then Viceroy was Said Pasha, a man of European culture and intelligence, and he expressed the belief, in which I then shared, that the trouble would be but a transient one; at the same time adding, with a laugh: "If your

1. De Leon wrote in his memoirs that when news of South Carolina's secession reached him, he was actually sitting on a fallen column at the temple of Karnak at Luxor. "It seemed strange to us," he recalled, "that sitting, as it were, among the tombstones of one of the oldest recorded empires, we should first hear the death-knell of the youngest of living nations." De Leon, *Thirty Years of My Life on Three Continents* (London, 1890), vol.1, pp. 294–295.

people stop the cotton supply for Europe, my people will have to grow more and furnish them."[2]

What he meant as a jest turned out to be a prophecy; for Egypt grew fat and flourished, while the Southern States, blockade-bound, waxed lean and impoverished from that very cause.

Long absent from my country, I had, nevertheless, always kept myself thoroughly informed as to all political movements; and pending the Presidential campaign of 1860 I distinctly saw, even from that distance, the black clouds lowering on the horizon, and threatening to break in storm and tempest over the country.

In my judgment, the best method to avoid a collision and to stem the tide of Abolition fanaticism on the one side, and of fierce resentment on the other, was to warn the North of the determined temper of the South, by nominating for the Presidency—in combination with the Democratic party of the North—a representative States Rights Southern man, instead of compromising on a Northern Conservative.

I considered Mr. Davis as our best and ablest representative man for that nomination, not so much for any supposed intellectual superiority over other Southern leaders, as from the fact of his eligibility, and from his moderation both of language and deportment towards the representatives of the North, and the Northern people generally.[3]

If after such nomination he could be elected by a combination of Northern and Southern conservatives, the evils which threatened the country under a sectional rule would be averted. I therefore wrote Mr. Davis, suggesting the boldest as the best policy, expounding my views with all the freedom of old friendship, and offering, if he approved of the idea, to resign my office, return home, and with pen and voice, aid in carrying out the proposed programme.

It is useless to add, that at this time the thought of the probability—or even the possibility—of a civil war had not entered my mind. While my long absence had not prevented my grasping the political situation, it and other

2. Egyptian cotton had not yet become a major competitor with American cotton on the world market, but the war, the Union blockade, and the Confederate cotton embargo would give Egyptian cotton a major boost.

3. Jefferson Davis was never a serious contender for the Democratic nomination for the presidency in 1860, but there were those who favored him as an alternative more acceptable to the South than Stephen Douglas, and more acceptable to some elements in the North than John C. Breckinridge.

causes had not allowed me fully to appreciate the mutual exasperation and fraternal hatred which culminated in that four years war—almost suicidal on the one side, fearfully destructive and demoralizing on the other, and almost fatal to constitutional liberty on this continent.

My letter to Mr. Davis was written in December, 1859.[4] His reply, bearing date a month later, was as follows:

Washington, D.C., Jan. 21, 1860.[5]

My Dear Sir—I have read your letter with sincere gratification, and return my cordial thanks for your kind offer. You express what I would have expected from you, but what I would have hoped from few men whom it has been my fortune to know.

I have no wishes or prospects which would justify you in making the proposed sacrifice; and for every reason object to your making it. My opinions, as you know them, would be sufficient to defeat any effort of my friends to nominate me at Charleston; *and should do so,* as they would impair the ability of the Democratic party to succeed in the next Presidential canvass. Since you left us there has been a great advance in public opinion towards the Southern Rights creed. We are now all powerful at the South, but are still in the minority at the North.

To get as many Northern votes as will insure the success of our candidate, it will be necessary to recruit largely from the conservative ranks; and you will at once perceive that the banner of a radical advocate of Southern Rights would not be sufficiently attractive in that quarter to produce the result. There will be a hazardous controversy in reaction to the resolutions declaratory of the position in relation to the rights of slaveholders in the United States Territories. The solution which will probably be the only possible one, will be to nominate some one who will be recognized in both sections as the true exponent of their opinions. Ex-President Pierce would probably best fulfill the conditions.[6] Mr. Dallas might do.[7] A Southern Rights man from a planting State would not be accepted by the North, without

4. The original of De Leon's letter has not to date been found.

5. The original of this letter is at Beauvoir in Biloxi, Mississippi. It is included in Lynda Lasswell Crist and Mary Seaton Dix, eds., *The Papers of Jefferson Davis,* vol. 6, *1856–1860* (Baton Rouge, LA, 1989), pp. 270–271.

6. Franklin Pierce, fourteenth president of the United States.

7. George Mifflin Dallas had been vice president under James K. Polk.

disclaimers and concessions not to be entertained for a moment; and a Southern man with Northern leanings, as Davy Hubbard expressed, would be a submission to which we could only consent as the alternative of submission to a "Black Republican."[8]

From both I pray that a good Providence and our own self-respect will preserve us.

* * *

The papers, which you no doubt see, will have informed you of the protracted and thus far fruitless struggle to organize the House of Representatives. No one can now see how the controversy is to be terminated; and the Southern members are becoming fast reconciled to their present unorganized condition.[9]

As we have little to hope and much to deprecate from the action of the present Congress, no legislation may be our best estate.

A few of your associates in the long siege of 1851 are still in the Senate, and all remember you with much regard. Let me hear from you as often as your convenience will permit, and believe me,

Ever most truly, yours.

Jeff'n Davis.

Consul-General Edwin De Leon, Alexandria, Egypt.

Deferring to the superior judgment of Mr. Davis, I accepted his conclusions, and events seemed to justify their correctness. But when the storm rose, nine months later, I again wrote an urgent request to know the actual state of affairs, and received in reply a letter, the material portions of which were as follows:

Washington, D.C., Jan. 8, 1861.[10]

My Dear Sir—We are advancing rapidly to the end of "the Union." The Cotton States may now be regarded as having decided for

---

8. David Hubbard, a Democratic congressman from Alabama, was a presidential elector on the John C. Breckinridge ticket in 1860 and a member of the 1st Confederate Congress.

9. When the new congress assembled in December 1859, neither Republicans nor Democrats held control of the House of Representatives. It would take two months and more than forty votes to select a speaker and organize the House for business, the problem throughout being the sectional controversy.

10. The original of this letter is in the De Leon Papers, South Caroliniana Library. It is published in Lynda Lasswell Crist and Mary Seaton Dix, eds., *Papers of Jefferson Davis*, vol. 7, *1861* (Baton

secession. South Carolina is in a *quasi* war, and the probabilities are that events will hasten her and her associates into general conflict with the forces of the Federal Government. The Black Republicans, exultant over their recent success, are not disposed to concede anything; and the stern necessity of resistance is forcing itself upon the judgment of all the slaveholding States.

The Virginia Legislature met yesterday, and took promptly and boldly the Southern ground. Mississippi is now in convention.[11]

I may leave here in a few days; though it is also possible the State may choose to continue its Senators here for the purposes of defence [*sic*] against hostile legislation.[12]

The confidence heretofore felt in Mr. Buchanan has diminished steadily, and is now nearly extinct.[13] His weakness has done as much harm as wickedness would have achieved. Though I can no longer respect or confer with him, and feel injured by his conduct, yet I pity and would extenuate the offences not prompted by bad design or malignant intent.

* * *

With great regard, I am,
As ever, your friend,
Jeff'n Davis.
Edwin De Leon, Esq., Alexandria, Egypt.

This letter I received on my return from Upper Egypt, in February, 1861; and it gives a clear picture, both of the actual situation and of the position and purposes of the writer. The publication of these letters is made at this time without the privity of Mr. Davis; the peculiar delicacy of his situation at

---

Rouge, LA, 1992), pp. 6–7. In the margin of his copy of this article in the scrapbook in the De Leon Papers, De Leon has noted "Davis's letter." It may mean that in a fuller memoir he intended to include the entire text of this letter from Davis. All subsequent references to De Leon's marginal notes are from this source.

11. South Carolina seceded December 20, 1861, and Davis's Mississippi would do so the day after he wrote this letter.

12. Davis would deliver a farewell address in the Senate on January 21, 1861, and leave for Mississippi the next day.

13. President James Buchanan, who deservedly sits near the bottom in virtually all polls of the presidents, sat by almost helpless as the country marched toward disunion. There was, perhaps, not much that he could do. His sin, however, is that he did not try to do something.

this moment preventing my consulting him in the matter, as I should otherwise have done.

Written with the freedom and frankness of private correspondence, these
letters prove how far Mr. Davis was from acting the part his enemies have assigned him, viz: as having plotted the destruction of the Union before and at
the time of secession, and rejoicing in the consummation of that long cherished scheme.

On the contrary, no one can read these letters dispassionately without being struck with the tone of sadness which sounds through them, and the unwillingness to accept conclusions, the weight of which was irresistible. In
the first letter, the hope and belief of averting the final issue of disruption is
strongly expressed, and extreme measures disapproved of. The last, so far
from breathing a tone of exultation at the collision which he saw, but could
not avert, is imbued with a sentiment of sorrow—pervaded with a spirit
blending almost prophetic foreboding with high determination to abide by
the decision of the State whose representative in the Senate he then was.[14]

"If this be treason, make the most of it!"

In the judgment of the American people Mr. Davis may have many sins to
answer for, and cruelly and pitilessly has the penalty been enforced for the
failure of his people to sustain by might what they regarded as their rights.
Yet, of this sin of having "plotted and planned the Rebellion," laid so often to
his charge, these letters prove him innocent, in the sight of man and of God.
Nor can that charge be laid at the door of any Southern statesman; for never
was a movement initiated and conducted with more defiant—with more indiscreet openness and publicity than that of secession. And to it it is false
and slanderous to apply the word plot, which implies secrecy, trickery, and
long preparation, before a declaration of purpose, or an overt act.

Mr. Davis, as Senator of the United States, and as President of the Confederacy, was but the crest of the mighty wave of Southern sentiment surging
below him, and was not only powerless to calm, but often to guide the swell
of its swollen waters.

Edmund Burke, speaking of our first Revolution, said he knew not how to
frame an indictment against a whole people.[15] The Government of the

14. When De Leon wrote his memoir, Davis was a prisoner at Fort Monroe, Virginia, awaiting a
trial for treason that never came. He would be released in 1867. De Leon's publication of the letters
was surely intended to counter the treason charges.

15. The eighteenth-century Irish-born statesman Edmund Burke spoke frequently on individual responsibility.

United States seems destined likewise to fail in attempting what the great English statesman shrunk from; for the trial of Jefferson Davis, for treason, embodies and embraces the act of the people, of whom he was and is the representative man.

CHAPTER 2
GENERAL OPINION IN EUROPE OF AMERICA
AND THE AMERICANS

On my arrival from Egypt, I found the whole of Europe in a ferment over the schism so unexpectedly breaking out in the Great Republic, whose quarrels and bickerings her nations have regarded only as family jars of no serious significance; and it was a long time before the magnitude or bitterness of the quarrel could be thoroughly comprehended abroad.

As an explanation of the condition of the foreign mind, and of the expression of its sympathies at the opening of the struggle, after secession and war became fixed facts, it may be useful to trace the current of thought and feeling a little in advance, as giving a clue to its subsequent development.

There were two nations only which ever took much interest in, or attempted to comprehend, the real character and facts of the great quarrel—England and France. Of the two, the first only succeeded in thoroughly understanding the question, the similarity of language, ideas and institutions giving her a clearer insight into our affairs than her neighbor could ever attain. In fact it may truly be said that the English estimate of the varying fortunes of the conflict was generally accepted by the continent as the correct one, and shortly after the opening of the struggle, by a tacit consent, the recognition or non-recognition of the "so-called Confederacy" by Europe was left to the decision of England and France. The other powers declined always to act until one or the other of these had taken the initiative.[1]

Americans are apt to complain now—as they did at the time with more vivid indignation—that Europe did not sympathize with the North, or denounce the South for its revolutionary attempt; but on the contrary, seemed rather to enjoy the strife and to encourage the combatants. This, they agreed, showed bad feeling and bad faith on the part of friendly nations, who should have frowned down the disunionists. But any American citizen, who, at this

1. De Leon's is an accurate summation of the European attitude toward support for the Confederacy.

time, calmly reflects or reasons on the subject, may well ask himself what reason had foreign governments or people to love America or Americans?

Why should they be expected to sympathize or affiliate with a government antagonistic to their own, and with a people who loudly proclaimed their superiority over the subjects of "European despotisms."

The whole history of the intercourse of the American Government with foreign powers, and especially with the "mother country," England, shows how little that people had to love us. And to a less extent there was not a foreign government which had not some old grudge against the aggressive and arbitrary spirit of the Young Republic which interfered to propagate its principles all the world over, in antagonism to the established opinions and institutions of Europe.

Take England for example. The diplomatic correspondence between the two governments shows a long series of disputes—often threatening war—on all imaginable questions of boundary, fishery, and other topics. No Fourth of July ever passed over without allusions to the old Revolutionary memories, to the War of 1812, and to the way in which we "whipped the British," and significant promises of our willingness to do it again whenever required, formed the staple of those annual celebrations, were printed in all our newspapers, and transferred, with flaming comments, to those English journals which dreaded the contagion of republicanism.

Anyone who recollects the Anglo-phobia created by the "Fifty-four forty or Fight" controversy on the Northeastern Boundary question—settled by the Ashburton-Webster treaty, in which the late lamented Sir Frederick Bruce took his first lessons in diplomacy—or the equally angry quarrel over the Northwestern Boundary, in which General Harney figured so conspicuously, can wonder little at the ill-feeling they created between two people equally arrogant and equally jealous of each other.[2] Then, too, Canada has always been a running sore in the side of England, which the stimulants applied by American sympathies have kept in a state of chronic irritation.

Besides these causes of annoyance, England saw with alarm the commercial competition which America was waging; and that the empire of the seas

2. De Leon is a bit confused here. "Fifty-four forty or fight" emerged as a political slogan during the controversy with Britain over the boundary of Oregon in 1845, which was on the *northwestern*, not the northeastern boundary of the United States. The 1842 treaty negotiated between Daniel Webster and Alexander Baring, Lord Ashburton, finally settled the northeastern international boundary between Canada and the state of Maine. General William S. Harney nearly caused a collision with Britain over San Juan Island when he was in command in Oregon in the 1850s.

was probably to be wrested from her hands by those "American Cousins," whose love was in an inverse ratio to their relationship, and whose language, in speaking of their venerable ancestress, was not always respectful.

This wounded pride, mortified vanity and self-respect, combined to make England feel anything but an ardent wish for the welfare of the American people. These respected neither her traditions nor her example, interfered seriously with her material interests, and at the same time gave her disaffected subjects at home a fruitful theme for agitation in the contrast between the two governments.

France, although bound to the United States by the old souvenirs of the Revolution, and the participation of La Fayette and Rochambeau in that conflict, was not forgetful of the arrogant tone in which General Jackson demanded—and obtained—the payment of an indemnity from Louis Philippe.[3] Nor was she oblivious to the ostentatious display of the sympathy felt for Russia in the Crimean war, in which both her pride and her interest were so strongly enlisted. Moreover, as representing Saxon in opposition to the Latin race—the Spaniard and Frenchman, who had vainly attempted to colonize the Mississippi—the American had no hold on the affection of the French people who regarded the Yankee as an unrefined, tobacco-chewing Englishman.

Spain, knowing how we coveted Cuba, and opposed her intervention in her revolted South American colonies, looked upon America as the lion in her path to a renewed empire.[4]

Austria remembered the Koszta case, when she was bullied in the face of Europe. Prussia had her diplomatic correspondence full of angry controversy as to the citizenship of returning refugees from her military conscription who all claimed to be American citizens.

The evidence of the feeling, both of England and France, was given in the treatment of our Military Commission, sent over during the Crimean war,

3. Marie Joseph Paul, Marquis de Lafayette, of course, was the most notable of the Frenchmen who took arms in aid of the colonies in the Revolution. Jean Baptiste Donathien de Vimeur, Comte de Rochambeau, commanded the French army sent to aid Washington in 1780 and that also took a prominent part in the decisive victory at Yorktown in 1781. Andrew Jackson risked war with France in 1834–1835 over French failure to pay a spoliation claim negotiated to recompense Americans who lost money due to the Napoleonic wars. King Louis-Philippe gave in to Jackson's scarcely veiled threat of hostile action if the debt were not paid.

4. Interest in the acquisition of Cuba went back more than half a century, especially among Southern leaders who saw its agricultural riches, its commanding position in the Caribbean, and its potential to make one or more new slave states.

and in which General McClellan figured. This Commission was received with effusion by Russia, but met the cold shoulder from both the English and French authorities.[5]

The general tone of the American Press has always been unpalatable to Europe; and in Congress, allusions to the "worn-out despotisms of Europe," and parallels between the enslaved condition of their subjects and our free and enlightened citizens formed the staple of many harangues.

Even in the better days of the Senate, when it was filled by able and veteran statesmen, instead of demagogues and stump speakers, men as marked for position and attainments as General Cass, did not disdain to pander to those prejudices, and indulge in wholesale invective of this description.[6]

Before the war, the differences of character, habits, and manners between the Northerner and Southerner, the Eastern and the Western man, were understood by very few persons abroad. The whole American population was classed under the general title of "Yankee," and supposed to have the same peculiarities, viz.: great loudness of speech and vehemence of assertion, especially in public places; eternal glorification of all American, and disparagement of all European things; and a desire to always wear clothes of glossy black broad-cloth, relieved by satin vests of bright hues, with the inevitable dress-coat for morning wear. Profuse tobacco-chewing and smoking, accompanied by copious expectoration on all surrounding objects in the absence of spittoons, which are not of European invention; and ignorance and contempt of all foreign usages and languages, and a violation of all established ceremonial. Add to these a nasal intonation and a swaggering defiance of all established usages—such as eating with the knife and picking the teeth with the fork—and you have, scarcely caricatured, the foreigner's idea of the typical American. For the quiet, well-bred American, who, like well-bred people from other countries, did not obtrusively assert his nationality, or did not otherwise fail to conform to the usages of those around him, was generally mistaken for an Englishman; while our loud and self-asserting compatriot bore away the palm of nationality, and caused the American to be generally regarded as a cross between Davy Crockett and Sam Slick.[7]

5. In 1855 George B. McClellan was appointed the junior member of a military commission to go observe the war then being fought in the Russian Crimea by Russia and Britain.

6. Lewis Cass had been a major general in the War of 1812 and later served in the Senate. His anti-British sentiments were well known and often enunciated.

7. David Crockett of Tennessee had become an American folk character even before his death in 1836. A fictional counterpart was Sam Slick, a crafty itinerant Yankee clock maker who passed acerbic

As our people began to travel abroad more than any others, their walk and conversation did not improve the foreign opinion. On the Continent, the Englishman was disliked for his silence and reserve, which were imputed to pride and arrogance. But the American, if not amenable to this reproach, sinned on the other side: he was not silent, or reserved, neither was he proud. On the contrary, his loquacity and his fearful gift of familiarity astonished the natives of the countries he visited; and his curiosity, insatiable as the grave, violated all the conventions of foreign intercourse and habits.

The "Live Yankee" was made a favorite character on the foreign stage, and caricatures of him superceded those of "Les Anglais" in Continental shop windows. In England, where he ought to have been most at home, he was least so; the points of repulsion being more numerous in consequence of his using the same language and acknowledging the same standard of taste.

Entertaining these views and feelings it is not to be wondered at that Englishmen did not cherish a fervent affection for America, or mourn over the probable disruption and division of the encroaching republic. On the Continent the traveling American, though less objectionable and antipathic to the population, was, classed with the traveling Englishman, only regarded as a more objectionable barbarian. His presence was looked on as rather a profanation in art galleries and the studios of artists, or amid the ruins of old empires that inspired him with no reverence, until he came to dispense his dollars with a lavish hand for objects of which they believed he did not comprehend the value.

But deeper than these surface causes; with reflecting men who had lived to see the lurid light of the French Revolution throw its baleful glare over Europe; who identified Republicanism with the excesses of that mad dance of death, and in the cap of Liberty, recognized only the red cap of French *Carmagnole*, with its refrain of "*Ca Ira!*" and the "Marseillaise," the supposed failure of the American experiment was a source of joy.[8] For Continental Europe regarded it as the trial of democratic institutions. She saw only a struggle between the "fierce democracie" and a privileged class who denied the great democratic dogma dear to Mazzini, Garibaldi, and to all foreign revo-

---

commentaries on the society of the era, created in a series of novels by Thomas Chandler. The Slick stories are credited as the origin of numerous American expressions and adages, such as "It's Raining Cats and Dogs," "The Early Bird Gets the Worm," "Don't Take Any Wooden Nickels," "A Stitch in Time Saves Nine," and "Quick as a Wink."

8. The *carmagnole* was a popular street dance during the Reign of Terror in France, deriving its name from the wide-lapelled jacket worn by Jacobin revolutionaries.

lutionists—that all men are and should be free and equal, irrespective of culture, color, or property; and should be entitled to social as well as political equality.[9]

Hence the only class in Europe really sympathetic with the North was to be found in the ranks of the Revolutionary party of France, of Italy, and of Germany. In England, the Radicals and Chartists—reinforced afterwards by the mill-owners and cotton spinners of Manchester and Birmingham—made the bulk of the well-wishers to the Northern cause.

It can neither be denied or doubted that the intelligence and wealth of these countries were ranged on the Southern side, considering it the conservative influence; and had the vote been polled at an early stage of the quarrel, the immense majority in any European country would have been found in favor of the Secessionists.[10]

As the struggle proceeded, partisanship on both sides became strong and acrimonious; but, until it was over, the relative positions of the masses did not alter much, although the partisans of the North were much the noisiest in proportion to their numbers. They reminded one of the striking image of Burke, applied to the English sympathizers with the French Revolution in his day: "The shrill grasshoppers," said he, "fill the field with their clamors, while the majestic oxen repose in peace beneath the shadows of the mighty oaks."

9. Giuseppe Mazzini was an Italian patriot and partner of Giuseppe Garibaldi and others of the "Risorgimento" that led, through a succession of fits and starts, to the successful creation of modern Italy.

10. De Leon's conclusion about majority sentiment for the South in Europe would be very open to debate.

CHAPTER 3
FEELING OF FRANCE AT THE OPENING OF THE WAR

I reached Paris in the month of May, 1861, and found Mr. Faulkner still fill-
ing his post as United States Minister there, conceiving it his duty to remain
until the actual arrival of his successor, Mr. Dayton.[1] Virginia had already seceded from the Union on the 17th April, 1861, and Mr. Faulkner, still declaring his intention of linking his fortunes with hers, at the same time
continued to represent the United States at Paris and introduce his successor at Court.

By curious coincidence, on the very day his State seceded from the Union,
and four days after hostilities had actually commenced by the attack on Fort
Sumter—the 17th day of April—Mr. Faulkner had an interview with Mr.
Thouvenel for the purpose of presenting him, as instructed, Mr. Lincoln's
inaugural.[2]

Some curious conversation took place at this interview in view of the
events then transpiring on the other side, and it is instructive as showing the
animus and opinions of the then Minister of Foreign Affairs, as well as those
of the Acting United States Ambassador.

"I said to him," reports Mr. Faulkner in his dispatch, "that the President
thought it not impossible an appeal would be made before long by the Confederate States to France, and to other foreign powers, for recognition of
their independence, and that it would meet with opposition from the Minister of the United States. The only request I would then make was that no
proposition recognizing the permanent dismemberment of the Federal

1. Virginian Charles J. Faulkner was Buchanan's pro-secession minister to France. He resigned
in January 1861, but remained in Paris until Lincoln replaced him with William L. Dayton.

2. De Leon is in error. The conference between Faulkner and Thouvenel took place on April 15.
Antoine Edouard Thouvenel was French foreign minister. On March 9, 1861, Secretary of State
William H. Seward sent instructions to all foreign representatives to present the Union's position
in the controversy and provide copies of Lincoln's March 4, 1861, inaugural. Seward to Ministers of
the United States, March 9, 1861, *Executive Documents of the Senate of the United States for the 2nd Session of the 37th Congress, 1861–1862* (Washington, DC, 1861), vol. 1, pp. 32–33.

Union should be considered by the French Government before the reception of the new minister already appointed."

Mr. Thouvenel replied that no application had yet been made to him in any form for the recognition of the independence of those States, adding his own belief that "the maintenance of the Union and its integrity was to be desired for the benefit of the people North and South, as well as for the interest of France," and that no precipitate action would be taken by the Emperor.

Thus far the official interview. But then ensued a freer conversation between the awkwardly situated Ambassador, whose convictions and instructions did not accord, and the astute Frenchman, who was thoroughly cognizant of that fact, and sought his private views as foreshadowing those of his Southern brethren.

Mr. Thouvenel interrogated the Minister whether there was not a division of opinion in the United States Cabinet on this question; to which an evasive reply was given, much to Mr. Seward's subsequent indignation.

In reply to another leading question, Mr. Faulkner stated that, in his opinion, "force would not be employed by the Federal Government. He thought the only solution of the difficulty was to be found in such mode of constitutional compact as would invite the seceded States back into the Union, or in a peaceable acquiescence."

Mr. Thouvenel emphatically declared that he thought the employment of force would be unwise, as it would cause a further rupture, and drive other Southern States to join those already in opposition to the Federal Government.[3]

To all persons acquainted with diplomacy it will be evident that utterances such as these—made unofficially, because officially they were impossible—carried great weight with them, and the more so because coming from a friendly source. Yet Mr. Seward's dispatch on this subject to Mr. Dayton conveys a rebuke to the Minister who held those opinions, and a reproach to the French statesman who concurred in them. After declaring emphatically there was no division in the Cabinet, and that Mr. Thouvenel must be so informed, it concludes with this swelling sentence, which surprised all parties interested very much indeed, and did not add to the Secretary's reputation as a "candid statesman," either at home or abroad:

3. De Leon's account is in the main accurate, clearly drawn from Faulkner's April 15, 1861, dispatch to Seward, now in State Department Correspondence, Diplomatic Dispatches, France, Record Group 59.2.2, no. 119, National Archives, Washington, DC. His quotations are inaccurate in places, though they do not alter the meaning.

"Tell Mr. Thouvenel," says Mr. Seward, under date of May 4, "with the highest consideration and good feeling, that the thought of the dissolution of this Union, either peaceably or by force, has never entered the mind of any candid statesman here, and that it is high time it be dismissed by statesmen in Europe."[4]

When Mr. Dayton read this to Mr. Thouvenel, that practiced diplomat only smiled blandly, shrugged his shoulders, and inquired if Mr. Dayton had seen the new opera. He considered comment superfluous, as, doubtless, did Mr. Dayton, a very sensible man, and one of the most respected representatives of his country.

At the same moment I found in Paris a representative of one of the seceded States in the person of Thomas Butler King, of Georgia. He had been charged by the Empire State of the South to represent her commercial interests—and, incidentally, her political—in England and France, and, if I mistake not, was the first Commissioner in fact, if not in name, sent abroad. Though Mr. King has been dead several years, I believe his services to his State and to the cause, in which he embarked with all the energies of his head and heart, were never either appreciated or rewarded. I desire now to do his memory the tardy justice of recounting his unrecognized labors.[5]

He was sent abroad by his State immediately after her ordinance of secession was promulgated, and remained until after the arrival of the Confederate Commissioners. Then, deeming the further exercise of his functions incompatible with theirs, as his State had joined the new Confederacy, he returned home through the blockade in the autumn of 1861, suffering shipwreck and almost capture in his transit via Havana and New Orleans.

On my return to Richmond, in April, 1862, I volunteered my testimony as to the value of his services to Mr. Benjamin, the then Secretary of State, and urged the recognition of them by sending Mr. King back to Europe to continue his useful labors.[6] I did not succeed in effecting this, much to my own

4. Seward to Dayton, May 4, 1861, State Department Correspondence, Diplomatic Instructions, France, Record Group 59.2.2, 15:530–533, no. 7, National Archives, Washington, DC.

5. Thomas Butler King of Georgia was a planter and one-time congressman appointed by the state of Georgia to promote trade in Europe shortly after secession.

6. Judah P. Benjamin was just barely secretary of state in April 1862. A former senator from Louisiana, Benjamin first entered the Davis cabinet as attorney general in February 1861. In September, lacking all qualification for the post, he succeeded to the position of secretary of war and endured a turbulent incumbency before being replaced in March 1862. Just before De Leon's arrival in Richmond, Davis named Benjamin secretary of state, the position he would hold until the death of the Confederacy.

disappointment, and as I candidly believe, to the detriment of the public service. He was not only a practiced politician in the American sense of the term—his long career in Congress having made him familiar with home affairs North and South—but what was more rare to find, a statesman also, a man of enlarged views, a polished manner and most winning deportment—well fitted "to shine at court" with unaffected grace.

Though a Northern man by birth, his life and fortune were dedicated to the State and section of his adoption. One noble son, whom none knew but to love, perished on the battlefield; another survives, who earned an enviable reputation in many a hard fought engagement.[7] He himself, worn out by anxiety of mind and sickness of heart, sleeps now where neither praise nor censure can touch him more.[8] But it is only strict justice to say that as he was the first authorized representative of the "Rebellion" abroad in point of time, so he was very far from being last in ability, in energy, or in personal influence.

In his own field, before the arrival of the Commissioners of the Confederate Government, he labored diligently and effectively, and had already prepared the foreign mind for their reception—by publications in the journals and by conversations with officials in high positions at Paris. He also published an able pamphlet, in French and English, chiefly devoted to the advantages which would accrue to France from a commercial treaty directly with Georgia, but incidentally explaining the grounds and reasons of her secession from the Union with great force and clearness.[9]

Manners, as well as morals and capacity, are needed for the fulfillment of such functions as these; and Mr. King possessed them all. Candor compels me to add that I could not truthfully pass the same eulogium on all his successors.

Although at that time the seceded States—afterwards to expand into the "so-called Confederacy"—had no other accredited representatives in Europe, except such as were sent to purchase supplies, or who had patriotically obtained fat jobs in the shape of contracts, yet there was no lack of unaccredited agents to be found both at London and Paris.

7. John Floyd King and Henry Lord King entered the Confederate service, and the latter was killed at the Battle of Fredericksburg, Virginia, in December 1862.

8. Thomas Butler King died May 10, 1874.

9. Paul Pecquet du Bellet noted in his memoir that "Mr. King had written a very able book upon the American War, with a review of the Northern policy and the full statistics of the Southern produce and commerce." William Stanley Hoole, ed., *The Diplomacy of the Confederate Cabinet of Richmond and Its Agents Abroad* (Tuscaloosa, AL, 1963), p. 32.

Many of the gentlemen, then so ardent and "patriotic," would probably not thank me now for the mention of their names. I shall, therefore, restrict myself to the unction of those who prove their faiths by their works, and who actually did and suffered something in addition to talking and writing something at a safe distance from the field of strife—self appointed foreign agents, whose commissions were their own autographs, and whose love for the South was of that peculiar kind which burns most fervently at a distance from the object of affection.

These I class with that swarm of pecuniary patriots who only ventured into the Confederacy to bring fat contracts out.

To both these classes I would apply the words of Dante: "Let us not speak of them, but pass them by in silence."[10] For they both did no good and much harm to the Confederate cause, by their indiscreet utterances and unauthorized statements in the one case; and by their peddling Southern credit idly and foolishly in European markets, in the other. That there were honorable exceptions to both classes above named, is true; but they were only numerous enough to constitute the rule.

Confederate credit—in both senses of the term—was seriously affected from the first, by the frauds and follies perpetrated in its name, both with and without authority; and much the same thing may be truthfully said of Federal credit also.

It is the curse, as it is ever the consequence of revolutions, that much of the scum is brought to the surface, and ours proved no exception to the rule. Even at this early stage of proceedings, something of this was perceptible, and—to the shame and sorrow of honest and honorable men on both sides— it raised itself to the proportions of a great nuisance, long before the four years war had terminated.

It would, of course, be impossible for me to chronicle the names of all the amateurs who did really good service to the Southern cause by pen, or otherwise; but a few of the noteworthy may be cited. One was that of a man, like T. Butler King, of Northern origin, but resident from early manhood in Savannah, Georgia, where for many years he edited the *Republican* newspaper. I refer to Joseph L. Locke.[11]

He had retired with a competency, and had been living in Italy some years prior to the secession of his adopted State. The first vindication of that move-

10. The actual quotation from the third canto of Dante's *Inferno* reads: "Let us not talk of them, but look and pass."

11. Joseph L. Locke sold the Savannah *Republican* in 1853 and shortly afterward moved to Italy.

ment, to my knowledge, came in a letter written by him, written from Rome to *Galignani's Messenger.*[12] In this, he expounded and explained with great clearness of language and cogency of reasoning, the States Rights doctrine and its corollary—the right of secession. That letter excited much critical comment, and was a model of good taste, good temper and close logic. He proved his faith afterwards by his works, returning home and taking an active part in the struggle in his adopted State. Like his friend, Mr. King, he did not long survive the war, dying suddenly at Savannah, immediately after its close.

There were others too, not bound to the South by either birth or residence, who at this early period espoused her cause with zeal and intelligence. Of these I can only note a few. Most active among them were M. Ernest Bellot de Minières, whose name is familiar to Americans in connection with the great Kanawha Canal Company, of Virginia, and Dr. Charles Girard, for many years Professor of the Smithsonian Institute, at Washington.[13]

The former published a most able brochure on the resources of the South, and on the political aspects of the question as affecting French interests.[14] The latter, as one of the co-laborators of the *Pays* newspaper, published a series of strong articles on the Southern side of the question, and subsequently visited the Confederacy and published the results of his investigation on his return.[15]

Several gentlemen of French extraction, who had resided in, or visited New Orleans, also contributed to the French newspapers in the same sense; and one, who had formerly been a pro-slavery advocate and unsuccessful editor in that city—Mr. Malespine—distinguished himself by the bitterness of his assaults on his former friends and patrons.[16]

But one conspicuous Frenchman volunteered to take an active part in the war. One morning, early in March, I met at breakfast a French gentleman,

12. Published in Paris, *Galignani's Messenger* was an influential newspaper with British readers in the mid-nineteenth century.

13. Parisian essayist and poet Bellot was also a merchant who would ship war goods through the blockade into the Confederacy later in the war. He wrote pro-Confederate propaganda during the war (see note 14 below). The naturalist Charles Girard was born in Mulhausen, France, but moved to Washington, D.C., and attached himself to the Smithsonian Institution, where he remained until 1859. He is far better known for his books and essays on reptiles than for his pro-Confederate writings.

14. M. Ernest Bellot des Minières, *La Question Américaine; Suivie d'un Appendice sur le Coton, le Tabac, et le Commerce Général des Anciens États-Unis.* Paris, 1861.

15. *Le Pays* was a popular and influential Paris newspaper.

16. A. Malespine wrote essays for the Parisian sheet *Opinion Nationale* and served as a deputy in the legislature.

who—emulous of the fame of Lafayette in the American Revolution—proposed acting a similar part in what he considered a similar quarrel.[17]

The Prince Camille de Polignac bears a name already historic. A noble scion of a noble stock, highly accomplished in mind and manners, although yet a young man, he had shown much military genius in foreign service. Actuated by the most unselfish motives, and under the spur of an enthusiasm, which even those who think it misdirected, must admit chivalric, this gay child of the Boulevardes left all the pleasures and luxuries of Paris to throw himself, heart and soul, into the Southern struggle. Coming through the blockade, he tendered his sword and his life to the Confederate authorities, and accepting a staff appointment, served so well and faithfully in the field as to gain a separate command, and, finally, by his merit alone, to rise to the rank of Major General.[18]

He adhered to the fortunes of the cause he had espoused to the bitter end, and, after the fall of the Confederacy, published over his own signature in the *Patrie*, a vindication of his former comrades in arms from some aspersions that had been cast upon them and on the cause for which they fought.[19]

It is true the Count de Paris and the Duc de Chartres made an ostentatious display of sympathy on the Northern side by taking the ornamental position of aides-de-camp to General McClellan; but their campaigns were bloodless—political, not military—as was the visit of the Prince Napoleon.[20] Prince de Polignac came to fight, and did fight throughout the war, though happily he survived it.

Although much struck by the generous ardor of the young prince, I deemed it but fair to warn him of the hardships and perils which awaited

17. Since Polignac enlisted with the Confederacy in 1861, by context De Leon can only mean he met Polignac in March 1861, which is puzzling, given that he says he did not himself reach Paris until May of that year. Polignac was in Central America previously.

18. Camille Armand Jules Marie, Prince de Polignac, came from a distinguished aristocratic French family and already had a laudable record in the Crimean War behind him when he went exploring in South America in 1859. At the outbreak of the Civil War in America, Polignac went to the Confederacy and was commissioned a lieutenant colonel in July 1861. By January 1863 he was a brigadier general and would spend the balance of the war with the Southern forces west of the Mississippi, rising to major general, until March 1865 when he left for France to try to enlist its aid for the South. He arrived too late to be of any aid and lived out his days in France, frequently writing of his war experiences.

19. *La Patrie* was one of the more respected of the Parisian newspapers in the 1860s. Polignac's 1865–1867 article has not been identified.

20. The Comte de Paris, a pretender to the French throne, came to America in 1861 with his brother, the Duc de Chartres, and their uncle, the Prince de Joinville. All three became aides on the

him in the South, and of which he could not be well informed. But these very things seemed only to strengthen his resolve and stimulate him more; and as I looked upon the frail figure and pallid face of this young elegant of the Boulevards, I could only wonder to find him so resolute and so reckless. He proved himself equal to the dangers and to the privations and won his spurs like a true knight. Concealing the hand of iron under the velvet glove, he was a true type of that old *noblesse* of France that wrote on all time, *"Bon sang ne peut mentir."*[21]

In the upheaving of his own country—now waiting only the removal of Louis Napoleon to burst into revolution—the name of Camille de Polignac will doubtless be heard again. He is a legitimist, and therefore does not seek the promotion he could surely gain under the present empire.[22]

Such was the external appearance of things at Paris, before the arrival of the accredited commissioners of the "so-called" Confederate States. A new impulse was given to inquiry and discussion by the announcement of the formation of the new Confederacy and the mission of its envoys, and I reached Paris just as this fermentation was taking place.

This step on the part of the newly born applicant for admission into the family of nations, brought her and her affairs immediately before the Emperor and his government.

Let us now see how he and they stood affected towards it in the initial stages; who were the friends and who the foes of the "erring sisters," as General Scott termed them, when it was now evident the Washington Government would not permit them to "depart in peace," as he advised.[23]

---

staff of now-General George B. McClellan, commanding the Army of the Potomac as it prepared to invade Virginia. The Prince Napoleon, cousin of Napoleon III, made a visit to Washington that same year, and for a time thereafter accompanied McClellan's army as a noncombatant observer.

21. "Good blood does not lie."

22. Polignac died in Paris on November 15, 1913, the last surviving major general of the Confederacy.

23. De Leon is mistaken. It was New York publisher Horace Greeley, not Winfield Scott, who early in the war declared that the North should "let the erring sisters go in peace."

CHAPTER 4
PEN PORTRAITS OF THE EMPEROR, OF HIS CABINET,
AND OF THE OPPOSITION

———•◦•———

In the very early days of the struggle but a languid interest was felt or expressed as to the merits of the conflicting parties, either in French journals or in French society—outside of the Cabinet, or of the opposition. The ignorance displayed, not only by private individuals but also by publicists, on all topics connected with the relative resources of the Northern and Southern States, with their geographical and statistical situation, and with the political questions involved, could scarcely be exaggerated. Instances, which, if cited, would appear actually ludicrous, were consistently falling under my observation.

For example, the Southern States *(Les Etats du Sud)* were generally supposed to be in South America; and the conflict was popularly believed to be between the States of North and South America.[1]

Even in high official quarters, the ignorance displayed in relation to the several States and the Federal Government, their reciprocal relations and relative power and resources, was absolutely astounding. This was the more remarkable from the fact that decidedly the ablest and clearest exposition of American Democracy, ever made in any language, was the well known work of the Frenchman, de Tocqueville, the English translation of which has been for many years the text book even of American statesmen.[2]

A noteworthy exception to this remark was to be found in the person of the Emperor himself, whose mind slowly and painfully elaborates every question submitted to it; and whose memory seems never to relax its tenacious grasp of any information it has acquired. For many years I watched

1. This erroneous view still prevails in some parts of the world, as was revealed to the editor by a BBC interviewer in London as recently as 1990.

2. De Leon refers to Alexis de Tocqueville's *De la Démocratie en Amérique*, or *Democracy in America*, first published in 1835. Despite some misconceptions and prejudices of the author's, it remains a brilliant observation on the character and personality of Americans and their political and social scene.

from a distance—and during the war more nearly—the workings of that subtle and powerful intellect, and of that all-pervading policy, which made Europe his chess-board, whose pawns were crowned kings.

Slowly that dull, but all penetrating eye, was turned towards our coming conflict; patiently was every move of the game on both sides watched and analyzed. If some of the sudden changes here baffled even his practiced insight, what wonder was it?[3] They surprised none more than the actors themselves in that great drama, who had loosed energies and passions they could not control; but which swept them along with the mad rush of the Mississippi when her levies have given way.

For like the great stream, the great American revolution found no Mirabeau—North or South—to master its wild power.[4] It swept on both men and measures in the mighty ebb and flood of public opinion in both sections, till the very end; and its retiring waves are now leaving the sprits that invoked it like stranded wrecks upon a desolate beach.

But what Napoleon looked to first and last—as he was bound to do—were the interests of his empire, and how they could be best subserved by the death grapple of North and South. No sentimental consideration—no personal preferences ever swayed his policy in relation to American affairs.

Egotist he doubtless is; yet is that egotism so intertwined with the glory and prosperity of France as to rise almost to the elevation of virtue. There is nothing mean or narrow in it: and if his policy sometimes make him seem faithless, pitiless and cruel—as in the case of Maximilian and in ours—yet, doubtless he justifies himself to his own inner consciousness by the belief that such is his duty, as the living embodiment of a dynasty and of an empire, in great part the creation of his own genius.[5]

As early as the spring of 1861—when I reached Paris, and when the issues of peaceful separation, or compromise restoring the separated States, occupied the public mind to the exclusion of the possibility of war, looming in the distance—the idea of the commercial advantages to accrue France, from treaties with the cotton and sugar States of the South, had already been

3. Historians regard Napoleon as an able statesman, with rather pro-Southern leanings, chiefly from policy looking to the advantage of France. Still he carefully avoided offending the North, and as a result remained noncommittal throughout the war. His chief concern was that the war in America interfered with the rebuilding of the French economy.

4. Honoré Gabriel Riquetti, Comte de Mirabeau, was a leading French revolutionary whose incendiary speeches helped to galvanize the populace to rise against the monarchy. In the margin De Leon has written "Richelieu Beloved France."

5. See chapter 19 for more on Maximilian.

suggested by Thos. Butler King to the then Minister of Commerce; and had, through him, been submitted to the Emperor.

One of the peculiarities of the Emperor is his secretiveness. His left hand never knows what his right hand is doing; and far less does he divulge to his ministers his real impressions or his intentions. The sudden changes in both his foreign and domestic policy, that startle France, are often equal surprises to his most trusted advisors and dearest friends. To a limited extent there were two exceptions, both of whom have since passed into the "silent land." They were the Duc de Morny, whose peculiar relations to him are well known and who was kindred in daring genius, as well as in blood, to the Emperor; and Monsieur Mocquard, his confidential secretary, whose characteristics of mind and person reminded the spectator more of Voltaire than any living man, and who equaled the Sage of Ferney in secretiveness, and gall profusely poured out on all except his master.[6]

So what the Emperor thought at this early period was told to none, save, perhaps, the favored few who never divulged, if they knew it. His ministers were as much mystified as the public. The official press abstained from meddling much with the subject, and the unofficial press displayed gross ignorance of the whole matter.

The Emperor himself made no sign, and although listening attentively to all that was said by all Americans, official and otherwise, who had access to him, fell back on the "great talent for silence" he possesses in an eminent degree, and said nothing to indicate a bias to one side or the other.

I have reason to believe that the personal sympathies of the Duc de Morny were inclined towards the Southerners from an early day, and he was consistent to the last in his preference; but he never permitted it for one instant to bias his judgment, or to close his eyes to the paramount interests of France. Still it cannot be doubted that his influence near the Emperor—as well as that of the Duc de Persigny, another trusted friend and counselor—was beneficial to the South, by confirming any prepossessions which the Emperor might secretly, as the Empress did openly, entertain for the weaker of the combatants.[7]

6. Charles Louis Joseph, Duke of Morny, was president of the French legislature. De Leon would later describe de Morny as "the brain of the Napoleonic Council," a man of "winning manners and graceful address." De Leon, *Thirty Years of My Life on Three Continents* (London, 1890), vol. 2, p. 55. Jean François Mocquard served as Napoleon's secretary, and in that position enjoyed considerable influence.

7. Fialin, Duke of Persigny, minister of the interior, exerted considerable influence on the French press. De Leon later described Persigny as impulsive, blunt, and very pro-Confederate, "one of the most honest and devoted men to the Emperor's person." *Thirty Years*, vol. 2, pp. 56–57.

For the Empress Eugenie, a true woman at heart, generous, impulsive, excitable, and with a hot Spanish blood coursing through her veins—found the reckless Southern spirit more congenial to her own than the cooler and more calculating character of the North. Moreover, she regarded the conflict in connection with her prejudices, both of religion and of race, as one between the Puritan descendent of the Anglo-Saxon in the North and the Catholic, or semi-Catholic Episcopalian of French or Spanish descent, in the South. And this view prevailed largely in France and the Continent, though not in England, where the matter was better understood. So the strongest and nearest influences near the Emperor were in favor of the South.[8]

As to M. Mocquard, he had no cosmopolite tendencies or affections. It is doubtful if he ever took much interest in either side of the question; but if he did he was too cautious to give public expression to his sentiments, or to venture on advising the Emperor on so delicate a subject.

The inner court influence in favor of the Northern side was that of the Prince Napoleon, a man of undoubted talent and equally distinguished audacity, who never hesitates to put himself in opposition to his imperial cousin, whenever it suits his own purposes or policy. Still, his influence, spite of repeated quarrels and even disgraces at Court, is certainly very great as a restraining, if not a convincing, one.[9]

Mr. Thouvenel, also, then Minister of Foreign Affairs—a statesman of the severest integrity and most unselfish patriotism, whose public and whose private character were both without stain—took much the same view as Prince Napoleon, though from very different motives. In the East I had known Mr. Thouvenel as Ambassador at Constantinople, and the impression which I then formed of him was heightened by subsequent observation of his character and course as Minister of Foreign Affairs.

He was as unlike the popular idea of what a Frenchman is as can be imagined. With a soldier-like bluntness of manner and bearing, a sharp, concise style of speech, and a directness of purpose which made him appear abrupt and almost rude, he was yet a man who inspired both respect and confidence. It was one of my great regrets at the time, that he, either from conviction or policy, inclined decidedly towards the Northern side, nor did he ever

8. The Empress Eugenie had considerable influence and occasionally presided over cabinet meetings in Napoleon's absence.

9. The Prince Napoleon stood second in line for the throne and wanted it. His support for the Union was unwavering and won much influence thanks to his time spent observing the war from McClellan's headquarters. He spoke through his own organ, the *Opinion Nationale*.

vary that attitude. It was probably to this, as well as to his obduracy in regard to the Roman question, that he owed his dismissal in 1862, when he was replaced by Drouyn de l'Huys, whose sympathies were different.[10]

Of the Prince Napoleon, who took a very decided part in the solution of this question in France, it will be necessary to speak frequently in the course of this narrative. For he not only took a lively interest in the matter, but from the commencement to the end of the war made himself the rallying point, and the Palais Royale, where he resided, the headquarters of the Northern party in France. It is but justice to him, however, to say that he was consistent in his attitude throughout; and even in the darkest hour of Federal fortunes, when the failure of the North and success of the South scarcely seemed doubtful, he never faltered in his opposition to the recognition of the Southern Confederacy, or wavered in his belief that the North would win.

Yet, although this championship operated upon the Court and Cabinet and rallied the old Republican party to its support—he, prince of the blood and highly endowed as such out of the public purse, being the acknowledged chief of the extreme Republicans there—nevertheless his personal unpopularity reflected on the cause he espoused. For, rightly or wrongly, there was and is no man in France more universally disliked—I may say detested—than Prince Napoleon, whose cant name, *Plon-Plon*, indicates the popular estimate of his character.[11]

To him, with equal justice, the Emperor might repeat what Charles II said to his brother James: "No one will ever kill me to make you king!" Those who do not love the Emperor still respect him, while his friends are devoted to him. But no man either loves or respects the Prince Napoleon, and the great mass of the French people believe him to be destitute of personal courage— an unpardonable sin in a country where life is held in such slight estimation, as weighed against glory or honor.

Moreover, many think and say that his pretended liberalism and championship of democratic ideas are but a blind; that he is only a decoy-duck for his imperial cousin, who has always the earliest information of plots and plans of the party most dangerous to himself and his dynasty. To give color to

10. The "Roman question" was how European statesmen referred to the threat of the revolutionary Garibaldi to capture the city of Rome, and the consequent embarrassment to France, which had recognized a new king of Italy in 1861. Thouvenel was dismissed on October 16, 1862, and Edouard Drouyn de Lhuys, a career diplomat and previous foreign minister, replaced him.

11. *Plon-Plon* was a popular perversion of the nickname *Craint-plon*—"Fear-bullet"—given to the Prince Napoleon as a result of his supposed hesitance to expose himself to fire in the Crimean War.

this idea, they cite the fact that his disgrace at court is always a very temporary affair; that even after most violent antagonism to, and apparent defiance of, the Emperor, his reinstatement to even greater favor and intimacy
is always rapid, and that he invariably gains, rather than loses, by his contu-
macy. This, under the present *regime*, is quite an exceptional case, for the
obduracy of the Emperor's resentments is as great as the tenacity of his gratitude. Suspicions have been excited by the exception, for it is evident neither
policy nor apprehension can have weight in the case of a man so unpopular
and personally so powerless for good or evil as the Prince Napoleon.

My own opinion, after long and careful observation of the relations between the Emperor and his cousin, differed from the popular one. Although
it is probable the Emperor preferred to see the Prince at the head of the Red
Republican party, rather than some real Democratic demagogue—knowing
that in the selfishness of the latter rested his own security that the plots
against him would not be carried to far—yet there was no love lost between
the two.

Inhabiting the Palais Royale, the Prince Napoleon inherited the policy of
his predecessor, the unprincipled Duc d'Orleans. Philippe Egalité made
himself a tribune of the people, and betrayed his family and his order, only
to perish on the guillotine by the hands of his own tools, who could not trust
a born aristocrat and prince, like himself.[12]

It suits neither the cautious character nor the selfish and sensual nature
of the Prince Napoleon to play this *rôle* too far; but that he has played it, and
is playing it in part, cannot be doubted. Compared with the Emperor, either
in courage, intellect, or craft, he was and is the Vulture as matched against
the Eagle.

The head and face of Prince Napoleon indicate his character, while both
remind one of the first Emperor in a coarse copy of the great original. You
see the same grand head and capacious brain, the same classic contour of
face and brow, only more gross and animal in expression. The coarseness of
the jaw indicates a stronger animality and more sensual nature; while the
iron will that sets its seal on the countenance of the first Napoleon is replaced by irresolute though cynical expression on that of his nephew.

I have dwelt thus long on the moral and mental characteristics of the
Prince Napoleon, because he played a most active and important part in the

12. Louis-Philippe-Joseph, Duc d'Orleans, was also known by the nickname Philippe Égalité.
He was an irresponsible wastrel who joined the revolutionaries during the Revolution and was for a
time their darling until he lost his head in 1793 during the Terror.

events I am about to record; and his political position and influence are so great in France, that he should not be passed over without such notice.

I give my own judgment of him for what it may be worth, as simply a personal estimate, but as I firmly believe an impartial one, which public opinion in Paris—whether justly or unjustly—will confirm.

Since the death of the Duc de Morny, the Prince Napoleon seems to have drawn nearer to the family circle, and to have exerted a greater influence than before.[13] It is even believed that he has replaced that much loved and trusted counselor in the Counsel of Regency—organized in the event of the death of the Emperor himself—in conjunction with the Empress, Count Walewski and the Duc de Persigny.[14]

The Imperial party being considered at an early day in the American quarrel as leaning towards the South, both from policy and principle, the opposition naturally espoused the other side. Although the rule of Napoleon over France is absolute, and his power truly imperial, in fact as well as name, yet is his bed not one of roses; and it is a grave error to suppose he ever dares to disregard and resist public opinion when decidedly expressed. The great end of all his policy is to found a dynasty based on public opinion and supported by popular sentiment; to identify his policy with the glory and prosperity of his people; and to be, as he claims, "Emperor of the French," rather than Emperor of France—a distinction with a difference, as the title he assumes clearly indicates.

Hence this great and growing distaste to his rule and reign—as evidenced by the existence of a powerful, if not numerous opposition party, whose headquarters are at Paris, and who have secured the entire representation of that city in the *Corps Legislatif*—has deprived him of that perfect freedom of action, on questions of external policy, which he is supposed to exercise. For, in fact, the President of the United States takes the responsibility of such measures with far less caution than does the absolute Emperor of France; and he cares far less for public resentment of the people he represents.

The Opposition in France is composed of three factions, agreeing on no other point than that of opposition to the Napoleon Dynasty. They are the Old Legitimists of the Faubourg St. Germain, who still cling to the old line and sustain the pretension of the Count de Chambord to the throne of his ancestors; the Orleanists, who see their constitutional king in the Count de

13. The Duke of Morny died March 10, 1865.

14. Count Alexander F. J. C. Walewski was a Russian who became a naturalized French citizen and served Napoleon as foreign minister, and then as minister of state.

Paris, the grandson of their citizen king, Louis Philippe; and the Red Republicans, who desire to make France a Republic on the American model.[15]

The first of these is effete and powerless. A shadow only of the memories of the past, clinging to its old traditions, and moving in a narrow and exclusive circle, it has no hold on the popular heart. The sentiment of loyalty to which it appeals has long since died into an echo in France. The eloquent old advocate, Berryer, is almost its last sworn champion in the *Corps Legislatif*, and it has no representative among the people.[16] It is a party which ever looks back—never forward; and its movements must, therefore, be crablike, not progressive.

Yet it is a party that records well-known historic names on its muster-role, and in the aristocratic precincts of the Faubourg St. Germain are to be found its head-quarters.

The second party is more youthful as well as more numerous; a party eminently conservative in character, and, above all things, respectable, in the English sense of the word. It numbers, in its ranks, many of the notables of the time of Louis Philippe, such as Guizot and Thiers, as well as the great body of the Bourgeoisie, or middle class, of whom the citizen king was the type and representative.[17]

But the most active, energetic and disturbing class of the Opposition, that which gives the Government the most anxiety, is the third—the Republican—composed, as it is, of all the ambitious and dissatisfied spirits of Young France, coupled with the survivors of the Government of 1848.[18] Added to these are many of the rising authors and contributors to journals, outside of the circle of court influence, who see in another revolution opportunities for that notoriety, which to a Frenchman—even more than to an American—is the very breath of life. For, although the Parisian loves luxury and respects money as a means to that end, yet he does not worship the golden calf near so devotedly as his Anglo-Saxon compeers on either side of the Atlantic. Glory and fame—to be in the mouths of men, and fill a place in their eyes, is with

15. Henri Dieudonné, Count de Chambord, was a dedicated champion of the pretensions of the Orleans. At the age of ten, in 1830, he was briefly proclaimed king, but then was forced into exile, from which he unrelentingly protested his right to the throne.

16. Pierre Antoine Berryer was a deputy and opposition leader in the legislature.

17. François Guizot had been prime minister in earlier days under the Orleans monarchy. Louis Adolpe Thiers was a journalist and historian who turned to politics and was for a time foreign minister before he fell out with Napoleon.

18. De Leon refers to the provisional government established after the attack on the Tuileries in February 1848.

him a stronger impulse; and hence Paris is, and ever has been, the focus of plots against the Government of the hour—whether that Government be under Bourbon or Napoleon—under a constitutional King without a charter, or an emperor chosen by universal suffrage.

Agreeing in nothing else, as before remarked, these three parties combine in opposing the policy of the Emperor and his supposed sympathies.

Many of the Republican leaders took the Northern side in our quarrel at the commencement, and adhered to it throughout. Still, the neutrality, which the French Government rigidly maintained through all its official acts and correspondence, gave them no just pretext for their outcry on this score; and they were compelled to urge the Government to show an actual sympathy with the North in order to keep that outcry up.

Thus stood matters in Paris when I reached that city in the early spring of 1861, before the arrival of the Commissioners, and immediately after the assembling of the convention to form a new Confederacy out of the States that had declared themselves out of the old Union, and free to form a new one.

In order to comprehend more thoroughly the foreign situation at this epic, a slight sketch of the state of public feeling, and of the attitude of parties on the other side of the British Channel, will complete this preliminary view.

CHAPTER 5
HOW COMING EVENTS CAST THEIR SHADOWS
IN ENGLAND IN 1861

The origin and causes of the war have been already treated by many able writers, among whom may be mentioned Mr. George Lunt, of Boston, and Mr. James Spence, of Liverpool.[1] An inner view is also promised from the pen of Mr. A. H. Stevens; so the subject may be regarded as exhausted, and certainly ought to be familiar to all American readers.[2]

To consider, or discuss it, does not fall within the scope or object of my labors; but it is necessary, occasionally, to refer to incidents connected with these topics, to show their bearing on the opinion of Europe. That wittiest of Englishmen, or of mortal men—Sidney Smith—has never been forgiven for asking the question, "Who reads an American book?"[3] But had he put the query in regard to an American newspaper, echo alone could have answered. In Europe, nobody does read them.

It was mainly to the London *Times* that the eyes of Europe were turned for early information of the struggle; for that great paper—which seeming to lead public opinion, really follows or anticipates it—is doubtless the great organ of English thinkers.[4]

It may justly be said that the *Times* was consistent only in inconsistency.

For more than a year preceding, that great mirror of British opinion had faithfully reflected the varying opinions entertained by thoughtful men, at the changing phases of American politics. Its editorials had pointed out to the British people, and to the Continental world, the strife of our sections,

1. George Lunt, *Origin of the Late* War (New York, 1866), and James Spence, *The American Union* (London, 1862).

2. De Leon refers to the forthcoming *A Constitutional View of the Late War between the States,* by Alexander H. Stephens, published in Philadelphia in 1868 and 1870.

3. De Leon refers to the English essayist Sydney Smith, who wrote in his review of *Annals of the United States,* by John Seybert: "In the four quarters of the globe, who reads an American book, or goes to an American play, or looks at an American picture or statue?"

4. In the margin De Leon has written "Telegraph," probably a reference to the London *Telegraph* and its role in the British press's discussion of the Confederacy.

and the probabilities of its prolongation or settlement—though the possibility of a civil war was never even hinted at. Some of these comments of the *Times* on the Boundary question, the John Brown raid, the Missouri Compromise, and slavery questions, are very curious and instructive, as are also the changes of its opinions on the secession, and the chances of the war in its earlier stages.

Before, and immediately after the commencement of the war, it supported the North and scoffed at the South. After the fall of Sumter and battle of Bull Run it turned to the Southern side; became its violent partisan after the Trent affair, and only deserted that line when the waning fortunes of the "so-called Confederacy" induced the belief that the cause was lost, and that through the blood and smoke of the struggle the North would emerge victorious. On the 14th of January, 1860, the *Times,* in a leading editorial, discussing the question of growing sectional hatred in the United States, uses this decided language, "That no disruption of the Federal Union will take place we certainly believe;" and reviewing the speeches of John Breckinridge and Henry A. Wise, on the situation, scoffs at the latter, while gravely deprecating the utterances of the former.[5] It likens Wise to "the Boston fanatics, who compared him to Pontius Pilate;" and thinks "they will set off each other, and no harm will ensue." On the 30th of the same month appears a leader on the importation of cotton, in which it sneers at the anti-slavery societies, and "prefers to have the cotton of slavery rather than not to have it at all."

These and similar declarations on the cotton supply question, tended greatly to produce and foster the Southern hallucination, that "cotton was king," and must secure the South a sure ally in Great Britain, whose principles were supposed to be deposited in her pockets.

The declarations and attitude of the outgoing and incoming Presidents were eagerly listened to, as indicating the actual situation and probable future. Mr. Buchanan took an early opportunity of enlightening Europe, and in his best diplomatic circular to the foreign agents of the United States, thus explained the circumstances concerned with Mr. Lincoln's election:

You are of course aware that the election of last November resulted in the choice of Mr. Abraham Lincoln; that he was the candidate of the Republican or anti-

5. On December 21, 1859, Vice President and Senator-elect John C. Breckinridge addressed the Kentucky legislature and raised the specter of disunion and civil war if the Republican Party were not stopped in the coming election. What made his speech disturbing was that theretofore he had been a noted moderate. Henry A. Wise, on the other hand, was an unabashed incendiary and secessionist, then sitting governor of Virginia.

slavery party; that the preceding discussion had been confined almost entirely to topics connected directly or indirectly with the subject of Negro slavery; that every Northern State cast its whole electoral vote (except three in New Jersey,) for Mr. Lincoln, while in the whole South the popular sentiment against him was absolutely universal.

This was accepted abroad as an authoritative exposition of the facts. The *Times* adopted the theory of Mr. Buchanan, that he "had no power to coerce," and heartily approved of his logic and his arguments, which it declared "conclusive." The earliest utterance of Mr. Lincoln only puzzled people at a distance, as they proved he had not definitely determined on his policy, but was drifting. But Mr. Seward was more explicit; and in one of his earliest dispatches to Mr. Adams uses this plain language, which did correctly indicate the purposes and policy of the administration, until the irresistible logic of events compelled a change of both:

> For these reasons he would not be disposed to reject a cardinal dogma of theirs (the Secessionists)—namely, that the Federal Government could not reduce the seceding States to obedience by conquest, even although he were disposed to question that proposition. But, in fact, the President willingly accepts it as true. Only an imperial or despotic government could subjugate thoroughly disaffected and insurrectionary members of the State. This federal republican system of ours is, of all forms of government, the very one most unfitted for such a labor. You will indulge in no expression of harshness or disrespect, or even impatience, concerning the seceding States, their agents or their people. But you will on the contrary remember that those States are now, as they always heretofore have been—and notwithstanding their temporary self-delusion, must always continue to be—equal and honored members of this Union.

And Mr. Greeley also, in the *Tribune*, at that time used language which, with the knowledge of his influence, and intimacy with Mr. Lincoln, induced the world to believe that coercion would not be attempted by the Washington Government.

Mr. Greeley's language was as follows:[6]

> And now, if the United States consider the value of the Union debatable, we maintain their right to discuss it. Nay, we hold with Jefferson, to the inalienable right of communities to alter or abolish forms of government that have become oppressive or injurious; and, if the Cotton States shall decide that they can do

---

6. In the margin De Leon further identified his subject as "H. Greeley."

better out of the Union than in it, we insist on letting them go in peace. The right to secede may be a revolutionary one, but it exists nevertheless; and we do not see how one party can have a right to do what another party has a right to prevent. We must ever resist the assertive right of any State to remain in the Union and nullify or defy the Laws thereof; to withdraw from the Union is quite another matter. And whenever a considerable section of our Union shall deliberately resolve to go out, we shall resist all coercive measures designed to keep it in. We hope never to live in a Republic whereof one section is pinned to the residue by bayonets.

Gen. Scott's famous advice to the President, that he might say to the seceding States, "erring sisters, depart in peace," coming from the great war oracle of the day, was construed as a preparation of the public mind for that policy. Mr. Lincoln's *obiter dicta*, in conversation and unofficial speeches, were regarded as not less decided in the same sense. Congress helped to foster this belief by the passage of the celebrated resolution, immediately after the first Bull Run, to the effect that the war was not waged for any purpose of subjugation or conquest, but simply to preserve the Constitution and the Union.[7] But long previous to these developments—as early as the 12th of March—the London *News*, the organ of the Reformers and Radicals, and friendly to the Washington Government, had thought it necessary, in view of this strong drift of public sentiment, to put forth a vigorous protest against any action by the British Government tending to recognize or countenance the Southern movement. In France, equal interest, though less anxiety was felt. The *Moniteur*, the official organ of the French Government, inserted conspicuously a most glowing description of the scene presented in the South Carolina convention at the signing of the Ordinance of Secession.

This was considered as very significant, that journal reflecting always the "inspiration" of the Government.

On the 6th of April, the *Times*, announcing the departure of the first Confederate Commissioners for England, for the first time suggests the idea that "there may be two separate confederacies on American soil."

On the 30th of April, Lord Wodehouse, replying to Lord Malmesbury, said that Her Majesty's Government did not intend to give advice on American affairs, and that Lord Lyons had been so instructed.[8]

On the 27th of the same month, the *Times*, in its leader on the fall of

---

7. The House of Representatives passed this resolution on July 22, 1861, the day after the battle.

8. John Wodehouse, Earl of Kimberley, was undersecretary of state in the Palmerston cabinet. James Howard Harris, the Earl of Malmesbury, had been foreign secretary as recently as 1859 and was a leading Tory. Richard Bickerton Lyons was minister to Washington.

Sumter, laughs at the want of carnage, and says: "If this be an omen of the result, the rich and unready North will be no match for the fiery forwardness of the South;" and *Punch* bitterly lampooned the telegrams sent by Mr. Benjamin, Mr. Walker and Major Anderson, apropos to what it regarded as a most farcical, because most bloodless, siege and capture.[9]

As early as the 9th of May, Sir G. C. Lewis announced in the House of Commons the forthcoming proclamation of neutrality, acknowledging the Confederate States as belligerents, a long stride towards formal recognition, which it was supposed would follow at an early day.[10] On the 15th of May the proclamation was promulgated.

France was known to have urged England to combine with her in the adoption of a more decided policy, proposing either joint mediation or intervention, by recognition of the Southern Confederacy, should the North refuse to listen to friendly counsel and reunion prove impossible. The latter contingency was one which both nations in their heart of hearts desired might prove true; for the American Eagle was a bird, they thought, whose wings would bear clipping—and an American balance of power, in the existence of two rival States on that continent, they regarded as a good thing for Europe and mankind at large.[11]

As for the parties litigant, they loved the one only a little more than they disliked and distrusted the other. Of all the foreign powers, but one alone at this early day felt a sympathy for the Washington Government, and formally gave it the assurance through its ambassador, ordering him also, not only to communicate "its feelings to that Government, but to leading and influential individuals also," a most exceptional intervention in the internal affairs of another nation. That power, strange to say, was the one apparently the most antipodal to the Great Republic—the Empire of Russia—whose natural alliance with the United States was first pointed out and urged by a Southern statesman, Roger A. Pryor, when editing the Washington *Union*, in 1852.[12]

For ventilating this idea, he brought down on his head much indignant

9. Confederate Attorney General Judah P. Benjamin, Secretary of War Leroy Pope Walker, and Union Major Robert Anderson, commanding Fort Sumter.

10. Sir George Cornewell Lewis was secretary for war and member of Parliament.

11. De Leon exaggerates French and British feeling. Napoleon would have been happy to see North and South permanently split but did not desire to involve France in a costly and perhaps embarrassing contest with the Union to achieve that end. Britain held similar views.

12. Roger Pryor edited pro-secession newspapers in Richmond and Washington, including the *Union*, and in 1860 was an outspoken proponent of disunion. He subsequently became a general in the Confederate army.

denunciation from Northern editors, who afterwards embraced the Northern Bear with a hug as strenuous as his own.[13] The language of the Russian
dispatch was as follows:

> This Union is not simply in our eyes an element essential to the universal politi-
> cal equilibrium; it constitutes besides A NATION, to which our august Master,
> and all Russia have pledged the most friendly interest. For the two countries,
> placed at the extremities of the two worlds, both in the ascending period of their
> development, appear called to a mutual community of interests, and of sympa-
> thies, of which they have already given mutual proofs to each other.

The brilliant successes of the Southern troops in the early stages of the
war, the rapidity and ease with which the Southern States took possession of
all the forts and arsenals within their limits, the bloodless bombardment
and surrender of Sumter, heightened this belief, and inclined the European
Governments and people to believe that the North would not fight, and that
the revolution would lead to a war on paper, with protocols for bullets.

Even the *Times*, contrasting the apparent readiness of the one side and the
readiness of the other, used these significant expressions already quoted.

England therefore made hot haste to recognize the South as a belligerent
in advance of every other power, and even before the arrival of the newly appointed Minister of Mr. Lincoln, Mr. Adams. France, on the contrary, reserved her action, until a month after the arrival of Mr. Dayton.

An incident which followed these two proclamations gave great hopes to
the Richmond Government and to the friends of the Confederate cause.

Immediately after they had been issued, the Governments of England and
France informally requested the Government at Richmond to recognize as
binding the principles of the Law of Blockade, as adopted by the Convention
of Paris, in 1858.

This was promptly acceded to by the Richmond Government, and was
considered almost as a quasi-recognition.

It has been charged on Mr. Dallas in certain quarters—and there may be
found persons silly enough to believe it—that he concurred in the propriety
of the action of the British Government, and that it was with his sanction the
step was taken, before the arrival of his successor. But no one who knew Mr.
Dallas personally—or had studied his character as exemplified in his life and
works—could for an instant credit the calumny.

13. De Leon clarifies in the margins of his copy that it was "R. A. Pryor" who brought down this
denunciation.

There are human ghouls—filthier and more cowardly than the creatures of Eastern superstition—whose delight is to take up the bones of the dead and disturb the repose of the tomb. Mr. Dallas has terminated his long career of public service, and sleeps well now where malice can not touch him farther; but it is only due to him to say that he was incapable of such treachery to the Government he still served, and would have disdained the idea that he, a Northern man, by birth, residence and all his affinities, should take a step which a sense of honor restrained Mr. Faulkner, a Southern man, from attempting or sanctioning in France. It is a proud boast, and one which no States in revolution ever before could make with truth, that neither in the Northern nor in the Southern service, military or civil, were there any traitors found, from first to last, except "base follows of the lewder sort," but no man of mark or high position. The side which each espoused was faithfully served throughout, and it is one of the highest and most honorable traits of national character drawn out by the war. Mr. Dallas, of all men, was the last to have constituted an exception to this rule, for he was a gentleman of the old school, and prided himself on his spotless honor, and more than Spanish punctilio in all points of morals as well as of manners.

While the interregnum in the diplomatic representations lasted, by the lagging on the stage of the reluctant veterans of Mr. Buchanan's ministers, before the new ones had arrived to represent the views and wishes of Mr. Lincoln's Administration, one Minister made himself wonderfully active, at both the English and French foreign offices; and in other places where public opinion was to be influenced. This was Mr. Sanford, then, as now, Minister to Belgium, but who gave himself a roving commission, and worked indefatigably, some said obtrusively, on the Northern side. So omnipresent and so brisk was he in his movements, that some wicked wag dubbed him the Diplomatic Flea; and though perhaps open to the charge of overzeal, of officiousness, he certainly was one of, if not *the* most efficient advocate of the Northern cause in Europe. His previous experiences in courts and cabinets, when, under the instructions of Mr. Mason, then Assistant Secretary of State, but now Confederate Commissioner, he astonished the French dress circle, at a reception, by his plain black small clothes, had taught him how and when to approach both effectively, and he did not do his work negligently.[14]

14. Henry Sanford, newly appointed minister to Belgium, was sent to Paris by Seward, arriving April 15, 1861, where he was to get acquainted and represent Union interests until minister Dayton could arrive. Even after he left for Belgium, he remained a useful representative of Washington in managing French affairs.

Mr. Sanford's ability as a diplomat has since been proved, by his having retained his position as Minister during all the changes of men and of policy which have marked the last six eventful years, but he certainly "won his spurs" in the commencement of the struggle, as I have reason personally to know.

Gen. Fremont, who was then in Europe, also threw the whole weight of his name and influence on the Northern side, as did also Gen. Phil Kearney, whose social qualities had given him influence in certain circles of France.[15] The great herd of Americans resident abroad possessed but little weight or influence, either from intelligence, culture, or distinction of any kind. They were chiefly people of good incomes, who left home because they found themselves—or imagined themselves—of more consequence abroad; and at the commencement of the war it was rather their style to affect sympathy with the Southerners, as representing the more aristocratic side.

As the conflict continued, and became more serious and more sanguinary, it touched the pockets and the persons of these—or threatened to do so—and then they became the most violent and implacable denouncers of the wicked conspirators, who not only raised the rates of exchange to such a degree as to diminish their incomes one-half, but compelled them, against their will, to go back to the country they loved so much at a distance.

The exodus from America was as great at the beginning of the war as it was in the opposite direction later; and all the fresh arrivals, breathing fury and fire, added to the excitement which began to manifest itself in Europe. "For," as these ignorant foreigners argued, "if the people who come away to avoid the war, are so ferocious and blood-thirsty, what must those be who stay to fight." Therefore, while these patriotic pilgrims fought the battles of their country over bottled beer in English, and over *vin ordinaire* in the best French hotels, an atmosphere of two different nationalities was perceptible: and the gulf that yawned between North and South, socially and politically, became evident to the foreign eye.

For that subtle and all-powerful atmosphere we call Public Opinion—which is the breath of life to Monarchs as well as Democracies—is generated more frequently thus in the open air, than manufactured in laboratories by those cunning chemists we call politicians; and the traveling Americans of

15. John C. Frémont had been the 1856 Republican nominee for president and was simply touring in Europe at the outbreak of the war. Philip H. Kearny had served in Napoleon's Imperial Guard since 1859, but after the outbreak of the Civil War returned to become a brigadier general for the Union.

both sections, disputing and arguing loudly in public places on the Continent, after their immemorial usage, gave an inkling of the actual division at home, long before it had formally been announced through State papers.

So straining their eyes and ears to catch the sights and sounds—slowly passing then by steam, not as now by lightning, across the Atlantic—the people of Europe watched and waited for developments from Washington and Montgomery, where two Congresses, instead of one, were legislating for a divided instead of an united people. Let us turn our eyes backward to the latter place, and look through English glasses at the shadows thence projected—which soon were to spread over both continents.

CHAPTER 6
THE FIRST ECHOES FROM MONTGOMERY

———•◦•———

Great as was the interest attached to the declarations of the new President, and the leaders of Northern opinion, at this early period, the utterances of the leading men in what was acknowledged to be a revolutionary movement, were yet more eagerly listened to. Montgomery became a centre of equal interest and curiosity with Washington, and the echoes of its voices resounded throughout Europe, while the acts and utterances of the South were scanned with a much more eager curiosity. The outgivings of her leading men were regarded as explanatory of the ideas and intentions of the Southern people, and the shadows projected abroad were often greater than the substance. They were also distorted by the bedlam through which they passed: the blockade at an early day sealing up the South from the rest of the world—so that many of the utterances attributed to leading men are in dispute to this day. My only duty is to state the versions of them generally accepted abroad, and to show the influence they exerted on public opinion there.

Truth compels the admission that the effect produced by most of the reported utterances of the representative men of the Confederacy, was injurious to the interests of the new claimant for admission into the family of nations.

When Locksley shot his arrow for the prize at the great tournament of Ashby de la Zouche, he "allowed for the wind," instead of aiming right at the bull's eye; but the Southern leaders did not take the same precaution, and missed their mark accordingly.[1]

Thus Mr. Benjamin's foresight was judged of by the reckless promise he was alleged to have made at New Orleans, that he "would drink all the blood which was spilt in the struggle"—which every thinking man in Europe regarded as an evidence of fatal blindness on his part, the moment the echo of the first gun from Sumter was heard.[2]

1. A reference to Robin Hood or Robin of Locksley's mythical archery.

2. In his marginal note here De Leon wrote simply "Benjamin," perhaps meaning that he intended in a fuller version of the memoir to expand on Benjamin's background and history. Actually

The boastful menaces made by Mr. Walker, Secretary of War, from a balcony at Montgomery, after the news of that event, in response to a serenade, that "he would prophecy that the flag (the Confederate,) which now flaunts the breeze here, would float over the old Capitol before the first of May, and it might float eventually over Faneuil Hall itself"—jarred equally on the foreign judgment and sense of propriety.[3] For it is not customary there, for men, of such position, to expound public policy, at such time and place, or in such terms, to an audience with music and banners.

Equally imprudent were the imputed utterances of Mr. Toombs, a little later, as reported by Mr. Hurlburt, then imprisoned as a spy at Richmond, and professedly a correspondent of a New York newspaper, never supposed to be very friendly to the Southern people.[4] The report of that conversation produced a great sensation in Europe, especially as the first Commissioners sent by Mr. Toombs, as Secretary of State, arrived only a short time previous to its promulgation. They were naturally supposed to represent the views and opinions so forcibly expressed by their chief, which were announced to friend and foe with a boldness and frankness characteristic of their author.

Mr. Hurlburt's report to the New York *Times* was, in substance, as follows:

Mr. Toombs professed the profoundest indifference to the opinion of the civilized world, on the subject of slavery, and its extension: avowed his intimate conviction that the policy of England and France must depend absolutely on the interests of the cotton trade, and would, consequently, be controlled by the Confederate States. France, particularly, he avowed and said, must be drawn into such practical alliance as would afford her the means of overtaking and outstripping England in the race of commercial expansion, and he had no doubt that France would rapidly recognize the importance of conceding to the new Republic aid in its extension towards the tropics. With Europe thus secured the Southern Secretary was quite at his case in regard to the pending struggle with the North.[5]

Benjamin probably never made this boast. It was widely made, and its origin is most commonly attributed to Armistead L. Burt of South Carolina.

3. Secretary of War Leroy Pope Walker made an impromptu speech to a Montgomery crowd on the evening of April 12, 1861, while the bombardment of Fort Sumter was still continuing and made a bellicose prediction that would later embarrass President Davis, whose posture from the first had been that the Confederacy sought no conquest, but only wished to be "let alone." William C. Davis, *"A Government of Our Own": The Making of the Confederacy* (New York, 1994), p. 316.

4. De Leon's marginal note "Mr. H" suggests that he intended to more fully identify Hurlburt in a later version. This was William Henry Hurlburt, later editor of the New York *World*.

5. De Leon noted in the margin next to this "See Hurlburt," the meaning of which is obscure.

Far more significant, as coming from one whose characteristics were well known to be those which distinguished his more impulsive colleague, were the deliberate avowals of Alex. H. Stephens, Vice President of the new Confederacy. His reputation at home and abroad was that of a man who weighed and considered every word he uttered. He was looked upon as possessing one of the coolest and clearest heads among the Southern leaders; and his habitual reticence, and calmer judgment, gave his words more weight than those of his more excitable compeers.

When, therefore, Mr. Stephens was reported as having openly and deliberately defied the sentiment of the world in relation to slavery, by declaring that to be the "corner stone," par excellence, of the new Confederacy, the shock it gave the public sentiment in Europe was a terrible one. It did more, throughout the struggle, to cool the friends and heat the enemies of the Southern cause, than all the arguments or denunciations of its most unscrupulous enemies. "Save me from my friends, and I will take care of my enemies!" never was more strongly exemplified than in this instance; in so far as the effect which I witnessed and vainly combated against for four years abroad. Lord Bacon, among the many wise things he said, never made a sager utterance than when he gave this famous aphorism: "I may have my hand full of truth, yet choose but to open my little finger!" Mr. Stephens opened his hand wide, and scattered what he regarded as the concealed truths it held, utterly unmindful of the Baconian maxim.[6]

The offensive doctrines, attributed to Mr. Stephens, were those he was reported to have advanced in an able and elaborate address to the people of Georgia, delivered at Milledgeville, on the 21st March, 1861. He was reported to have said on that occasion, in denial of the doctrine set forth in the Declaration of Independence, that "all men are created equal:"

> Our new Government (the Confederate,) is founded on exactly the opposite ideas; its foundations are laid, its corner stone rests upon the great truth that the negro is not equal to the white man—that slavery, subordination to the superior race, is his natural and moral condition. This, our new Government, is the first in the history of the world, based upon this great physical, philanthropical and moral truth.[7]

6. De Leon refers to philosopher and statesman Francis Bacon (1561–1626).

7. The speech by Alexander H. Stephens was made in Savannah, not Milledgeville, Georgia, March 21, 1861, and became known as his "cornerstone speech." De Leon was right about the embarrassment it caused Davis, who had hoped to distance the Confederate cause from slavery.

And this error of judgment took its rise in this way. These representative men, in turning their attention solely to the task of "fixing the Southern heart," and appealing to the prejudices and the passions of the men who were to carry the muskets, forgot to look beyond the narrow range of their own immediate neighborhood, and seriously compromised the success of the negotiations which were to secure foreign recognition. Without that, they should have known how vain and fruitless were all the valor, the sacrifices and sufferings through which they led their people, not even within sight of the promised land of independence; but into a "slough of despond," deeper and drearier than that dreamed of in the dismal imagination of Bunyan.[8]

I cite these ill-advised and imprudent utterances, and refer to their evil effects, in no carping sprit towards the public men who made them; who doubtless meant well, and believed they were advancing the cause by so doing—never reckoning on the recoil. But the truth of history demands that these great stumbling blocks in the way of foreign recognition, from first to last, should be pointed out, since they never could be removed entirely from the path of the diplomatic agents abroad, and were reproduced with wearisome iteration, by the indefatigable agents of the North, at every place and at all times, when the prospects of recognition seemed to brighten, and always with a most damaging effect.

For these three first fallacies:

1st. That the North would not fight.—Benjamin and Walker;

2d. That cotton was king.—Toombs;

3d. That slavery was the corner stone of the new Confederacy—Stephens; not only prevented the adoption of early and vigorous efforts for obtaining munitions of war and supplies from Europe, before the blockade became effective, but paralyzed also the efforts made at a later period to supply those omissions, and helped to frustrate the efforts made to obtain recognition or intervention from Foreign Governments, which else had been easier.

For they arrayed against us not only the prudence and the policy, but also the prejudices of the European populations, and rendered powerless the most friendly feelings and best intentions of Governments and Rulers, who dared not adopt a child whose godfathers had given it so evil a name. Hence it was, that although the great mass of the French and English people preferred the Southern to the Northern combatants, sympathized warmly with

8. The "slough of despond" is among the more famous quotations from John Bunyan, *A Pilgrim's Progress*.

the successes of the former, in the stricken field, and hoped they might finally with the day; yet they did not desire that their Governments should
recognize a Confederacy whose "corner stone" was ostentatiously proclaimed to be slavery; and whose chief public men boastfully announced
their ability to compel such recognition, basing their ability on the meanest
of all motives of human action, self-interest.

Therefore, England said: "Let the looms stop, we will not let the operatives starve, but cotton shall be no king of ours;" and France, true to her traditions, cried out: "We respect your fight for freedom, but make it entirely
so, by liberating your slaves, and we then may listen to your appeals for
recognition—and for aid—if need be." And to neither of these appeals did
any answer come from Richmond—for, strange to say, it was in France more
than in England that slavery was the bugbear. The latter was governed by
policy in her action—the former swayed by a sentiment too strong even for
the will or wishes of the Emperor to disregard.

England had everything to gain and nothing to risk by the policy of inaction; even the *mare clausum* of the blockade was but a slight impediment to
her trade. France, on the contrary, sacrificed great material interests in the
future, and resisted still greater temptations in the present, in adopting the
same course. This is a fact, which has never hitherto been appreciated or understood in this country; but which shall be proven, in the course of this
narrative,—the episode in Mexico to the contrary notwithstanding, which
carried its own punishment with it.

The earlier messages of Mr. Davis show that at first, he, at least, was fully
awake to the importance of laying down a basis acceptable to the world at
large; to the necessity of conciliating foreign opinion, and of securing recognition, if not intervention, through all the devices of honorable diplomacy.
In his message of 29th of April, 1861, he refers to the mission of the first
Commissioners sent to Europe, in terms which evince his lively sense of its
importance. But, unfortunately, his recommendations were not followed up
by equally vigorous action; his own mind, as well as those of his advisers,
having been seemingly diverted from this subject, by the presence of the
war, which rapidly loomed up in larger proportions and grander dimensions
than even the most despondent had dreamed of. This is the language used by
Mr. Davis in his message:

> The State Department has furnished the necessary instructions for those Com-
> missioners who have been sent to England, France, Russia and Belgium, since

your adjournment, to ask our recognition as a member of the family of nations, and to make with each of these powers treaties of amity and commerce.

Further steps will be taken to enter into like negotiations with the other European powers, in pursuance of the resolution passed at your last session.

Sufficient time has not yet elapsed since the departure of these Commissioners for the receipt of any intelligence from them.

As I deem it desirable that Commissioners or other Diplomatic Agents should be sent at an early period to the independent American powers south of our Confederacy, with all of whom it is our interest and earnest wish to maintain the most cordial and friendly relations, I suggest the expedience of making the necessary appropriations for that purpose.[9]

It is but just to say that while the flippant pledges of Mr. Benjamin, the idle vaunts of Mr. Walker, and the over-confidence of Mr. Toombs, reflected the popular delusions of the hour, there were in the South men more far-sighted and sagacious, who did not share them, but foretold the people of the wrath to come. Not into this delusive mirror gazed the anxious eye of Jefferson Davis—nor the cold clear gaze of Alexander Stephens;—unblinded by this glamour was the penetrative vision of Pierre Soulé, or the troubled regard of Robert Hunter—the Falklands of our Revolution—ever pining for peace, in the midst of the mad game of war.[10] Many others, also, there were, among Southern statesmen, who foresaw the dread ordeal through which the South must pass, after her new birth; but the roar of the cannon, the rattle of musketry, and the shouts of the combatants drowned their voices, and carried them along, vainly striving to be heard upon the surging tide of the Revolution.

Such men, were Soulé in Louisiana, Forsyth and Seibles of Alabama, Sharkey of Mississippi, Jenkins and Hill of Georgia, Boyce and Perry of South Carolina, Wm. C. Rives of Virginia, and a host of others.[11] Yet these

9. In the margin De Leon writes "Davis on recognition of first message," a suggestion that he intended to elaborate on reaction to Davis's address. The original text of the message appears in many places, including U.S. Congress, *Journal of the Congress of the Confederate States of America* (Washington, DC, 1904), vol. 1, pp. 160–168.

10. Pierre Soulé, a native of France, was a one-time senator from Louisiana and later minister to Spain. He opposed secession, but embraced the Confederate cause afterward. Robert Mercer Taliaferro Hunter was a prominent Virginia statesman and one of her first delegates to the new Confederate Congress. He became Confederate secretary of state in July 1861 and served until succeeded by Benjamin in February 1862. De Leon's high opinion of him was not shared by many others, who found Hunter to be a self-serving fence-sitter.

11. In his marginalia De Leon notes that these men were the "first commissioners." John Forsyth was one of Davis's commissioners to Washington prior to the firing on Fort Sumter.

men, who originally resisted the forcible disruption of the Union, and who sought to settle the vexed questions inside instead of outside of it, were truer prophets than Toombs or Benjamin. Though like Cassandra, they wandered in vain, and were repaid by reproaches, not by thanks, for their unheeded prophecies—they were faithful to their section to the bitter end—bore uncomplainingly their full share of the sorrows and sufferings they strove vainly to avert, and since the disfranchisement of the South have stood up more staunchly for the remnants of Southern rights, than many of their noisier and more boastful brethren.

But the voices of the more moderate men never reached Europe; their echo died away within the limits of the Confederacy, and the louder and harsher tones alone reverberated across the ocean, and were accepted as the enunciation of Southern sentiment. Nor can it be doubted that such was the truth. The Southern people, as a mass, regarded the election of a sectional President by an exclusive Northern vote, as leaving them but two alternatives, either separation, or submission then and forever after to Northern domination in their Federal and State Governments. Rightly or wrongly they believed this, and resolved peaceably if they could, forcibly if they must, to leave our Union, whose "blessings" they regarded like those of the evil genii, as curses only. The men therefore who gave expression to this sentiment in the strongest terms, and who most widely miscalculated both the resolve and the resources of the North, and the necessities of Europe, pleased most the people, who believed what they wished to be true.

While the echoes of these wild words were ringing through Europe, the three first Commissioners were just commencing their delicate and difficult negotiations, and I shall introduce them to my readers in the next chapter, giving the personal characteristics of each and all of them, before explaining what work they did, and how they did it.

----

charged with trying to negotiate a peaceful separation and turnover of federal property in the South. John J. Siebels was a leader of Montgomery society at the outset of the war. Judge William L. Sharkey of Mississippi remained steadfastly opposed to secession throughout the war, in spite of the condemnation of his Mississippi neighbors. Charles Jones Jenkins was another judge opposed to secession, who would become Georgia's first postwar governor. Benjamin Hill of Georgia, like Stephens, opposed his state's secession right to the moment the issue was decided, then served in the Confederate Congress. Benjamin F. Perry of South Carolina remained an outspoken opponent of secession before and during the war, and William C. Rives of Virginia opposed secession as a foolish measure but served his state in the Confederate Congress. De Leon errs in placing William W. Boyce among these men, for he was an ardent secessionist from the outset.

These three Commissioners, were Judge Pierre Rost, Wm. L. Yancey and A. Dudley Mann, who reached Europe the end of April, in 1861.[12]

12. Like so much else, Davis's appointment of these commissioners was heavily influenced by politics. Pierre Rost of Louisiana at least spoke French but had absolutely no diplomatic experience, though he was well acquainted in French upper social circles. William L. Yancey had been one of the leading exponents of secession, yet was such a radical that his own Alabama did not send him to Montgomery as a delegate to the convention that created the Confederacy. As a leader in the movement, and as a citizen of Montgomery, he was entitled to some kind of recognition, and Davis unwisely chose this most undiplomatic of men to head his European commission. Ambrose Dudley Mann of Virginia was a friend of Davis's who had some foreign service experience, and that got him his appointment. None of the three was qualified, which only sealed the fate of an already doomed mission. They left for Europe March 31, 1861.

CHAPTER 7
THE THREE FIRST COMMISSIONERS—
MESSRS. ROST, YANCEY AND MANN

About the end of April, 1861, the three Commissioners, to whose mission Mr. Davis had alluded in his message of April 29, arrived in England, accompanied by the Secretary of the Missions, Mr. Walker Fearn, of Mobile.[1] Having enjoyed a close connection and personal intimacy with these gentlemen, who favored me with their confidence from their arrival up to the hour of my return to the Confederacy, in January, 1862, I propose giving a sketch of the moral and mental attributes of these first representative men of the new Confederacy in Europe.

Judge Rost, the senior in age, although an eminent and well-known jurist in Louisiana, had never before taken any very active part in national politics, although he had attained the ripe age of sixty years. His reputation for high qualities, both of head and heart, had preceded him; and, although not a professional politician, he proved himself a most adroit and able diplomat, while the polished amenity of his manner, and the frank cordiality which seemed natural to him, won him friends from first acquaintance. His years sat lightly on his head, which was frosted over externally, but not frozen within; and it has seldom been my fortune to meet with so attractive and winning a person and presence as his. French in origin and early education, he combined the polish of his birth-place with the rougher readiness of the country he had adopted in youth, and in which the greater portion of his life had been spent.

Like his compatriot in both hemispheres, Mr. Soulé, he loved his adopted country with all the warmth of his heart, and made for her sacrifices such as many of her native-born sons shrunk from encountering. He left a high and lucrative position in Louisiana, and large plantations, to accept the difficult and thankless duties of the new mission, by which he had much to lose and

1. Walker Fearn's only apparent qualification for this mission was his kinship with Thomas Fearn, congressman from Alabama.

nothing to gain. For he was not ambitious of public office, and his fortune made him independent of it.

In my judgment the South sent abroad no better nor more creditable representative both of its intelligence and character, no better type of its genuine manhood, than Judge Rost, who did his duty in such a way as to extort reluctant praise and respect from those who differed most widely from him in sentiment and opinion. I never heard any man speak ill of him, either as to the purity of his life, the sincerity of his convictions or the noble means by which he sought to obtain what he regarded as noble ends. He staked on the issue of Southern independence all the earnings and emoluments of a long life of labor; and now, in the evening of his days, sits amidst the wrecks of his splendid fortune; but he is a man equal to any fortune, and can console himself with the knowledge that he will leave as a heritage to his children an honored and a noble name.

Coming over to Paris soon after his arrival in Europe, he made that city his headquarters and the seat of his labors, leaving his colleagues in London; and during the whole course of the struggle among the many missionaries sent to that political Mecca, no man impressed the French statesmen or society so favorably as he. The Southern cause lost by far its most popular advocate there when the Confederate Government transferred him to Spain, replacing him in Paris by Mr. Slidell, who, whatever his merits as an American politician might have been, certainly did not contrive to conciliate the French Government or people nearly so well as his predecessor.[2] Judge Rost's knowledge of constitutional law was very extensive, and he had the happy faculty of presenting his ideas and his authorities with that clear precision and terseness so peculiar to the well-trained judicial mind. His energy and industry, also, were both indomitable and untiring, and his tact equal to his talent, while both were surpassed by his rare modesty. I have seldom met a man so little vain or self-asserting; and the tricks of the demagogue or mere politicians he scorned to stoop to. In short, both in his public and his private life, he was a thorough gentleman in the highest meaning of that much abused term. His strict sense of honor was proven in his retirement from the post he held, when convinced he could do no further good at the place to which he was sent, though he had kept no position in reserve to fall back upon. Few men of his class and character figure much in revolutions.[3]

2. Here and elsewhere De Leon never misses a chance to criticize John Slidell.

3. De Leon's appraisal of Rost is chiefly personal, and he carefully says little of Rost's effectiveness as a diplomat, which was essentially nil. Du Bellet, by contrast, thought Rost essentially

The name and mental and moral attributes of William L. Yancey are too well known to the whole American people to need any elaborate description of them at this late day. Now that death has set its seal upon that marked individuality, stilled that fervid heart and silenced that eloquent voice, more justice will be done his memory than was accorded to him in life, for he was not a winning or persuasive man, like his colleagues, but a bold, antagonistic and somewhat dogmatical one; abrupt in manner, regardless of the elegancies and small courtesies of life, a refined man in feeling, but not in deportment, not at all impressive in personal appearance, and decidedly negligent in dress. But as Dr. Johnson said of Edmund Burke, "if you were caught in a shower, and accidentally took refuge under the same shed with him, and there conversed half an hour, you would come away impressed with the idea that you had been talking with no common man." He was a wonderful talker as well as an almost inspired orator—the Patrick Henry of the new revolution—whose first sparks his breath had fanned into flame, and whose ashes rest lightly upon his grave. His enthusiasm was contagious, his knowledge of American politics more thorough, even to the minutest detail, than that of any man I ever met. He used that knowledge, too, very skillfully, and his vivid imagination illustrated and adorned the dryest facts and figures in such a manner as never to make them tedious to the listeners. He was a great talker and a strong reasoner, and when brought into contact with Englishmen of marked note, never failed to make a strong impression on them. His own conviction of the truth of his own assertions was so stamped upon all his utterances, that no one could doubt his sincerity. But as a diplomat abroad he was not a success, as he himself said and acknowledged. It was not his sphere; neither his education, his training or his life-long habits had adapted him to "shine in courts" or to figure either in foreign society or in foreign diplomacy, for both of which a special experience is required.[4]

A man may be a first-class American—nay, even a statesman—and yet be utterly unfitted for the foreign service, and if he be not a young man when sent to the new field the transmutation becomes impossible. The very ways and means employed to secure success in American politics are the last which can be resorted to abroad—where neither the press, the stump, the

---

useless. Frank L. Owsley, *King Cotton Diplomacy: Foreign Relations of the Confederate States of America* (Chicago, 1959), p. 52n.

4. Yancey has not had a definitive biographer to date, though Eric Walther's mammoth biography is currently in press and anxiously awaited.

caucus, nor the popular vote can control great political issues nor influence courts, cabinets, and social circles.

Hence the particularly small figure cut abroad by men who had played a conspicuous part at home, and whose advent was heralded by a flourish of trumpets as loud as that which blew down the walls of Jericho. But despite these drawbacks Mr. Yancey did accomplish some good and did no mischief in his mission; and he had the good sense to see that he was better fitted for another sphere of action. Within a year of the time he had left the country he returned to it to take his seat as Senator from Alabama in the Confederate Congress.[5]

I shall never forget the last interview we had in London, on the Christmas Eve of 1861, just before my own departure for the Confederacy, via Havana and the blockade. He called at our hotel to bid us good-bye and send some messages by us to his family. It was a genuine London December afternoon, and the fog was so thick that we had to light the gas at three o'clock to see to read. It was cold and raw, and we had fire, also. Mr. Yancey came in, sat down by the fire in an abstracted and moody manner, as though the gloom without was reflected on his mind and face, and talked long and earnestly on Confederate prospects at home and abroad. He was less sanguine and hopeful on that occasion than I had ever seen him before, and I rallied him upon it— especially as the Slidell-Mason capture difficulty was unsettled, and many persons believed (Mr. Mann, his colleague, among them) that the Commissioners would not be given up, and that war between the United States and England would arise, which would be equivalent to our certain success.[6]

Mr. Yancey would not take a hopeful view, even, of the possibility of any serious complication arising from this source. He said he knew Mr. Seward too well to hope he would commit so suicidal a blunder, and that the difficulty was sure to be tided over. In this opinion he differed with his colleague, but judged from his own standpoint and personal experience. He added that he despaired of obtaining foreign aid, either moral or physical, and had made up his mind to return home at an early day. Then suddenly raising his head, and turning towards me, he said, "De Leon, do you know I have learnt one thing since I came here?" To my natural inquiry as to what that one thing was, he responded: "That I ought never to have come here. This kind of thing does not suit me. I do not understand these people or their ways well

5. De Leon's appraisal of Yancey as a diplomat is fair and on the mark. He did neither good nor harm and got out of a service for which he was quite unqualified.

6. This refers to the *Trent* affair, which will be dealt with in a subsequent chapter.

enough. It requires a different kind of training from any I have had, but it has taken me nearly a year to find this out. Now I know it, and am going home as soon as I can. My proper place is there."

I regard this incident as illustrating a very characteristic trait of the man. Few would have had the good sense to appreciate a situation so clearly; a fewer still would have had the manliness to avow it.

Mr. Dudley Mann, the third of the Commissioners, was better versed in foreign politics and foreign manners than Mr. Yancey. He had been much abroad, spoke and wrote French, and was a gentleman of pleasing address and polished manners. He was also a high-toned and dignified man, incapable of anything low or vulgar, and not even a whisper against his integrity was ever breathed. He had been sent, during General Taylor's administration, as Special Commissioner to Hungary; had figured in the Ostend Conference, and acted as Assistant Secretary of State to Mr. Marcy, when he was supposed to be the author of the celebrated costume circulars which stripped the gold lace off of American Ministers abroad and reduced them to the necessity of black small clothes, causing the Minister and his two Secretaries at one of the Queen's receptions to be dubbed as the "three black crows" by a sarcastic British journal of aristocratic affinities.[7]

If not a brilliant man, he was a safe one, and his industry and zeal in the cause were untiring. The selection of Mr. Mann was, I imagine, chiefly due to his supposed familiarity with men, measures, and manners abroad, on all of which topics most of our prominent politicians, North and South, were and are fearfully and wonderfully ignorant—rapid tours over the Continent— in which they do not read as they run—to the contrary notwithstanding.[8] This profound ignorance of foreign men and things is often as lamentable as it is ludicrous, for in the history of nations the greatest effects have often arisen from apparently the smallest things. The subtle Talleyrand embodies this truth in his famous comment on an affair of state: "It was worse than a crime—it was a blunder." The crime might be forgiven—the blunder never could be remedied.

---

7. Zachary Taylor served as twelfth president of the United States. William L. Marcy was secretary of state in the Franklin Pierce administration. The Ostend conference took place at Ostend, Belgium, in 1854, among three American foreign diplomats, including Soulé and James Buchanan, and its result was a declaration that if Spain would not sell Cuba to the United States, then the nation would be justified in seizing it by force if necessary. It was a national embarrassment immediately repudiated by Pierce and brought no credit to anyone involved.

8. De Leon's characterization of Mann as safe but not brilliant is a perfect description.

The credulity of the Southern People on these topics was proportionate to their ignorance, and it would have been matter for laughter, had it not been sad enough for tears, to see how that credulity was imposed upon at a later period by the dissemination of the most outrageous fictions in relation to the reception, standing, and intimacies of Confederate agents abroad, tending in some cases to most mischievous results, as far as the interests of the cause were involved.

The Commissioners were very fortunate in the selection of the Secretary assigned to them in the person of Mr. Walker Fearn, a gentleman whose cultivated mind and polished manners fitted him equally for the labors of the study or for the pleasures of society. With an exceptional acquaintance with foreign languages—several of which he both spoke and wrote fluently—full of energy and zeal—Mr. Fearn was of infinite value to the Commissioners, and afterwards filled the same post successfully in the late missions to Spain and to Mexico.

Soon after their arrival the Commissioners separated, Judge Rost going over to Paris, where his son Emile acted as his Secretary, and Messrs. Mann and Yancey remaining at London, and retaining Mr. Fearn.

These gentlemen were unofficially received by Lord Russell, who gave them a patient hearing, and neither encouraged nor discouraged them.[9] He received them only as private individuals, it is true, and declined receiving and acknowledging their commission as the regularly accredited Commissioners of a new Government; but he corresponded with them, and that correspondence was afterwards sent in to Parliament with other diplomatic correspondence, and published, also. What was regarded as a still more significant symptom was the fact of the formal issuing of the Queen's Proclamation of Neutrality and Belligerent Rights so shortly after this interview.[10]

The refusal of Lord Russell to recognize them in their official capacity was easily explained, as being rather premature; but in those earlier days the Commissioners themselves, and all the Confederate sympathizers in England, regarded the recognition as merely a matter of time, and of very short time, too. And the Commissioners—both in England and France—had apparently good grounds for their confidence. While the Government officials, both in England and France, exercised a prudent reserve and reticence of language and action in their dealings with these new envoys from a new

9. John Russell, Earl of Russell, was a distinguished career politician who served Lord Palmerston as foreign secretary during the Civil War.

10. The proclamation was declared on May 14, 1861.

Government, which was to be expected, yet the current of diplomacy and the tide of public opinion abroad, both seemed setting in strongly towards the new Confederacy; and all the more so because the belief was almost universal that the North had not the power, even if it had the wish, to retain the seceding States by force—and by persuasion it was now known to be impossible. For this belief the press and politicians and Government of the North were responsible, for Europe accepted their admissions and declarations as the reflections of the Northern mind and purpose, which subsequent events proved to be a false light on both sides of the Atlantic.

Let us cross the Channel now and see how Judge Rost sped in his mission to the crowned sphinx who has revived even more than the glories of old Napoleonism in the great Capital of the civilized world, Imperial Paris!

CHAPTER 8
JUDGE ROST'S FIRST MOVEMENTS AT PARIS—
MR. DAYTON—CASSIUS M. CLAY

Early in the month of May, 1861, Judge Rost reached Paris, and took up his quarters at the Grand Hotel du Louvre, near the Palais Royal, where I had apartments also. We soon became intimate; and as I found him at first sight, so did I find him ever afterwards—the soul of honor himself and never distrusting that of others, and as incapable of conceiving small suspicions as he was of harboring petty jealousies. By birth a Frenchman, and having many connections as well as patrimonial property in France, he soon revived the old ties of kindred and acquaintanceship, and obtained ready access to the private bureaux of the Ministers and to the best society in that gay capital.

At the moment of his arrival Judge Rost was very sanguine of the early recognition of the Confederacy, both by England and France, for which he had good and sufficient reasons, as already explained. In fact, throughout Europe it was looked upon as a mere political struggle, to result either in the peaceful return of the seceded States, with new and stronger guarantees as to the balance of power, or in a friendly division of the country between the two sections, still linked to each other in a kind of league, offensive and defensive, against the outer world, on the other continent.

This delusion was first dispelled by the call of Mr. Lincoln for 75,000 men, by the collision in the streets, and by the sudden change in tone and policy manifested by the President in his home, and Mr. Seward in his foreign policy.[1] Then every one saw that the war of words was to be succeeded by one of a sterner kind, and that the country was to be convulsed and torn asunder by a civil war, greater in its proportions and more disastrous in its effects than any similar struggle since the time of the French Revolution.

---

1. De Leon refers to Lincoln's April 15, 1861, call for 75,000 volunteers to put down the insurrection after the firing on Fort Sumter. The "collision in the streets" was the rioting in Baltimore, Maryland, four days later when a Massachusetts regiment of volunteers on its way to Washington was attacked by a mob as it marched across the city from one railroad depot to another.

In view of this altered aspect of things, the English and French Government found it necessary to take counsel together to decide on conjoint action. But after conference and free interchange of opinions, it was evident that French and English opinion did not accord as to what that policy should be; for while France thought it best promptly to proffer joint intervention, for the purpose of mediation, in the hope of averting bloodshed, England was in favor of the more cautious policy of declaring absolute nonintervention by proclamation of neutrality, coupled with a recognition of the Southern States as a belligerent but not as a government. Her reasons for adopting this course arose from no scruples as to the Law of Nations, nor from any fondness for the North, but were based on purely selfish considerations; and the egotism of nations, unlike that of individuals, may often be praiseworthy.

Over Great Britain commerce was king, as much as cotton ever was over the South, and well bred statesmen know that the sea would swarm with privateers to prey on that commerce whose sails whitened every sea the moment the pretext was given by any recognition of the Southern Government, which the authorities at Washington declared they would consider a *causus belli* and adhesion to the side of the Southern combatant.

So the British lion from the commencement to the close of the controversy was held like a hound in leash by this silken string in the hands of Mr. Seward, and the empire of the sea during that period was unsparingly asserted and exercised by the armed cruisers of the North, who paid but scant respect to the "meteor flag of England" on the ocean, or to the same emblem when floating over British possessions suspected of harboring Confederate vessels or property.

France was not troubled with these fears, and possibly might not have been unwilling to witness the conflicts of the rival cruisers on an element where her interests were smaller than theirs, but which it was the desire of the Emperor to increase. Hence in these international conferences on the American question, France was for pushing forward, and England for holding back—the result of which was the compromise declaration of belligerent rights and refusal of recognition of the Southern Confederacy or formal reception of their envoys.[2]

Still this did not discourage the Commissioners. I have reason to know that Judge Rost's intercourse, semi-officially, with the Ministers and distinguished personages near the French Court was as cordial and encouraging as

2. The French and British proclamation of belligerent rights came on May 14, 1861.

he could have hoped for; while after his arrival the press took a more decided tone in favor of the South, in spite of the very favorable impression which the new United States Minister, Mr. Dayton, personally had produced.

After Mr. Dayton's arrival in Paris as the representative of the Northern Government, Judge Rost found in him "a foeman worthy of his steel." He, too, was an elderly man, and belonged to the old, rather than to the new, school of American politicians, in his mind as well as his manners. He belonged to that higher class of public men who figured in our counsels when Webster, Clay and Calhoun were the great leaders and the models for imitation. He neither ranted in public nor blasphemed in private conversation, and did not recognize the necessity of ceasing to be a gentleman when he became a politician.

The contest, therefore, between the two earliest representatives of the two sections in France was characterized by a courtesy and dignity which reflected honor on the men themselves and on the people they represented. Even his political foes respected and honored Mr. Dayton, and no truer eulogy was ever uttered over any man's grave than the testimony rendered by Mr. Bigelow—afterward his successor, then Consul General—who made this feeling tribute:[3]

> Mr. Dayton possessed in a conspicuous degree that first of all Christian graces—truthfulness. He could not act falsely; he scorned all indirection. This may seem too common a quality among statesmen to be selected for spoken eulogy. Those who think so have had either a more extensive or a more fortunate experience than mine.

Between these two representatives, therefore, so similar in many points of character, and each so strong in his own convictions, the diplomatic war was conducted like one of the conflicts of ancient chivalry—both knights being without fear and without reproach. Still, as before mentioned, Judge Rost had the advantage of the ground. French sentiment was then decidedly in favor of the South.

The course adopted by Judge Rost was calculated to make this sentiment stronger. While he neglected no honorable means of advancing the interests of the cause, and labored indefatigably in so doing, he did not permit parasites to blow his trumpet so loudly in the newspapers as to notify his adversary of all his movements. On the contrary, he thought less of himself than of

3. John Bigelow was United States consul at Paris and after 1864 would be minister to France.

his work, cheerfully adopting the suggestions and encouraging the efforts of any one who could advance the cause. Neither was he moved by that petty vanity which seeks ever the exclusive credit of originating measures, and which scorns to adopt the most useful ones, because of their parentage. Thus, Judge Rost, seeing at once the importance of the negotiations opened by J. [*sic*] Butler King, (of which mention has already been made,) took them up at the point where Mr. King had left them, and pressed the same considerations as vigorously as possible, in the interests of the Confederacy, instead of confining them exclusively to Georgia. In this work he was effectively aided by Mr. Bellot des Minières and other gentlemen, who had access to the Ministers, and who plied their busy pens to persuade the French people, through the press, of the value and advantages of such special treaties in their favor. Actively employed in this and kindred labors, and in the exercise of social influences, which are very potent in France, his time was carefully employed, and at his special solicitation I was induced to linger at Paris, to aid in disseminating correct information on our side of the question, and in exerting the influence which long residence abroad and familiarity with its men and things had given me. We found the feeling at Paris most cordial to the new Confederacy, and especially so to its representative men. The position and views of the different political parties I have already depicted in a previous chapter, and these favorable tendencies were heightened and confirmed by the favorable impression produced by the first representative of the Confederacy at Paris. Judge Rost was quietly but patiently and indefatigably occupying himself at this task, when the even tenor of his way was broken by the first blast of the Northern war trumpet blown abroad through the London *Times,* by Cassius M. Clay, then on his way to Russia, as Mr. Lincoln's Ambassador, the echoes of which resounded as loudly in France and in England. As this was one of the most important episodes at the opening of the diplomatic campaign in Europe, I shall devote some little space to a detail of the incidents which accompanied the promulgation of this, the first Northern, manifesto abroad. This movement on the part of Mr. Clay had an important bearing on Southern diplomacy abroad, because it gave the opportunity the unrepresented South coveted, for a discussion in the public prints as to the merits of the question at issue, and the impartial hearing of both sides before the tribunal of the foreign public. Coming directly from Washington, the accredited representative of the President to the only Court in Europe, ostentatiously and avowedly friendly to the North,

Mr. Clay's utterances were supposed to be but the echoes of Mr. Lincoln's views and purposes, and hence excited great interest and greater curiosity.[4]

It is true that foreign diplomats and people generally, unaccustomed to "the free fight" system of Western politics, marveled much that the Minister to Russia should assume the functions of his regularly commissioned colleague to the Court of St. James, who had by that time reached his post; but Mr. Clay's pronunciamento for that very cause—like the reel in a bottle—was all the more curious.

It was stated, also, that Mr. Adams was not grateful for this officious interposition of his Russian colleague in the politics of Great Britain, discussed, *en passant*, as ordinary people would swallow and digest an oyster, although the diplomacy was of a louder kind than that which he practiced, and took the entire public into confidence, with an attitude like that of "Ajax defying the lightning!" But the languid interest of the British people was roused by the publication of Mr. Clay's letter, in which he gave the Northern view of the coming conflict, its causes and consequences, and incidentally attacked the policy of England, in language more forcible than flattering.

This letter, when published, was accompanied with a most caustic rejoinder from the *Times*, in response to the reflections on England, but with alight allusions only to the American phase of the question. But it seemed to me to be due to my Southern fellow-countrymen that that letter should be answered in such an authoritative manner in the same journal as to give the Confederate view of the same issues; to confute, if possible, the dogmatical assertions and confident predictions of Mr. Clay, putting in his plea as advocate of the Northern side.

Judge Rost concurred in this opinion; but although he agreed in the propriety and necessity of such a reply, did not agree with me in thinking that it should come from the Commissioners. Neither did he think it should be anonymous, but suggested that one who had just resigned office under Mr. Lincoln was the proper person to respond to his new appointee. His colleagues concurring in this judgment, I did, therefore, write a letter, under my own signature, in reply to Mr. Clay's, which also appeared in the *Times*,

---

4. Cassius M. Clay of Kentucky had just been appointed minister to Russia by Lincoln, a necessary political gift to a founding father of the Republican Party who had sought but lost the second spot on Lincoln's ticket. Clay published a letter in the London *Times* on May 20, 1861, in which he quite undiplomatically told the British people who their friends ought to be and offered the veiled threat that Great Britain must be careful not to alienate the United States.

after having submitted it to the Commissioners, who fully endorsed it as a fair statement of our case. As the first issue joined on this great controversy abroad, through the public press, in an appeal to a European tribunal, these two letters now possess an historic interest extrinsic to their merits as literary or political productions, and may be regarded somewhat in the light of public documents, setting forth clearly the opposite case, finally tried and decided by wager of battle.[5]

Mr. Clay afterwards made an after-dinner speech at the Hotel du Louvre at Paris, on the occasion of a Fourth of July celebration there, in which he reiterated the same views and opinions set forth in his letter, highly lauding France at the expense of England. This speech was reproduced with much sarcastic comment in the English press, gave Mr. Adams much trouble, and excited an angry and unfriendly feeling in England towards the section Mr. Clay was supposed to represent in these railing accusations against English feeling and policy, and threats of an Americo-French alliance against her. These letters made a great sensation at the time, and served as the textbooks for the advocates of North and South respectively, until the public listened more eagerly to the clash of arms than to the war of words on either side.[6]

Immediately succeeding their publication came the movement of Mr. Gregory in the British Parliament, for the recognition of the Southern Confederacy. As that scene was one of historic interest, and the first fruit of our secret diplomacy, I shall describe it as I witnessed it. It seemed to us as tempting as the apples of Paradise, but it proved as fatal, encouraging false hopes, and like the Dead Sea apples, turning to ashes on the lips.

The motion itself, once of such vital interest, has long since passed into the limbo of lost things, and many of the principal personages who figured on the stage have since passed away. In the succeeding chapter I shall attempt to summon back the shadows of both from the shadowy realm of the Past.

---

5. As De Leon says, the *Times* editors published their own angry rejoinder to Clay's letter in the same issue that contained the offensive missive and then published De Leon's unsigned May 23 reply, which appears herein in appendix 1. "That reply was the first gun on our side," De Leon told Davis later. De Leon to Davis, October 24, 1861, Lynda Lasswell Crist and Mary Seaton Dix, eds., *The Papers of Jefferson Davis*, vol. 7, *1861* (Baton Rouge, LA, 1992), p. 374.

6. De Leon makes much more of the Clay episode, and his own letters, than it merits, and later historians have virtually ignored the whole affair.

On the 4th of March, 1861, W. H. Gregory, Esq., Member for Galway, introduced into the British Parliament a motion for the recognition of the Southern Confederacy.[1] This was promptly met by a counter motion from Mr. Foster, Member for Bradford, one of the earliest and most consistent advocates for the Northern side.[2]

When Mr. Gregory's motion was first presented, the Confederate States numbered only the seven Cotton States. The motion was postponed from time to time until the 7th of June, when it came up and was finally disposed of—Mr. Foster's also sharing the same fate on the same day.

I had come to London for the purpose of publishing my reply to Mr. Clay in the *Times*, about ten days previously, and having frequently seen Mr. Gregory in the interval, was aware of his intention of pressing his proposition to a vote, and remained in London to witness the denouement. I speak from positive personal knowledge, in declaring that Mr. Gregory's intervention and efforts in behalf of the Southern cause from first to last in the British Parliament and elsewhere, was entirely disinterested, and based on his own strong convictions of what English policy ought to be, and what Southern rights really were.

Solitary and alone he set that ball in motion before the arrival of the Commissioners, and viewing the struggle, and the relations of England to it, from the standpoint of a British Member of Parliament.

He was the consistent friend and champion of the Southern side in its darker as well as in its brighter day—because he believed that cause a just one in the first place, and because he deemed it to the interest and honor of England that she should recognize what Mr. Gladstone, one of the shining

1. William H. Gregory was one of the leading critics of the Lincoln blockade in Parliament.

2. This is a misprint. De Leon refers to William Edward Forster, a former Quaker, newly elected to Parliament from Bradford. He would later be prominent for education legislation.

lights of the Administration, had declared to be "a nation."[3] The charge has been made—reiterated in the face of positive proof—and widely credited on this side of the water, that Mr. Gregory had a pecuniary interest, at a much later day, in advocating the side he had espoused.

He was even charged in public prints and quasi State papers, as being a holder of the Confederate cotton bonds—but this I know to have been untrue.

Mr. Gregory never did, and never would take such an interest, for many reasons, chief among which was the notorious fact of his having taken the initiative in pressing upon Parliament the right of the Southern Confederacy for recognition.

He was at that time a young and rising member of the Lower House, and his early promise has since been fulfilled, as he now occupies an influential position in Parliament. He was tendered the Secretaryship of Ireland but a short time since—an office of great power and patronage—second only to the Vice Royalty of that unfortunate and unhappy portion of Her Majesty's Dominions. Himself an Irishman by birth, and representing an Irish constituency, the compliment was a high and a tempting one to Mr. Gregory—but his peculiar political affinities at the time did not permit him to accept it.

When it was known that he had determined to bring up and press his long deferred motion in Parliament, on the 7th of June, for the immediate recognition of the Confederate States, then numbering many more than at the time of his original proposition—it occasioned a great fluttering in Government and opposition circles, and among the friends of the Northern and Southern sides respectively.[4] Mr. Gregory was a Whig, an independent member of the party which then controlled the Government, and more significance was given to his movement on that account, while it was generally supposed the great Tory leaders of the Opposition were more friendly to the South than to the North. It really appeared as though the Washington Government had but few and feeble friends in Parliament, while the South appeared to be the favorite of both parties.

Although the British Peers observed a discreet silence on this exciting theme, men's minds and tongues were busy with it, and at clubs and coffee

3. William E. Gladstone served as chancellor of the exchequer and was a leading reformer in Parliament who inadvertently made public statements interpreted as favoring Confederate independence in spite of Britain's officially neutral position.

4. By this time there were eleven seceded states in the Confederate States of America (CSA).

houses, and in social circles, the matter was discussed, almost always in a manner favorable to the South.

While the friends of the South were animated, elated, and confident, the advocates of the North were uneasy and apprehensive. For up to that time, Messrs. Cobden and Bright, and the Manchester party—afterwards the mainstay of the North—had not "pronounced," and were believed to be more friendly to the South than to the North, owing to their supposed cotton supply necessity.[5] The real condition and true interests of the British manufacturers at that time, which was to stop the supply, as they then had on hand an immense surplus of unsalable manufactured goods, was not known, and this was one of the facts which it took time to reveal.

As before stated, Mr. Gregory was a Whig—an independent member of the party then in power—whose coalition ministry was as "tessellated a pavement" as that of Lord North in former times.[6] A large number of that party in the Lower House were supposed to share in Mr. Gregory's unwillingness to follow the lead of Lord John Russell, the most unpopular of ministers and of men. It was believed also that Lord Palmerston, who was in everything the reverse of Lord Russell, would not have been inconsolable at the retirement of his former rival and present colleague, were his policy overruled.[7] The Tory party was confidently counted upon to sustain this movement, the opinions of many of its leading members being no secret.

So the Commissioners, then at London—Messrs. Yancey and Mann—had every reason to indulge in the illusions of hope with regard to the favorable reception, if not the actual adoption, of Mr. Gregory's notion. That gentleman was himself very sanguine; in fact—after a conversation with him, the day before he made his motion—I arrived at the conclusion that he expected an attentive hearing of his presentation of the merits of the Southern cause, and possibly the improvement of the chances of recognition, but did not anticipate any definite or decisive action on the question, which was yet too little understood, and too new to the majority of members, to be hastily decided upon.

5. Richard Cobden of Manchester was a giant among parliamentarians, and an ardent champion of the Union. For a quarter-century he and John Bright were inseparable partners in representing industrial interests.

6. Frederick, Lord North, was prime minister of Britain during the American Revolution.

7. Henry John Temple Palmerston was an Irishman who dominated British politics for half a century and became prime minister in 1859. He granted recognition to the new kingdom of Italy but remained steadfastly neutral on American affairs.

In his judgment, the difficulties of adjusting the blockade question, the rights of neutrals on the high seas, and the reciprocal rights of belligerents and neutrals, was engrossing more of the attention of her Majesty's Ministry and the Opposition, than the political question of recognition.

The former was of more immediate and vital importance to British commerce and interests than the latter; and England found herself in the new position of a neutral, apt to suffer from the precedents she had established in a long series of years, in which she had ever figured as a belligerent. Dealing with so eminently practical and astute a people as the Yankees, British statesmen saw the dilemma in which they were placed, and feared to provoke too rigorous an adherence to the principles and actions which had been their own contributions to international law. They feared, if they insisted on a rigorous adherence on the part of the North to the principles of international law, which regulated blockades, and recognition of *de facto* governments, that the rights of belligerents at sea, according to their own code, would be forced upon them, to the immense injury of their commerce and carrying trade, which so obligingly conveyed shot, shell and rifled cannon to the Northern, and powder and supplies to the Southern belligerents, all under the same neutral flag.[8]

It is true that "the meteor flag of England" equally "braved the breezes" of the Gulf Stream, and of the Gulf of Mexico; and was to be seen on the coasts of New York, as well as that of Louisiana and the Carolinas; but it "braved the battles" of neither section, except involuntarily, when a Yankee cruiser sent shot or shell into or after it on the high seas, or off blockade-bound ports, on suspicion of suspecting its intentions.

All these things Mr. Gregory had carefully considered, and regarded them as so many drawbacks to the success of his motion, the adoption of which the North had declared it would consider as a quasi declaration of war against it; threatening reprisals in the shape of privateers, and other thorns in the side of fat, comfortable, easy-going, contented John Bull, less taxed, more prosperous, and less warlike than he had been for many generations.

The eventful evening of the 7th June, the day fixed on the docket for the consideration of the motion, at length arrived. It was a lovely, bright evening, illumined by such sunshine as London basks in, on its May days, but which Americans distrust the existence of on the "limited side" of the

8. De Leon notes in the margin that these shippers who worked both North and South were "double cannon carriers."

Atlantic, and I walked down with the two Commissioners, Messrs. Yancey and Mann, from Piccadilly across the Green Park to the Parliament House.

Mr. Mann was very sanguine, and in high spirits; Mr. Yancey thoughtful, and rather somber, and by no means so hopeful as his colleague. My own anticipations were not so sanguine as those of Mr. Mann, tinged partially by the fact of my previous conversations with Mr. Gregory, and the careful abstinence from the topic which I noted in the *Times*, which ignored the matter altogether. As the *Times*, at that moment, notoriously reflected the views of the Government, I considered its silence as evil omen.

We sent in our cards to Mr. Gregory, and other members of Parliament, and were, by special privilege, admitted to the reserved seats on the floor of the House, termed "the Peers' benches," a row of benches fronting the wool sack or Speaker's chair, and facing the members' seats, whence we could see and hear all that was going on. And here, to give a clearer understanding of the scene which ensued and of the actors in it, a slight sketch of the place and persons, and of the features wherein the British Parliament differs from the American Congress, may not be out of place.

CHAPTER 10[1]
MR. GREGORY'S MOTION—
SKETCHES OF LEADING ENGLISH STATESMEN—
FALL OF CURTAIN ON THE FIRST ACT

———••••———

The British Parliament—both in its external and internal aspects, and in its forms of procedure and their accompaniments, as well as in the publicity given to its debate—differs very widely from the way in which things are managed in this country. Every one knows that the House of Lords is in all respects a select circle, composed of hereditary lawgivers, ruling the country by right of birth, and entitled to seats through their titles of nobility, with a chosen few from the ranks of the people elevated to the peerage, and its perquisite a voice and vote in the Lords, by that patent of nobility proceeding directly from the Creator, which men call genius.

Thus Copley, son of the Boston portrait painter, called Lord Lyndhurst, sat in that Chamber side by side with the heir of all the Percys, and Harry Brougham, the cannie Scotch laddie, who mediated the muse on a little oat-meal in Edinburgh garrets in early youth, as Lord Brougham now filled a chair in the close vicinity of a person of title, whose ancestors came over with the Conquerors.[2] But these are the exceptional cases. As the Conservative body, in imitation of which our Senate was devised by the Fathers of the Constitution, as a check and balance to the Lower House, drawn directly from the people—it had, and still has, its uses. But the most loquacious men are silenced, and the most disputatious calmed, on dwelling long in that atmosphere—as witness the transformation of Lord Brougham.

The drowsy decorum of its debates, (in the days of which I speak,) unless enlivened by a tilt at the Whig banner bearer, Lord Russell, by the Earl of

1. De Leon or the publisher erred here by designating this chapter 9, inasmuch as in the preceding issue of the *Citizen* a chapter 9 had already appeared. The mistake would not be corrected, and all subsequent chapters were sequentially misnumbered. In this edition they have been renumbered properly.

2. John Copley, Lord Lyndhurst; Henry Peter Brougham of Edinburgh, Lord Brougham and Vaux, was an outspoken opponent of slavery.

Derby, seldom attracted auditors.[3] Therefore, very small provision was made for them in the smallest and narrowest of possible galleries, perched high up in niches for the accommodation of the families of the Peers, or of their country cousins, to whom they wished to pay cheap civilities. To obtain an order for admission to them was almost as impossible, except for the favored few, as it was here, but a short time since, to secure a seat to witness the performance of Ristori or the "grand Duchess," or as it now is to see Dickens convert his "American Notes" into greenbacks, by preaching international good will at sixteen thousand dollars the course.[4]

But the American world naturally supposes that the Lower House, or Commons, which is supposed to be the direct representative of the British people, would afford ample space and verge enough for the admission of a goodly number of the outside world, to hear its debates on subjects immediately touching the public interests or the public heart. But those who so suppose, forget that John Bull is not like his cousin Jonathan; and that his habits are not gregarious. He loves silence more than speech, however frothy, or however highly seasoned that speech may be; and he looks to facts rather than to figurative expressions of "sound and fury signifying nothing."[5] Therefore, John Bull very sensibly prefers reading in his morning paper, with his tea and muffins, at breakfast, the debate of the previous evening, or night, in Parliament, to sitting in a hot and stuffy seat in a small and crowded gallery, in the midst of a closely packed crowd, where he can see nothing, and hear but little of what is going on. He, therefore, avoids the Parliament Houses, unless he has a little job in the railway or contract line to put through with the assistance of his best friend, (for they grind axes at Westminster as well as at Washington, though in a more quiet way,) and in his *Morning Times*, or *Herald*, or *Telegraph*, gets a full and accurate report of the debate, which he digests with his buttered rolls.

The British Parliament ever was a model of decorum and decency, when compared with the American Congress, even in its better days, probably on this account more than any other. For there is no gallery full of wire-pullers,

3. Edward Geoffrey Smith-Stanley, Earl of Derby, immediately preceded Palmerston as prime minister, and was a leading conservative in Parliament.

4. The Italian actress Adelaide Ristori was one of the most flamboyant female players of the era, sometimes called the Grand Duchess, and Charles Dickens needs no introduction. De Leon here refers to Dickens's sold-out lecture tours of the United States in 1842, and again in 1867 to 1868 while De Leon was writing his memoir.

5. De Leon quotes from the doomed regicide's famous soliloquy in the fifth act of Shakespeare's *Macbeth*.

male and female, white and black and parti-colored, to "rain influence down and judge the proofs," to members making speeches, not to their colleagues, nor even to their constituencies, but to the galleries—packed juries for the occasion, and whose noisy demonstrations of applause or censure the presiding officer is often powerless to check.

On the contrary, a rather drowsy decorum, a severe business-like method of procedure, is adopted in the British Parliament, in both its branches, and demonstrations of applause, beyond a few languid "hear, hears," from the body of the House, are never heard or permitted. From the galleries there comes no sound, and the occupants are almost invisible to the eye of the members on the floor, as they are enabled to catch but few glimpses from their airy perch, of what is transpiring below.

The galleries of the House of Commons are so very contracted, hold so few persons, and the tickets of admission are so difficult to get, that their occupants exert no influence on the proceedings of the House; and strangers who are fortunate enough to have acquaintances among the members are sometimes, as a special favor, introduced into the body of the House, and assigned a place on "the Peer's benches," a row of elevated seats at the entrance, fronting the woolsack and the members' seats, on a level with them, where everything can be perfectly seen and heard. Into these seats we were inducted on the evening of the 7th of June, by the courtesy of Mr. Gregory, and there I saw and heard the first opening act of the drama of recognition on those boards, ending in a postponement, which afterwards proved to be final; though other and successive scenes of the same performance were repeatedly rehearsed on the same boards at subsequent periods, without arriving at the great denouement. As a special compliment to Mr. Gregory, whose success in the best London society was as great as in the less pleasing field of politics the galleries exhibited, on this evening, an unwonted array of bright feminine presences, and an unusual alacrity of demeanor on the part of the members, coupled with mysterious disappearances from below, followed by sudden reappearances above, proved the rarity of these fair apparitions in these upper regions.

The younger members seemed chiefly affected by these reflected lights, but even the veteran Premier, Lord Palmerston, and the godly Gladstone, turned their eyes upwards oftener than usual, though not celestially; while the O'Donoghue, handsomest and most *debonnaire* of Milesians, (who excited the jealousy of Napoleon when Prince President, by his successes at Paris, and was banished therefrom,) proved by his appreciative glances that he had not forgotten those souvenirs, nor read Tom Moore's melodies for nothing.[6]

Mr. Gregory sat serenely below, undisturbed apparently by this bristle of preparation for his *début* on the Parliamentary stage, in the character of Confederate champion that evening, and conversed freely with myself and other friends, pointing out the notorieties to us, while the motions that had precedence of his were taken up and disposed of. Mr. Gregory is a man of middle age, but of most youthful appearance, with a head and face which indicate both talent and energy in every tone and feature. His eye is bright and penetrating, his features regular, with a prominent pose and clear cut lip. He wore no moustache, but long side whiskers of a dark brown color, of the received English pattern. His dress was faultless in its fit, and its choice of colors, though devoid of foppery; his form tall and graceful, and his movements easy and unrestrained.

His pronunciation was entirely without any suspicion of Irish accent, and like most highly educated Irishmen, he spoke the English language with a purity and correctness of pronunciation uncommon even in London-bred men, who have a hard accent peculiarly their own, intermingled with slang expressions, and accompanied by a drawling hesitation of speech, which many English writers have parodied.

His opponent for the evening, and the introducer of the resolution repudiating any recognition of the Confederate States, Mr. Forster, member for Bradford, was a thin, angular, bilious-looking man, very plain in appearance and dress, harsh in voice and abrupt in speech. He looked and talked more like a New England man—one of the members from Maine—than the representative of an English town. Yet he carried with him the respect of his audience from his obvious earnestness and sincerity in the cause he espoused. Indeed, while later and more noisy converts to the Northern side in England—such as reverend solicitors for spire-building, &c.—have earned "golden opinions" (literally) from the gullible people here, this man, who took the responsibility of advocating the cause when most unpopular in England, before Bright or Mill, or any of the Smiths and Halls took it up, has had neither solid pudding nor empty praise, nor even Protestant "Peter's pence" from the American people.[7] The member for Bradford may well cite

6. Daniel O'Donoghue was a member of Parliament from County Tipperary, Ireland. In Irish lore, the Milesians were the ancestors of the Irish people. Thomas Moore, of County Kerry, wrote *Irish Melodies*, which was one of the most popular song books of the era.

7. De Leon refers to John Stuart Mill and Sydney Smith. Hall is unidentified.

himself as another instance of the truth of the aphorism as to the ingratitude of republics; for on the evening of which I speak he stood solitary and alone, as far as I could see, in his support of the Northern cause, and received but courtesy from the House, while his adversary, Mr. Gregory, was treated with "the most distinguished consideration."

Looking below, the peer's benches, as well as the members seats, were seen to be filled, and even the aisles were crowded.

The occasion had called together all the notabilities of the Upper, as well as of the Lower House, and many outside celebrities also. There might be seen the snowy head and serenely noble countenance of the Nestor of English statesmen, Lord Lyndhurst, and the marvelously ugly and unmistakable face of the veteran Brougham, full of sagacity and pugnacity still, with a nose like his head, unmatched of men. Near him towered the burly form of Lord Robert Cecil, now Lord Cranborne, the hardest hitter and most gifted orator of the new *régime*—a staunch supporter of the Southern side; and the long, thoughtful face of Lord Campbell, afterwards introducer of a similar resolution, and emulating the fame of his father, who took the lives of Chancellors.[8] There, too, passionless and serene as a marble bust, in its thoughtful repose, was the marked face of Gladstone, on whom the mantle of Macaulay seems to have fallen, and whose mellifluous lips distil honey too sweet for the common taste—a man of clear and comprehensive intellect, but not coarse enough for common fare, although he has tried to play the tribune of the people against John Bright, and been distanced, of course.[9] There, too, like a small boy perched on a high stool, sat Lord John Russell, with the large head, crabbed countenance and dwarfish person, with which *Punch's* caricatures have made the world familiar, but the reality of which it were impossible to caricature. The expression of a roguish little bull terrier given by *Punch* as the predominating one on that worn and haggard face was also very perceptible; even in its repose the snarl seems ready to preface the snap.

Next him, as though to afford the most striking contrast, his antipode in everything, mind, manners and appearance, a head and shoulders higher, towered the erect figure and well balanced head of Lord Palmerston, whom all men affectionately dubbed "Pam"—most popular and most powerful of Englishmen he, since the death of the Great Duke, and on his every limb and

8. Robert Cecil, son of the Marquis of Salisbury, was a leading Conservative. George John Douglas Campbell, Duke of Argyll, was a leading Liberal and keeper of the privy seal in Palmerston's government.

9. Thomas B. Macaulay, essayist, poet, lawyer, historian, and leading abolitionist.

lineament nature had stamped manhood.[10] Jaunty in his movements, scrupulously neat in his dress, youthful in figure, if old in face; his hat perched a little on one side of his head, yet not concealing the broad, bold brow and the shrewd, commonsensical face, the veteran Premier seemed far more contented and more at ease than his colleague. Though, as head of the Administration, supposed to feel a lively interest in the matter, he is evidently bored and in a semi-somnolent condition while waiting for the resolution to be called up.

On the Opposition benches were to be seen the noble face and portly presence of Earl Derby, the great Tory chief, a born Prince of God's gift of genius, as by the accident of birth; a ripe scholar, whose leisure is occupied with the translation of Homer; a ready debater, a powerful orator, and one whose heart is as capacious as his head; one of the last and best types of "England's old nobility," against which the surging tide of radical reform is now dashing, threatening to bury it under a mad deluge. A true representative he of what soon must be an extinct species, if social follow political revolution, and what Carlyle terms "Beales and his 50,000 ragamuffins," backed by practical John Bright and impracticable Stuart Mill carry out their programme of universal suffrage, and cause the aristocracy to be "improved away" from the face of the earth.[11] He seems wide awake, and talks closely and earnestly to a man, the profusion of whose brown hair and beard almost hide his features, except a nose so very Norman in its arch as to defy concealment. Evidently hard of hearing, but with an eye that indicates intelligence and observation, dressed in the extreme of fashion and in garments much too youthful and bright for his worn face and wasted limbs, there is an affectation of juvenility about the man, which makes you smile as you survey him; but the smile is succeeded by a stare when you are told that you look upon the man who has illustrated every walk of English literature, the equal in many, and without a peer in his own special department; poet and orator; politician and dramatist, historian and essayist, translator and romancer—

---

10. The Great Duke is Arthur Wellesley, Duke of Wellington.

11. Thomas Carlyle published a caustic article on the state of democracy and government in London in April 1867, mentioning therein the action of a mob that tore down the railings of a royal park in the city to gain access to Queen Victoria. It was republished in America as "Shooting Niagara—and After," *Littell's Living Age* 94 (1867), p. 687. Carlyle closed the article with the words: "What are Beales and his 50,000 roughs against such; what are the noisiest anarchic Parliaments, in majority of a million to one, against such? Stubble against fire. Fear not, my friend; the issue is very certain when it comes so far as this!"

you look on all in the person of the man I have sketched—Edward Bulwer Lytton.[12]

Sitting near him, with hat drawn down so low over his eyes as entirely to conceal his frontal developments, with eyes half closed, self-absorbed, saturnine, speaking and spoken to by none, with legs stretched out before him to their full length, with spare and nervous figure, and long raven locks curling down and shading a sallow, bloodless cheek, and rigid, clear cut features of a decidedly Oriental type (Caucasian, as he himself terms it)—sphynx like in the repose of his imperturbable countenance, sits Benjamin Disraeli. Today he is the coming man of England. At that time he was, both personally and politically, unpopular; but seemingly scornful and indifferent then, as now, to public opinion, which he has ever treated as his puppet, and whose strings he knows well how to pull at the proper time.[13]

I was intently surveying these world-wide celebrities, clustered together in this narrow space, when a stout, clumsily built man of medium height, with a heavily molded face—precisely like that of the Model John Bull in *Punch's* pictures—whose countenance was redeemed from stupidity only by a clear bright eye, but which was withal stolid and surly looking, came up to where we sat, and took Mr. Gregory aside, and spoke earnestly to him for a few minutes.

There was a Quaker cut, an affectation of simplicity in his clothing, as well as in his broad brimmed hat, which he carried in his hand, and his manner seemed brusque and abrupt. When he finished his conversation, and Mr. Gregory returned to my side, he seemed somewhat anxious and perplexed, and turning to me said, "Bright urges me not to press my motion, but to withdraw it. He says he is quite sure the House is not willing or ready to act on the subject, and does not even wish it discussed. He further says that all parties concur in the propriety of avoiding the matter for the present."

"Does he speak as a friend or an enemy," was my inquiry, to which Mr. Gregory replied that he thought he was sincere in his advice, and that the general sentiment of the House seemed to be an unwillingness at that time to meddle with the matter. He then left me, conferred with several other members, and withdrew his resolution, to the evident relief of the House, the members of which all seemed to regard touching the topic at that time, very much as they would handling a red hot ploughshare. In fact, this timidity,

12. Edward Bulwer-Lytton was an enormously popular novelist, as well as having served in Derby's cabinet prior to the rise of Palmerston.

13. Benjamin Disraeli was a leading Tory and longtime adversary of Gladstone.

which the *Times* next day elegantly termed "the reticence" of the House, impressed me very much at the moment, and the impatience manifested towards Mr. Potter, who sought to press his resolution in the Northern interest, contrasted very strongly with their gratitude to Mr. Gregory, for relieving them of the discussion. Mr. Gregory managed the matter more gracefully than one would have supposed possible, under so great a disappointment; for he had made elaborate preparation, and was ready to present a very strong case for the consideration of the House. But he saw—as we all did who were present—that it was injudicious, and would be injurious to press the matter in the then temper of the House, and it is very doubtful that he would have been permitted to proceed, even had he persevered. For the British House of Commons, a model body in many respects, and generally preserving its dignity and the decencies of debate, much more than our Congress, yet does, on rare occasions, present scenes of "noise and confusion," greater than those which once checked the utterances of Gen. Cass on the eve of an election. If a member will persist in addressing the House, when it has clearly signified its disinclination to hear him, the chorus of crowing cocks, coughs and catcalls, that accompany such speech, soon silences the most obstinate lips, and overpowers the strongest lungs. The Chamber becomes a very Babel of discordant sound, and the unhappy member is compelled to give in at last from sheer physical exhaustion.

No such demonstration was made, since none was needed, on this occasion. Mr. Gregory rose in his place, when his motion was called up, and in few but appropriate words, announced his intention, in deference to the wishes of the House, not to press the adoption of his resolution, but to postpone it. Loud cries arose from various parts of the House thereupon, "withdraw it," "postpone indefinitely." Those were the only interruptions.

The few words uttered by Mr. Gregory proved that had the opportunity been accorded him, he would have acquitted himself ably—his distinct enunciation and graceful manner proving him to possess oratorical powers far above the ordinary Parliamentary level.

Unlike most members of that body, Mr. Gregory has no hesitation of speech—none of the "hemming" and "hawing" which characterized the majority of men in that body, when on their legs, and from which, even Lord Palmerston himself—practiced and ready debater as he was—never was wholly free.

Lord Derby, Mr. Gladstone, Mr. Disraeli and Mr. Bright, as well as Mr. Gregory, could, and did speak fluently, without break or interruption; but they were the exceptions to the general rule, most Parliamentary speakers freely interspersing their remarks with a drawling, hesitating ejaculation, very hard to form an idea of, and breaking the thread of their discourse to an ear unaccustomed to it. It must be a great relief to the reporters, nevertheless, since fully half of most of their speeches consist of these drawling interjections, which neither Thackeray nor Dickens have caricatured in reproducing.[14]

As a matter of permanent historical interest, I append the authoritative account of this most interesting incident:

THE AFFAIRS OF THE AMERICAN STATES

Col. W. Patten said that before the order of the day for going into the Committee of Survey was read, he wished to make an appeal to the honorable member for Galway, (hear, hear,) and ask him if it was absolutely necessary he should proceed with the motion of which he had given notice. (Hear, hear.) He believed he was speaking the opinion of a great number of persons who were well acquainted with everything which related to the United States of America, and who were deeply interested in our maintaining friendly relations with those States, when he said it would be very inexpedient at the present moment to enter upon such a discussion. (Cheers.)

Mr. Gregory said, in answer to the honorable member, he could assure the House he was the last man who would willingly involve the country in any embarrassment, or take any course which would in any degree be prejudicial to the maintenance of friendly feeling with America. He thought it only fair that one section of the States should have an opportunity of justifying the course which they had taken; and the only object which he had in view, in bringing forward the subject, had been to endeavor, if possible, to give a perfectly impartial statement of the differences which existed between the two sections in that country. (Hear, hear.) Although they had heard only one portion of the question, although the information which had been published came almost exclusively from Northern sources, and although he was almost pledged to persevere in his motion, yet, seeing that there was such a strong feeling in the House on the subject, he was unwilling to do anything which could, in the slightest degree, aggravate or embitter the dispute. (Cheers.) He would not put himself in opposition to the wishes of the House so generally expressed, and therefore, he would postpone the motion to some future opportunity. (Cheers.) His honorable friend, the member from Birmingham said "Withdraw it." (Hear, hear.) He would postpone it *sine die*, with the hopes that he should have some opportunity before the close of the session of

14. William Makepeace Thackeray and Charles Dickens.

bringing forward the subject, because he must say that it was most unfair and un-just that publications should be circulated throughout England, in which the Southern Confederacy should be accused of unwarrantable secession, and its members were called traitors and perjurers, (Oh, and hear, hear,) and that he should have no opportunity whatever of putting forward their case in a manner in which it could be dispassionately considered. (Hear, hear.)

Mr. W. Forster, who was received with loud cries of "Order" and "Agreed," said he wished to know whether the honorable gentleman meant to bring the subject forward on another occasion, or to postpone it altogether.

Lord R. Cecil said he hoped it would be understood on behalf of those who did not take the same view as the honorable gentleman who had just spoken—(Loud cries of "Order" and "Chair.")

The Speaker—I must remind the noble lord that there is no question before the House. (Hear, hear.)

Mr. M. Milnes—I wished to ask the honorable member for Bradford whether it was his intention to proceed with his motion.

Mr. W. Forster entirely agreed in the feeling of the House, that it was most un-desirable there should be a discussion on the merits of the quarrel between the States of America, (Hear, hear.) He should never have thought of putting his no-tice on the paper, had it not been for the motion of the honorable member for Galway. If it were only the intention of the honorable member to postpone his motion for a short period (loud cries of *sine die,*) he believed it would conduce to a better understanding of the relations with America, and to preventing miscon-ception, were he to bring forward his motion to-night. (Cries of "No" and "Agreed.") With the understanding that the motion of the honorable member was postponed indefinitely, he would withdraw his motion altogether. (Cheers.)

Mr. Crawford asked the honorable member for Galway whether his notice would remain on the paper. (Loud cries of "No—he said *sine die!*")

The subject then dropped.

Mr. Gregory never renewed his motion, but one year afterwards, Mr. Lindsay renewed substantially the same proposition, which was supported vigorously and ably by Mr. Gregory and other members, but which met the same fate as the original motion.[15]

Mr. Gregory, however, published a letter in the *Times,* in which he summed up with great conciseness the main points of the argument he had intended addressing the House. This letter produced a very powerful effect

15. William Schaw Lindsay was a prominent shipping magnate and Member of Parliament al-ready on record for strong pro-Confederate sympathy. On October 2, 1861, he made a strong speech in his home district advocating British and French recognition of the Confederacy.

upon public opinion, and is well worthy the attentive perusal of all who take an interest in the judgment passed by an impartial foreigner on the merits of the question—a question which has not yet found its definite solution, and on which posterity has yet to pass its verdict.

The Confederate States, it is true, have passed away like an exhalation of the morning—but the lessons which may be derived from the incidents connected with its short existence may prove profitable to our people, since our only safe guide for the future is to be found in the lessons of the past.

And so we drop the curtain on the closing scene of the first act of this tragedy, in which the formal attempt to obtain foreign recognition was made and abandoned.

In the next chapter, the effect of the Trent case and the influence of King Cotton on Confederate diplomacy, will be our theme.

CHAPTER 11
THE INFLUENCE OF THE BATTLE OF BULL'S RUN,
THE COTTON FAMINE, AND THE TRENT CASE
ON CONFEDERATE DIPLOMACY ABROAD

———•◆•———

The fate of Mr. Gregory's motion excited a great sensation in France as well as in England, proving as it did the fixed intention of the British Government to preserve its neutrality between the belligerents, and to give no aid and comfort to the South by Parliamentary action. The Commissioners were disappointed at the result of this movement, but they were not dispirited. They, as well as almost every one else, regarded it only as a postponement of an act for which England was not yet quite prepared.

The news of the battle of Bull Run, which shortly after reached England, confirmed the foreign impression that the South was more than a match for its larger, though more unwieldy antagonist; and both the *Times* and *Punch* in England, and the French press, magnified the results of that battle to the Confederates and the disparagement of the Federals. It was even thought that this first battle would be the last; and even the Prince Napoleon, sworn ally of the North, and fresh from Mr. Lincoln's table, allowed one of his aids to publish in the *Monitour* a contrast between the Northern and Southern forces, especially the cavalry, which was as uncomplimentary to the former as it was flattering to the latter.[1]

Russell's famous account of the flight, in which he bore an active and a frightened part (according to the testimony of others) was accepted as the correct version of the whole battle, and foreigners fell into the same error which paralyzed Southern preparation, that the North would not fight.[2]

The ideas we have referred to were embodied in a very able leader in the

1. On July 21, 1861, the Union army commanded by General Irvin McDowell was defeated by Confederate forces under Generals Joseph E. Johnston and P. G. T. Beauregard. It was a close affair, mismanaged on both sides, but the arrival of fresh Southern regiments at the perfect moment and spot started a Union panic that ended in rout.

2. De Leon refers to the correspondent for the *Times* of London, William H. Russell, who wrote a vivid account of the battle that earned him the nickname "Bull Run" Russell. It was highly flattering to the South and outraged people in the North.

Times, under date of July 19, reviewing Mr. Lincoln's message to the extra session of Congress, in which the statement is broadly made that "the South must succeed."[3] In a leader on Mr. Chase's report, apropos to a foreign loan, the same tone is taken, and the belief is expressed that the financial difficulties of the Washington government will break it down.[4]

On the 5th of August came a leader, in which it pronounces the Bull Run defeat to be "the Austerlitz" of the North, but in its resumé of the action of Parliament it seems to approve of the course adopted. At this time appeared Russell's famous Bull Run letter, which produced an immense sensation at the time. Any one who reads it now will be surprised that it did so; for though the narrative is a spirited one, and the flight graphically described, yet it does not pretend to describe the battle, which the writer admits he was not in a position to witness.[5] At the same time the *Times* gave a summary of Jefferson Davis's message, and laughing at Bull Run and Northern threats against England, assumed a tone of great contempt.[6] That mirror of public opinion also dwelt on the suspension of the Habeas Corpus Act, and warned the North to make friends with the South.[7]

About this time the question of the cotton supply came also to the aid of the South, and strengthened the remonstrance of Mr. Davis and his Commissioners against the blockade, which stopped that supply and had begun to occasion great distress in the manufacturing districts in England, as also in France.

The public mind began to be much exercised on this important subject, and the probable course the Confederate States would adopt was eagerly canvassed. It was known that there existed two opinions there as to the course best to be pursued; and it was believed the predominant one was

3. On July 4 Lincoln convened a special session of the U. S. Congress and sent them a message outlining the events leading to the attack on Fort Sumter and his subsequent call for volunteers to put down the rebellion. In the margin De Leon has written "Times" and "see today," perhaps a reference to the *Times*'s comments on the state of the United States in 1867.

4. Salmon P. Chase was Lincoln's secretary of the treasury, and De Leon here refers to his first report to Lincoln on the state of the Union's finances and its effect on the ability to prosecute a war, including the necessity for foreign loans.

5. This is Russell's letter to the *Times* of London, dated July 22, 1861, which soon found its way into the press North and South.

6. The Provisional Congress of the Confederacy convened in its new capital, Richmond, Virginia, on July 20, 1861, the day before the battle at Bull Run. Davis sent them a message announcing the admission of new states and assuming a defiant stance against Northern aggression.

7. The Lincoln administration suspended the privilege of the writ of *habeas corpus* on April 27, 1861, out of fear of insurrection in Maryland and the consequent isolation of Washington.

based on the belief that "cotton was king," and that by withholding it the South would extort recognition from England.

There was great uneasiness felt and expressed on this subject, and of course the Confederate agents, through the press and otherwise, urged the matter on public attention.

The *Times* expressed the prevailing sentiment in England at that period, when on the 16th of October, alluding to the deadlock of the two armies in Virginia, it broadly intimated the impossibility of the North's subjugating the South, and adduced a long list of facts and arguments to prove that "slavery had not been the motive cause of the war on either side."

Lord Russell's opinions on the situation were embodied in his pithy saying, which gave so much offense and rankled so long in the Northern mind, viz: that "the South was fighting for independence, and the North for empire." He embodied the British belief in this summary of the struggle.

In August, Mr. Bright, in view of the increasing distress in Lancashire, was obliged to express an opinion, and came out openly on the Northern side.[8] He took no sentimental grounds in doing so, nor did he base his position on the merits of the struggle. He took his position purely with reference to the manufacturing interest, of which he, as a mill owner and manufacturer, was a part, and declared that "the speediest and surest mode of obtaining cotton was through the success of the Government of the United States." This was the only important accession the North received. Then came an incident which overshadowed all others, and encouraged the Southern agents to renewed and more strenuous efforts. I refer to the famous Trent case, which brought the North and England much nearer to actual war than most people imagine. It were idle to speculate now on the consequences of such a collision, which at the time seemed almost inevitable.

The Trent case, in all its phases, is so familiar to the American mind, and so fresh in its memory, that I shall not attempt to recapitulate its incidents, but only touch upon the effects on the formation of foreign opinion.[9]

8. De Leon's marginal note refers to "Bright's Reasons," no doubt a reminder to explore Bright's motivations for taking the stand he did.

9. Briefly, on November 7, 1861, James M. Mason and John Slidell, Davis's new commissioners to England and France, left Havana aboard the British steamer *Trent* for the circuitous journey to England to take up their duties. The next day they were stopped and arrested by Captain Charles Wilkes of the USS *San Jacinto*. Wilkes took them to Boston to be held, while an international furor arose over a U.S. warship forcibly boarding and seizing legitimate passengers from a British merchant vessel. There was much talk of war, but little real chance of it. Britain demanded the release of the prisoners, and Lincoln acquiesced, thus calming the furor.

I was in London when the news of the capture of Messrs. Mason and Slidell, with their secretaries, Messrs. Eustis and McFarland, reached that city.[10] If Commodore Wilkes designed making a sensation he succeeded to his heart's content.[11] The usually apathetic Englishmen were roused to a sudden frenzy by this insult to their flag, such as I had never witnessed in them before. The feeling was so strong and so universal that it was impossible either for the Government or the most casual observer to mistake it. The whole nation almost as one man rose up and called for immediate rendition of the captured Commissioners, or for war. No other alternative was presented; none other would have been accepted. This incident did more to create a friendly feeling toward the South, and an unfriendly one toward the North, than all previous incidents combined. The Administration, averse as it was to increase the irritation of the Washington Government or the Northern people, was compelled to take decided steps, and peremptorily to demand rendition of the Commissioners, a request which it was supposed, in the inflamed condition of the Northern mind, the Washington Cabinet would not grant. For the conviction abroad was very strong on this point; and England prepared for war by immediately dispatching troops to Canada, the vulnerable point at which it was supposed the North would strike. Indeed many thought that the declaration and the act of war against that Province would be simultaneous.[12]

But one Englishman of note had the boldness to oppose this rushing tide. John Bright undertook the defence of the American Government, and brought down on his broad shoulders the merciless lash of the *Times*, which dubbed him "the devil's advocate."

Mr. Cobden also wrote a letter designated by the papers as "a prayer for peace," in which he proposed arbitration; but this the English Ministry and the English people would not listen to. Their demand was imperious and without alternative—"Deliver up the Commissioners or fight." Apology for the act was also claimed, but this Mr. Seward avoided, substituting in its place what was very much like insult.[13] But practical John Bull having secured the substance, paid little attention to the phrases in which the skillful

10. George Eustis was Slidell's secretary, and James E. Macfarland was Mason's secretary in London.

11. Captain Charles Wilkes, commander of the USS *San Jacinto*, who took Mason and Slidell from the *Trent*.

12. De Leon's portrait of English outrage is generally accurate, though the sentiment for war was never fully developed.

13. Lincoln and Seward knew they had to release Mason and Slidell but did not wish to appear to be backing down before British demands. Their final expedient was to release them because of

Seward covered over his surrender, and received the rescued Commissioners with a coldness and an indifference, which chilled the glowing hopes of the Confederates.

General Scott had been some time in Paris, and his name and reputation carried more weight with the public there than at home. He was regarded as a confidential agent of his Government, and was well received by the high functionaries and politicians. Yet he was unable to produce any change in French sentiment, and hurried home when the Trent question looked most threatening, with the avowed intention of preventing a collision.[14]

Mr. Thurlow Weed, who was then in Europe, as was supposed on a secret mission, took up the cudgels for his old friend Seward, and for the North, in a letter addressed to the *Times*, which was published in that journal, accompanied by the most caustic comments.[15] Two ex-diplomats of the old régime—Mr. Randolph Clay and Mr. Fay—undertook the same task, and fared no better.[16] The thunderbolts of the Jupiter of the press fell hot and heavy on their devoted heads, and the English people chuckled over and applauded the punishment.

On the other side, as may be supposed, the occasion was improved to the utmost by the agents of the Confederacy, through the press, and in all other ways.

France was in thorough sympathy with England, and sent assurances of her readiness to aid in enforcing a due observance of the Law of Nations upon the Yankees, but received a curt reply from Lord Russell, that England was fully competent to take care of her own honor and to protect her own flag without assistance. This reply was, of course, couched in diplomatic language, but

---

Britain's protest over the commissioners being seized from the vessel of a nation that was neutral in the American conflict. Seward reminded the British that such seizures by Britain from American vessels helped lead to the War of 1812, and now Seward expressed his pleasure that Britain recognized that America had been right and Britain in the wrong. In short, Seward made it appear as if the United States had forced Britain to admit its own earlier error, and in consequence was happy to let the prisoners go.

14. In his marginal note De Leon further identified his subject as "W. Scott." General Winfield Scott arrived in Paris for a visit immediately after the *Trent* affair arose, though not as an agent of his government. He attempted to calm the rumors that the United States seized the commissioners with the intention of inciting war with Britain.

15. Thurlow Weed was a prominent New York politician whom Seward sent abroad to work to persuade England and France to remain neutral.

16. John Randolph Clay of Pennsylvania was a career diplomat, until recently minister to Peru. Theodore S. Fay had most recently been U.S. minister to Switzerland.

such was its purport; and this did not tend to strengthen the *entente cordiale* between the two governments, for it wounded the pride of France.[17]

Though this caused France to love England less, it did not cause her to love her enemy the more, and the press of that country occupied itself much with questions relative to the blockade and the rights of neutrals, assuming both the English doctrine on these subjects, and the English from whom they had borrowed it, to be in defiance of the established Law of Nations.

M. de Hautefeuille, the ablest French writer on International Law, contributed to this *Revue Cotemporaine* a most remarkable article on these topics, which was marked by great hostility to England, whom he accused of arbitrarily taking her own interests as the supreme law.[18] He urged the meeting of a Congress to settle the rights of belligerents at sea, and the formation of a league of armed neutrals to protect their commerce in the event of a maritime war.

As this proposition was supposed to proceed from the inspiration of the highest authority in France, high hopes were entertained of its adoption and consequent diminution of the rigors of the blockade, if not its dissolution.

But these hopes were of short duration. The settlement of the difficulty in the Trent case, and the coolness between the two Governments consequent on Lord Russell's snappish answer to a friendly overture, prevented such co-operation; but the curious spectacle was at the same time witnessed of the peaceful sojourn of two ships of war—the Tuscarora (Northern) and the Nashville (Southern)—in the same harbor (that of Southampton), where they lay almost side by side for some time.[19] A better commentary on English neutrality than this could not be afforded. Yet the consequence was that both belligerents were dissatisfied, and England out of patience with both because of their unreasonableness.

17. De Leon's description of this episode is considerably at odds with the findings of Lynn M. Case and Warren F. Spencer, *The United States and France: Civil War Diplomacy* (Philadelphia, 1970), pp. 238–239.

18. Laurent Basile Hautefeuille was an authority on international law. De Leon notes in the margin "Revue Con.," probably an intention to quote from the actual article in a later version of the memoir.

19. The CSS *Nashville* arrived at Southampton on November 21, needing repairs after damage at sea, and did not leave until early February 1862. The USS *Tuscarora* was there keeping an eye on the *Nashville,* and port authorities ordered both to leave after being convinced that each was engaged in espionage against the other. James Mason to R. M. T. Hunter, January 30, 1862, U.S. Navy Department, *Official Records of the Union and Confederate Navies in the War of the Rebellion* (Washington, DC, 1894–1922), Series 2, vol. 3, p. 323.

This feeling made her people more surly and resolved when this Trent question came up.

It is a very significant and a very striking fact, and an illustration of the very different way in which parties act in the English and American legislative bodies, that no attempt was made to manufacture political capital out of this Trent affair. Lord Palmerston's Ministry found no more powerful supporters of their decided policy than in the opposition ranks headed by Earl Derby and Mr. Disraeli.

No factious or party efforts were made to embarrass the action of the Government; on the contrary, a cordial and zealous support was given to all measures intended to uphold the dignity of the British flag, which they considered had been wounded by the act of Commodore Wilkes, and which they believed the Northern Government intended to sustain. The *Times* blew up the embers of popular wrath to a white heat, and indulged in language of bitter scorn and derision. It denounced the conduct of the war by the North for the first time, and in unmeasured terms, and raked up every act which could lower it in the eyes of the civilized world. It dwelt on the famous stone fleet intended to block up the harbor of Charleston, and denounced it as a barbarism unknown even to the dark ages and to the most uncivilized warfare in ancient or modern times, and used equally strong language with regard to the Greek fire.[20] It declared that the "gradual brutalizing of the North" was one of the most marked features of the struggle, and scoffed at Mr. Seward's sixty-day predictions.[21] In fact, its tone blended hostility and scorn in equal degrees—the latter perhaps predominating.

Punch also improved the occasion by some of the most powerful cartoons from the pencils of Leech and Tenniel.[22] "Britannia Waiting for the Answer" and "Britannia's Message," were two of the most striking of the serious ones.

But the most significant was one which represented the Yankee troops in

20. The "Stone Fleet" was a flotilla of thirty-five old whaling ships purchased by the Union navy, loaded with several thousand tons of granite, and sent to be sunk in the entrances to the main shipping channels into Charleston harbor, presumably to close the port. They simply sank in the mud and Confederate blockade running continued virtually as before. Greek fire was a solution of phosphorus and other ingredients that burst into flame on exposure to the atmosphere, designed to be contained in hollow exploding shells and lobbed into forts and cities. It was little used, and chiefly in the bombardment of Charleston in 1863, but Confederates experimented with it, too.

21. In 1861 Seward had predicted that the Confederacy would be conquered within 60 days, an estimate that proved to be off by about 1,630 days.

22. Sir John Tenniel and John Leech were popular illustrators for *Punch*, who also illustrated some of the works of Dickens.

precipitate flight from Bull Run, arms thrown away, running breathlessly in one direction, and Mr. Bull calmly inquiring of the fugitives where they were going. "Going to take Canada," cries out the leader of the fight, rushing on as he replies.

On the 2d of January, 1862, while the question was still unsettled, the *Times,* then known to represent the views of the Administration, devoted three articles to the declaration that the quiet of England arose from fixed resolve, and that she would have satisfaction, and the statement was made that the cotton famine had not proved so difficult to deal with as had been anticipated.

On the 9th of January came the report of Mr. Seward's answer to Lord Lyons, which was treated in a tone of bitter contempt, though the fact of the surrender of the Commissioners was accepted as sufficient atonement for the injury done the national pride and dignity by the previous proceedings. The American press was treated by the Thunderer with as scant courtesy as Mr. Seward; for its changes on this question were compared to Mr. Thackeray's celebrated and not over-estimable character, Barry Lyndon, a gentleman whose scruples never were permitted to stand in the way of his interests or convenience.[23] I cite these illustrations to show the English animus at the time, which they faithfully represented.

How this threatening matter was finally settled by Mr. Seward's delivering up the Commissioners in the least courteous manner possible, accompanied by despatches intended to deprecate the sacrifice he had to make as an alternative of escaping worse evils, is familiar to every one.

A thrill of joy ran through prosperous England when the tidings came that she did not need to vindicate her honor at the cost of war. The French Emperor, not so much delighted, twisted up his moustache as is his wont when excited, and smoked some extra cigarettes. The French and Italian Revolutionists, or Reds, were bitterly dissatisfied that "Perfide Albion" should not have been democratized by a war which might cripple her commerce and destroy her prestige.

In Parliament the feeling was one of satisfaction. The *Times* signalized the surrender of the Commissioners by an editorial intending to throw cold water on the rising hopes of the more ardent secessionists, accompanied by a purely gratuitous insult to Messrs. Mason and Slidell, for whom it declared

23. The "Thunderer" was a nickname for the *Times* of London. Barry Lyndon, the eponymous protagonist of Thackeray's novel, was an unprincipled cad, coward, and seducer who stopped at nothing to advance his social ambitions.

the British Government and people cared no more than it did for two of their own negroes, and warning the Confederate Government that it must not mistake English feeling, which was not sympathetic, but purely based on a selfish jealousy of their own honor, wounded by the illegal and violent proceedings of Commodore Wilkes, and its apparent endorsement by his Government. Lord John Russell was severely blamed for the readiness with which he accepted the tardy and scanty amende made by Mr. Seward, whose manner of delivering up the Commissioners, with the reasons he assigned for it, were justly regarded as the reverse of satisfactory; but the small Premier having made up his mind to avoid a quarrel if possible, and appreciating the immense concession which Mr. Seward had made in "eating this leek," was not inclined to be captious or over-exacting, and let the discourtesy pass.

It is but just to Mr. Seward to say here, that his action in the premises was sagacious and statesmanlike, and it required no small share of moral courage to assume the responsibility of surrendering up the public prisoners in the midst of the wild excitement and popular approval of the act. A weaker or less sagacious man in his place would have braved the consequences, and those consequences would have been a war with England in thirty days, the recognition of the Southern Confederacy by England and France, followed by all the lesser Powers, and the rapid and effective breaking up of the blockade. The combination of these causes would have insured the independence and the success of the Confederacy beyond a doubt.

Placed in a position of infinite difficulty and delicacy, the representative of the Washington Government at London had no common task to perform. Yet it is due to Mr. Adams to acknowledge he played well his part, and by his singular moderation of language and of action tempered down the rough edges of Mr. Seward's rougher diplomacy. Both friend and foe admitted that in these trying circumstances he sustained his own dignity and that of the people he represented, as far as it was within his power to do so, and won reluctant admiration from many who loved not the cause or the Government he sustained. Had an indiscreet or less sensible man filled that post at that time, all the astuteness and all the dexterity of Mr. Seward could not have prevented war. The credit for having averted it, even at a price galling to national vanity and humiliating to national pride, must be shared between these two. Mr. Lincoln seemed to have carefully avoided the responsibility, as the very remarkable omission of any allusion to the matter in his message proves—an omission which excited much sarcastic comment abroad.

The Confederate Commissioners and all the friends of the South, of course, made as much capital out of this affair as they possibly could, through the press and otherwise. But the storm of angry feeling raged so fiercely that they had little need to do aught else than stand by and wait for developments.

The rapidity with which that angry feeling subsided was marvelous to witness, but it was succeeded by a sensation towards the North compounded of aversion and contempt, which it took many subsequent victories, and its final success, to eradicate from the English mind. That John Bull ever did or ever will love his cousin Jonathan is a pleasing fiction invented by after-dinner orators on international celebrations in either country. They are so radically dissimilar in all things, but more than Roman in ambition and love of extended territory, that it is the most difficult thing in the world to keep the two on terms of common civility; and the scar of the Trent affair adds but one more to the many sore points yet throbbing painfully and still unforgotten.

The Commissioners were divided in opinion as to the probable issue of the controversy and the action of the Washington Government. Judge Rost thought the chances equal. Mr. Yancey believed the prisoners would be surrendered. Mr. Mason was sanguine as to their retention.[24] So much so that he remonstrated with me on my determination to sail in the Southampton steamer of the 2d January for Havana, thence to take a blockade runner to New Orleans, which he considered a useless waste of time, believing that English war vessels would have opened intercourse with the sealed-up Southern ports before the expiration of the three weeks which it would take me to reach Havana.

Persisting in my determination on reaching St. Thomas on the 16th of January, 1862, I found that the released Commissioners had sailed thence for Southampton two days before.[25]

And thus that pillar of cloud for the North, and of light for the South, faded away from the vision of both, and was lost to the sight of all men, though it darkened the path of the former and illuminated that of the latter for a long time afterwards in England and over Europe.

How I broke the blockade in a steam-tug loaded with gunpowder—sailing from Havana to Baritara Bay—two days south of New Orleans, and reached

24. De Leon misspeaks here, meaning to say Mann when he wrote Mason.

25. Mason and Slidell were finally released December 26, 1861, and left for Europe on January 1, 1862, arriving at the end of the month. In the margin here De Leon wrote "Ed's blockade," presumably a reminder to write more on the blockade.

that latter city after many moving accidents by floods and bayous, including a chase and bombardment by the blockading fleet, which struck our little boat three times, it is not necessary to dilate upon here.[26]

Suffice it to say that I reached Richmond—the then capital of the new Confederacy—a few days after the 22nd of February, the day on which Mr. Davis was formally installed as President.[27]

What I saw there, and how it impressed me at the time, shall be the theme of the next chapter.

26. De Leon refers to Barataria Bay, the one-time haunt of smugglers and privateers like Pierre and Jean Laffite, and still a landing place for ships evading the Union blockade.

27. Davis's presidency at first, like the congress that elected him, was "provisional," meaning temporary until regular elections could be held under the permanent constitution framed and adopted in March 1861. In November 1861 elections were held, Davis running unopposed, and he was inaugurated as regular president of the Confederacy on February 22, 1862, the same day that the first regularly elected congress convened. De Leon notes "date at Richmond" to himself in the margin, a reminder to find the actual date of his arrival.

CHAPTER 12
INSIDE OF THE CONFEDERACY—IMPRESSIONS OF THE MEN AND THINGS I SAW THERE—PRESIDENT DAVIS AND HIS CABINET

———•◦•———

I reached Richmond the end of February, 1862, just after the inauguration of Mr. Davis as President of the Confederacy, and found Congress in session and busy at its work.[1] My reception by the President was most cordial, and I promptly renewed my long interrupted relations with my old co-laborers in the Southern cause in 1850–53, whom I found controlling the machinery at Richmond, as they formerly had done at Washington, with but a very small infusion of new or of younger men. And this at first struck me as one of the peculiarities of the revolution. Everything seemed to run in the old grooves. The old Constitution had been adopted with a few modifications; the old rules of Congress enforced by the same men I had been accustomed to see twelve years before, were governing the Richmond Capitol; and even the same speakers on very similar subjects were to be listened to within those walls.

The giants had passed away, and the men who had been dwarfed by grow-ing up beneath their shadows, had succeeded them, even as you see a thick forest of scrub oak trees replace the mighty monarchs of the forest, when time or storm have uprooted them from their thrones in the Old World.

It was natural to expect to see the Senate filled by the older politicians who had left their soft seats at Washington to come here, and who had been mainly instrumental in taking their States out of the Union; but in the House of Representatives the same facts were observable. Not only was there an ab-sence of new blood in this body, but I noted the presence of many lobby members whose advent was of evil augury. Many faces familiar under the gaslight in the old halls of Congress, and whose presence boded no good for the public—men whose only interest in the new Confederacy, as in the old Union, had been the scent of the spoils, and who, engorged by their feast at

1. De Leon states that it took him fifteen days to reach Richmond. *Thirty Years of My Life on Three Continents* (London, 1890), vol. 1, p. 321.

Washington, swooped down upon the new tables spread at Richmond. So that when I was asked by Mr. Davis, a few days after my arrival, whether I had attended the sessions of Congress and what my impressions were, I could not forebear replying that when I closed my eyes it carried me back twelve years. So like the old Congress did it sound, even to the familiar voice of irrepressible Senator Foote, and the crashing sound of the crushed peanut shells which strewed the floor—and when I opened my eyes the delusion was scarcely dispelled—so similar were the two scenes, with the exception of ours being on a smaller scale.[2]

Mr. Davis smiled grimly at my answer, and made no reply, probably having expected a more enthusiastic response. But the fact was as I stated it; and even at that early period of the struggle the camp seemed to attract the young blood of the country far more than the Council Chamber, and the energy and genius invoked by the hot breath of revolution wasted itself on bloody battle-fields, instead of carving out the destinies of a new country, leaving the task of legislation to the old politicians who never could depart from the beaten tracks in which they had always traveled, and who rehearsed on the new stage the same old state performances they had previously figured in at Washington.[3]

Thus Wigfall, whose genius and fury of irregular energy and glowing eloquence made him the Mirabeau of the revolution, first went into the field, and only returned to Congressional duties when failing health compelled him.[4] Roger A. Pryor, who was capable of playing a high *rôle* in the Council Chamber, both by his eloquence and his well-trained intellect, exchanged his seat in Congress for the tent, leaving a void which none was found to fill; as did also the impulsive and gifted Barstow, who "went to illustrate Georgia" on his first battle-field; where he perished, leaving only one of his compeers in that State able to "illustrate" her in statesmanship as he could have done.[5] So, too, of my own dear friend Maxcy Gregg, of South Carolina, and his more fortunate compeer, Wade Hampton, who still survives, both of

2. Henry S. Foote had been a senator and governor of Mississippi before the war, then served as a congressman from Tennessee.

3. De Leon noted in the margin here "Congress at Richmond," clearly evidence of an intent to elaborate on the Confederate legislature in a future version of this memoir.

4. Louis T. Wigfall of Texas had been an ardent secessionist and was a fiery hothead in congress who would become a leader in the opposition to the Davis administration.

5. Francis Bartow of Georgia served his state as a delegate to the original provisional congress in Montgomery, then resigned to command a Georgia regiment in the Battle of Bull Run, where he lost his life and became a Confederate martyr.

whom were the best representative men their State could have sent to the Congress, yet who both flung down the pen and took up the sword.[6]

And so in every State of the Confederacy the new blood which should have given tone to the new regime, was poured out on the battle-field, instead of infusing new vitality to the young State which sprang, Minerva like, from the brain of the old.

And this was one great secret of the failure of the Confederacy. No great political convulsion like this, heralding a new birth, ever yet was successful, unless it took its origin and derived its chief sustenance from young and vigorous brains. The child was born lusty and vigorous, but it was "spoon-fed" by ancient politicians, with their narrow notions, who could not and would not look beyond the narrow range of their own previous experience, and it "languishing did live" and die of a premature decay politically, even before the clash of arms had ceased, with the surrender of the great Southern General under the apple tree.[7]

There were exceptions, of course, to that general remark, but only sufficient to prove the rule. I believe now, as I did then, that no better nor wiser selection of a chief to control the destinies of the new State could have been made, than that which by popular acclaim elevated Jefferson Davis to that giddy height; but in the councillors he omitted, as well as those he chose, I equally believe he made mistakes, though how much of the blame for such omissions or such choice attached to him personally, I had no means of judging, during my short sojourn in the capital.

I chronicle only the fact that in many of his advisers, as well as in the absence or opposition of other men of mark in the South, (such as Pierre Soulé, John Forsyth, Louis Wigfall, W. W. Boyce and others) the country suffered, as well as the chief, who over-tasked brain and body in the desperate effort to accomplish more than unassisted human energy could perform.

I very soon perceived that the President and his policy, popular as they seemed with the great masses of the Southern people in and out of the field, yet had to encounter a powerful, though as yet unorganized, opposition in

6. Maxcy Gregg was a South Carolina politician who became a Confederate general, being killed at the Battle of Fredericksburg in December 1862. Wade Hampton was one of South Carolina's largest planters, but left his fields in 1861 and ended the war a lieutenant general in command of the cavalry of the Army of Tennessee.

7. A reference to the myth that Robert E. Lee surrendered his Army of Northern Virginia to General Ulysses S. Grant under an apple tree at Appomattox Courthouse, Virginia. The ceremony took place inside the home of Wilmer McLean.

Congress; while both Congress and people looked past his advisers up to him for the responsibility of every measure, the members of his Cabinet being supposed simply to register his decrees, as absolutely and as blindly as those of the Emperor Napoleon, whom he assimilated to in the iron will and inflexibility of purpose which stamped his character and administration.

I found, then, that there existed in Congress, chiefly among its younger members, much dissatisfaction both as to the selection of Mr. Davis's Cabinet officers, and other appointments, as well as to the general conduct of affairs— domestic and foreign. This nucleus of disaffection afterwards ripened into a strong and determined opposition party, which long before the close of the war rendered the executive and legislative branches of the Government repellant and discordant, and complicated the difficulties of a situation difficult and desperate enough even with perfect concord and concert of action.[8]

On my arrival in February, 1862, Mr. Toombs had left the Department of State and was understood to be in disaccord with the Administration, and he was by no means an enemy to be despised either from the weight of his name or his influence in Georgia, where it was at that time greater than that of his life long colleague, Mr. Stephens, who was also believed not to be enamored of the Administration, in which he did not take an active part. Second in intellect and in statesmanship to no man at the South, Mr. Stephens in the beginning of the struggle did not inspire the enthusiasm of the people, nor in many instances enjoy their full confidence. More far-sighted than the great majority, he foresaw and prophesied the difficulties and dangers attendant on the disruption, and was regarded as luke warm to the cause because he uttered unwelcome truths to an excited people, and coldly accepted, without being animated by a kindred enthusiasm to theirs, the high position they assigned him, next to that of the President.

All who knew the two men intimately also knew that cordial and sympathetic union between them was impossible, owing as much to the points of similarity as to those of repulsion in their mental and moral characteristics. Both were men of indomitable pride and of boundless ambitions. Both concealed beneath a cold and somewhat repellant exterior a love of popular applause, and that "infirmity of noble minds," the desire of fame. Neither was

---

8. The Confederacy was not a two-party system. Essentially there was the Administration, or Davis Party, and an amorphous and disorganized opposition, united if at all chiefly by personal antagonism to Davis himself. Led by men like Wigfall, Boyce, Robert Barnwell Rhett, and Stephens, the Opposition never seriously threatened Davis's legislative program and proved in the main to be an ineffective embarrassment.

fitted, either by temper or habits of thought, to play a subordinate or second part and each could play a grand solo, but neither could figure in a duet. Moreover, their standpoints were entirely different, and their beliefs equally so.

The President, after the first plunge was made, went heart and soul into the cause, dismissed from his mind all thought either of the prudence or propriety of the step, and never permitted himself either to despond or to doubt the issue. His previous habits of thought and of political belief had prepared him to accept the disruption as a legitimate conclusion from the postulates he had laid down for many years in Congress and at home. He neither regarded slavery nor secession as evils *per se,* or, at least, if such, as compensated by greater good.

Mr. Stephens's standpoint, as well as his antecedents, was different. He had resisted the current setting towards secession, and was no enthusiast for the institution of slavery; in fact, his soundness on both points had been doubted. His judgment was decidedly opposed to extreme measures, and he had as decidedly stated that opposition. After the secession of his State, he accepted it as a fixed fact, and acted, as he openly avowed, from a sense of duty only to his State in embracing her cause and sharing her fortune; but he made even this great sacrifice so coldly, and in a manner so devoid of enthusiasm in the beginning, as greatly to detract from the merit of his action in the eyes of a people excited almost to frenzy.

Once embarked in a cause however, it was not in his strong nature to adopt half measures, and his speeches and utterances were among the ablest and the strongest during the struggle, and certainly the most so, since the failure of the cause to which he has shown more devotion in its downfall, than during the hours of its supposed triumph. So little interest did he seem to take in the proceedings of Mr. Davis's administration, while I was in Richmond, that I never saw him in the company of the President; never heard of his assisting at Cabinet meetings; nor did he preside over the Senate as *ex officio* he was entitled to do, but under the plea of ill health kept himself much retired from all public affairs, except those of his native State, where Governor Brown was always a thorn in the side of the Richmond Government, and this reflected upon Mr. Stephens, who, justly or unjustly, was supposed to inspire the Governor.[9] Whatever Mr. Stephens's faults may be,

9. After the first few months of the war, Stephens did, indeed, essentially remove himself, spending most of his time at home in Georgia and gradually becoming more and more involved with the Opposition. He and Governor Joseph Brown were one-time foes who made occasional—and uncomfortable—common cause in their antipathy to the president.

however—and I do not consider him as faultless by any means—indirection and intrigue are not among them; he was a bold and direct if a bitter and prejudiced man, and I do not deem him capable of meanness.

The testimony is the more valuable, coming from one who, in his party combinations during many years, was generally in opposition to Mr. Stephens, and as times then went, very bitter opposition, especially during the Compromise agitation of 1849–50, and the contest between the separate State action and cooperation parties in the South.

One member of the Cabinet only appeared to have or to exercise much influence over Mr. Davis, and that one was Mr. Benjamin, then Secretary of War. As far as I could see, however, the President exercised autocratic power over all the Departments, and supervised and directed everything.

The State Department had recently been vacated by Mr. Toombs, who was supposed to verify his own declaration to the letter in his management of that post—viz: that he carried the Department of State in his hat, requesting once to know whether an importunate applicant for a place fitted to him, "could get in there?"[10] It was under Mr. Toombs's administration, however, that the first three Commissioners had been sent to Europe, and, if I mistake not, the second Commission, composed of Messrs. Mason and Slidell, also.[11]

What his purposes or ideas of foreign policy were I have no personal knowledge, for he had vacated the office when I reached Richmond, and I saw him only at the head of his mounted brigade some time after, his head covered with a slouched hat capable of containing archives, and his shoulders protected by a blanket-rug, as he rode through Richmond, bearded like a Pard, and looking more like a head-hunter than a diplomat.

Robert M. T. Hunter was acting as Secretary *pro tem* when I first visited the Department, and in conversations with him I soon perceived that he was not so blindly confident as most of the men I met. On the contrary, he seemed to me to be more despondent and less hopeful than circumstances warranted, and inclined to take rather a gloomy view of the future in every aspect. To his ripe experience and thoughtful mind the importance and necessity of

10. There are several versions of Toombs's remark, a statement thoroughly typical of the man. The most common version has him saying to an applicant for office, "can you get in here, sir," taking off his hat. "That is the Department of State, sir." Coincidentally, the quotation comes from De Leon's brother Thomas C. De Leon's *Four Years in Rebel Capitals* (Mobile, AL, 1890), p. 33.

11. In fact, Toombs resigned as secretary of state on July 24, 1861, months before the appointment of Mason and Slidell.

obtaining foreign recognition and intervention if possible was very evident; but, at the same time, he seemed very hopeless of our obtaining it.

The treatment of our Commissioners abroad, who were compelled *faire antichambre*—that is to say, wait outside for an unprivileged audience, while the Washington Minister went in at the privileged door, and admitted but once even on those terms—exasperated Southern pride. The concessions made by Lord Russell to the threatening language and arrogant demands of Mr. Seward relative to the reception of the Commissioners, and the humble apology of the former that, although he once admitted the Confederate agents, he should never offend in that way again, and the failure of the Trent case to inure to our advantage—all seemed to convince Mr. Hunter that foreign aid was not to be secured, although he evidently entertained painful doubts as to the probability of our final success without it.

My own report of things on the other side (as cheerful and hopeful as I could truthfully make it) did not succeed in removing this impression.

Using the privilege of an old friend, I strongly urged him to remain at the head of the State Department, as he certainly was the best qualified man we had for that post, and might effect more good there than in the Senate. But he declined doing so, not being willing to assume the responsibility, and shrinking from assuming a share of the unpopularity of the Cabinet, daily increasing, and with slight prospects of diminution.[12]

I have no doubt that it would have been far better for the President and for the Confederacy had his objections been overruled; for Mr. Hunter was a statesman, which his successor, Mr. Benjamin, with all his talents industry and subtlety, never was and never could be—but only an astute politician of the Plaquemines school.[13] So, with far less ability and information, was his confrere and colleague Mr. Slidell; and had the President searched throughout the whole Confederacy to select the two most unpopular men in it, he could not have succeeded better than in selecting the two Senators from Louisiana, who, justly or unjustly, never did, at any period, possess the con-

12. As already stated, Hunter was a slippery trimmer who pretended friendship to Davis's face, but worked to undercut him behind his back, his eye chiefly on his own ambitions to succeed Davis as president. Nothing in Hunter's actual record would warrant De Leon's high opinion of him, a good example of De Leon's frequent failure to see men and events clearly.

13. De Leon misses no opportunity for a jab at Benjamin, his *bête noir*. There was no "Plaquemines school," though Plaquemines is the parish where Benjamin lived. De Leon's reference is merely an unsubtle denigration of Benjamin as a quasi-corrupt local politician, adept at wire pulling and self-interest on the order of Louisiana's local politicians then and later.

fidence of the country, and whose influence was limited to a very small compact clique of political wire-pullers in Louisiana.

Giving these gentlemen the benefit of the best possible intentions, and crediting them with the desire of doing their best and not denying the undoubted genius and industry of one of them at least, I did at the time, and still do concur in the popular verdict that they were not the right men in the right places, but quite the reverse; and I am quite sure, however competent they may prove themselves to manipulate American politics at Washington, that they were totally unable either to comprehend the foreign situation or to advance the Confederate cause abroad. Thus, at the very moment when it was almost our *dernier resort* to secure French assistance, Mr. Benjamin wounded the pride of that Government and people by dismissing its consul from Texas, accompanying the insult with the injury of charging complicity in a plot to make it a French possession of that Government.

So, when an issue of veracity between Mr. Roebuck and the Emperor, and of good faith on the Emperor's part to the British Ministry, further alienated his feelings from the Confederacy, justly or unjustly, it was regarded as the fruit of an intrigue of Mr. Slidell's.[14]

And so on *ad infinitum*; for the worst possible reputation a diplomat can have is the suspicion of his being too diplomatic. I had had no previous personal acquaintance with either the Secretary or the Commissioner, both of whom had come on the political arena subsequently to my leaving the country in 1853—so was not prejudiced against them. Knowing that common rumor was often a common liar, and the popular judgment in their regard might be unjust, I applied myself diligently to the task of approaching them without prepossessions either way. I hoped that something might be done through them, and resolved to cooperate cordially with them—which I did until I found it impossible longer to do so.

When I first met Mr. Benjamin, so great was the charm of his manner, so winning was his address, so apparently open and frank his conversation,

14. In October 1862 B. Théron, French consular agent at Galveston, was suspected of attempting to maneuver Texas into leaving the Confederacy and resuming its independence, in order to provide a relatively weak and unthreatening northern boundary for Mexico, which Napoleon had determined to conquer and operate as a vassal state of France. President Davis instructed Benjamin to expel Théron from the Confederacy, which he did. Benjamin to Slidell, October 17, 1862, U.S. Navy Department, *Official Records of the Union and Confederate Navies in the War of the Rebellion* (Washington, DC, 1894–1922), Series 2, vol. 3, pp. 556–559. John A. Roebuck supported Palmerston staunchly in Parliament.

so bright and quick his intelligence, that I was charmed with him, and comprehended his society must be [a palliative] to the overtasked body and mind of Mr. Davis.

Moreover, his zeal and energy in the cause were indisputable, and he adhered to it unflinchingly to the bitter end. I spoke, therefore, to him with the same freedom as I had to my old friends, Mr. Davis and Mr. Hunter. He evinced the deepest anxiety and the warmest interest in our foreign relations, and seemed to place great reliance on Mr. Slidell's tact and management especially—a delusion which he persisted in professing to the end—and with which he even inspired Mr. Davis, who had served with Mr. Slidell in Congress, and knew him to be almost the only man connected with Southern politics, who had never spoken or written a word on any subject, which any one remembered; and whose only reputation—which preceded him abroad—was that of an adroit intriguer.

Sydney Smith once said of Lord John Russell, that his confidence in himself was so great that at an hour's notice he would have assumed the command of the Channel fleet with perfect composure. The rapid transitions of Mr. Benjamin suggest the same reflection.

The remarkable versatility of Mr. Benjamin's talent is proven by the fact that he occupied successively three seats in the Cabinet, and to the last moment exerted a greater personal influence over Mr. Davis than any other of his counselors. He was first Attorney-General, a post for which his legal training fitted him—then Minister of War, for which his whole career disqualified him—and finally Secretary of State, where, in my judgment, his record will not add to his reputation—for of State papers from his pen, worthy of comparison with the statesmanlike and powerful messages of Mr. Davis, we have none.

His published dispatches during the struggle were not characterized by the ability he possesses and manifests in other branches of composition—were generally *mal apropos*, and did much mischief frequently. Of his unpublished dispatches (of which I have some yet,) I do not propose to speak. The only Confederate State papers worthy of the name, were the messages of the President. The future student of the great struggle which has so convulsed this country, will find in them the clearest and most concise history of the causes of the war, its progress, and the chronicle of events as they transpired, which that war has bequeathed us. The so-called histories of the war on either side do not contain a tithe of the information they give, or of the light they throw on the incidents and principles of those stirring times. Mr. Davis unconsciously wrote history while framing messages—while his Secretary of State penned only messages of temporary interest while writing dispatches.

It was the earnest desire of the President, as well as of his advisers, that advantage should be taken of the favorable state of feeling in Europe, engendered by the Trent affair, to secure recognition at least, if not more.

My long experience in foreign affaires, and my recent residence abroad and familiarity with all that had transpired, induced the President and his advisers to place some confidence in my judgment, and we had very frequent conversation on the subject, the President being by no means hopeless of managing the matter, and Mr. Benjamin as sanguine and confident as his successor was despondent. In fact, it was the kind of thing he liked—the difficulties put him on his mettle, and he busied himself devising new plots and plans to secure new allies for the Confederacy, with sleepless energy and untiring industry.

Just about this time, in March, 1862, Mr. Yancey returned from Europe, landed at New Orleans, and made a speech, in which with his usual headlong openness he relieved his mind, and took the entire people into his confidence as to the failure of his mission, with the decided assertion of his knowledge and belief that no better success would attain any one who succeeded him, declaring openly that the dignity and the interests of the Confederacy required the immediate withdrawal of all the Foreign Agents—in which opinion one of his colleagues, Judge Rost, was understood to concur; Mr. Mann's opinion, if given formally, never having been seen by me—though I think he took the opposite view.[15]

After the two new Commissioners had been sent, a move to which very indiscreet publicity had been given, the old Commissioners were removed to new fields of labor; Judge Rost was assigned to Spain, taking Mr. Fearn with him; Mr. Mann to Belgium, Rome and Denmark, at which latter place he had at a subsequent period some negotiations about Confederate matters at St. Thomas; Mr. Slidell took Paris.

Mr. Mason remained in England, for which place his habits of thought and life, and want of familiarity with foreign languages, best fitted him. He was liked and respected personally by those who came in contact with him. His proud old Mother State had her dignity fully sustained by him.

With reference to his diplomatic abilities men may and do differ, especially in his foreign agency—a new field to him. The stern-lights of experience

15. Yancey actually arrived March 13, 1862.

are of little value in navigating new waters, and old men are slower to learn hard lessons than younger ones. The diplomacy of the young Confederacy was manipulated by older men and on more ancient traditions and prejudices, than that of the Washington Government, which was one great source of weakness and failure to the former.

As I said, in one of my intercepted letters to President Davis—giving great offence at the time—"Our old political leaders, like the Bourbons, seem to have learned nothing and forgotten nothing." Mr. Yancey was an exception; he had learned something, but could not forget enough to comprehend the actual situation, or renounce long cherished illusions as to cotton and slavery.[16]

But Mr. Yancey's return, his report, the measures he proposed, and those which were finally adopted, demand a separate chapter.

16. This is a reference to De Leon's October 1, 1863, letter to Davis, captured on a blockade runner at Wilmington, and soon thereafter appearing in the Northern press, including the Washington *National Intelligencer* on November 17, 1863. In it De Leon lambasted Confederate politicians and speculators, whom he called "swaggering shufflers from danger who call themselves Confederates," and also expressed his opinion that there would be no forthcoming recognition either from England or France. He also expressly told Davis that he could "buy golden opinions" in the French press. Lynda Lasswell Crist, Kenneth H. Williams, and Peggy L. Dillard, *The Papers of Jefferson Davis*, vol. 10, *October 1863–August 1864* (Baton Rouge, LA, 1999), p. 3.

———•◆•———

Mr. Yancey returned to New Orleans, through the blockade, the beginning of April.[1] As he was a man who never went half way either in his utterances or his acts, and came back with a fixed idea in his mind, he publicly avowed his belief and his policy within twenty-four hours after his arrival.

This course was not that of a diplomatist, but it was very characteristic of William L. Yancey, and it confirms the judgment of him pronounced in an earlier chapter. His conduct, however, was not more indiscreet than the publicity and notoriety given to the mission of the gentlemen who succeeded him as Commissioners, and the ostentatious parade at Havana, which led to the imbroglio. In fact, it was less so; for his functions were completed, while the others were just commencing theirs.

The evening of his arrival, on entering the rotunda of the St. Charles Hotel, after dinner, a large crowd met Mr. Yancey, and insisted on his addressing them, which he did, in a speech of half an hour's length. He remarked on rising that—

"He had been absent for a year endeavoring as Commissioner to secure the recognition of that independence for which his countrymen were so gallantly contending.

"He should doubtless surprise his auditors when he told them they had no friends in Europe; that they must depend on themselves alone. And what he said of European feeling in regard to this Confederacy was equally true of its feeling toward the North, whose people, whose Government and whose press, the statements and writings of whose public men, and literary writers, they believe to be altogether mendacious.

"The sentiment of Europe was anti-slavery, and that portion of public

1. As earlier stated, Yancey in fact arrived on March 13, 1862.

opinion which formed and was represented by the Government of England was abolition.

"At the same time it was very well understood and believed that the pretexts on which this war was inaugurated and carried on by the North against us were utterly false.

"They would never recognize our independence until our conquering sword hung dripping over the head of the North.

"They believe we are a brave and determined people, resolved in obtaining our independence. But they would like to see the two Confederacies crippled by war, and so would give aid to neither.

"As to the blockade, he said that the nations of Europe would never raise it until it suited their interests. In his own private opinion he believed that necessity would occur at a very early day.

"He said it was an error to say 'cotton is king.' It is not. It is a great and influential power in commerce, but not its dictator. He referred to the idea in England of getting cotton from other quarters, but thought it a fallacy. He thought the blockade was a blessing to the Confederate States, by compelling them to rely solely on their own sources.

"Mr. Yancey counseled a firm, united and generous support of the Government, which had been just inaugurated.

"We had placed them at the helm. They might commit errors; but all history teaches that where there is mutiny in the crew the bark must go down. He concluded by expressing the strongest confidence in the final success of the cause, and at the close was greeted with the most enthusiastic cheers."

Mr. Yancey followed up this speech by his personal presence at Richmond, where his arrival and opinions created a great sensation.

He repeated the same views in conversation with the President and leading men, and threw the consideration of the matter into the Senate by the introduction of a resolution in secret session recalling all the Commissioners. A very animated discussion arose upon this resolution in that body, and a very wide discrepancy of opinion was seen to exist; but Mr. Yancey's fiery eloquence and the logic of facts which he brought to bear with the authority of his late experiences, made many proselytes to his opinions. I had many and earnest colloquies with him on the subject, and we only "agreed to disagree" on the policy and propriety of the measures he proposed.[2]

2. No record of Yancey introducing such a resolution to the Senate survives, but since it was in secret session, that may explain it. There seems little reason to doubt De Leon's account of Yancey telling him he had done so.

Both the President and Mr. Benjamin were anxious about this movement, and leading Senators, such as Orr, Wigfall, Hunter and others, thought there was danger of the adoption by the Senate of the policy of isolation suggested by Mr. Yancey, of which they disapproved.[3]

I therefore actively employed myself to combat Mr. Yancey's views, in conversations with Senators, and by suggestions to the editors of Richmond journals.[4]

Having finally submitted my views in writing to the President and Secretary of State, at their request, I caused their publication in the *Whig*, a paper not over-friendly to the Administration, but whose editor, Mr. Mosely, being a patriotic man, not only inserted my vindication of the foreign policy of the Government, but also warmly approved of the new programme proposed.[5]

This communication was published without my signature, but its authorship was known.

The immediate practical results of Mr. Yancey's motion were: The failure of his attempt to withdraw all the Commissioners from Europe, and the initiation of fresh and more vigorous efforts to act upon foreign cabinets and public opinion abroad.

My own programme, as opposed to his of entire inaction, was one of vigorous action—embracing an attack on all points simultaneously. It sought to organize a plan by which a combined effort might be made at once to secure recognition and active intervention, if possible, from governments, and to fortify them in taking this step by creating a public opinion in Europe favorable to the South, through the medium of the foreign press, and by special publications adopted to that end.

The only step which had been taken in the latter direction was the appointment of Mr. Hotze as commercial agent to London, with instructions to act on public opinion, through the press, as far as possible. Shortly after this time Mr. Hotze established at London a journal called the *Index*, in May, 1862, avowedly as an organ and exponent of the Confederate cause. The establishment and conduct of this organ I did not then approve of, for no

3. James L. Orr was a senator from South Carolina. Wigfall was now a senator from Texas, and Hunter a senator from Virginia.

4. Significantly, a year later De Leon had come around to Yancey's point of view on withdrawing diplomatic agents from Europe, and on May 9, 1863, proposed to Davis that he recall all of his commissioners in order to shock England and France into reconsidering their position toward the Confederacy. Lynda Lasswell Crist, Mary Seaton Dix, and Kenneth H. Williams, eds., *The Papers of Jefferson Davis*, vol. 9, *January–September 1863* (Baton Rouge, LA, 1997), p. 177.

5. Alexander Mosely was editor of the Richmond *Whig*.

reasons relating personally to its manager and contributors, who labored with indefatigable industry and good taste in its management; but because I foresaw that the Confederate label placed openly upon it would mar its utility and confine its circulation to the class who already sympathized with us and did not need convincing.[6]

My investigations had also satisfied me that the same labor and the same expenditure turned into other channels already existing and reaching the public ear, would effect infinitely more good. Hence the *Index*, though valuable as an authoritative exponent of the views and wishes of the Confederate Government, and as a medium of communicating abroad facts and measures connected with the action of Congress and the incidents of the war, never could produce much effect on the foreign mind, whose views were colored by the reflections from its own journals.

Therefore, my idea was to infiltrate the European press with our ideas and our version of the struggle, and to secure cooperation of foreign governments by making an appeal, not to sentimental considerations, but to their substantial interests. A firm believer in the sentiment that the "pen is mightier than the sword," I did not think that the American conflict was to be decided almost exclusively by the latter, nor do I believe that such has often been the case in the world's history. In ours it may have been because the second condition was not complied with, and the Confederacy did not entrust that "pen" to hands "entirely great," without which States cannot be saved by that or any other weapon.

My views and ideas, as submitted to the President and Secretary of State, were substantially as follows:

> Thus far we have practiced what might be termed a waiting diplomacy. The Confederacy has relied on foreign countenance and assistance, momentarily proffered without holding out any extraordinary inducements, or making any liberal offers to secure recognition or intervention. You have believed that the cotton famine abroad—the design of dividing and thus weakening the power of this aggressive democracy and the justice of your cause—would command European countenance and aid. Consequently, you have sent abroad your diplomatic agents, in the belief that it was only necessary to ask recognition to insure it; and though you have given them a wide discretion and liberal powers, yet your policy is too vague. What is needed is some specific proposition, of exclusive advantages, to one or more foreign powers strong enough and bold enough to make an

6. Henry Hotze and the *Index* are the subjects of Charles P. Cullop's *Confederate Propaganda in Europe 1861–1865* (Miami, FL, 1969).

alliance offensive and defensive with you, against your opponent, who with his superior resources and open ports finds foreign neutrality almost equivalent to foreign alliance. Moreover, you have hitherto believed that your resources and the warlike character of your people, would allow you to fight out this battle unaided, and that you could dispose with foreign aid.

Mr. Yancey's report—which my own experience confirms—has established the falsity of all these hopes and all these views. It is clearly necessary to take a new departure. What shall the new policy be? Mr. Yancey says, "withdraw your commissioners, and trust to the issue of battle and to the coming necessities of Europe, industrial and political." In this I differ in toto from Mr. Yancey, and regard the diplomacy of the Confederacy so far from having been exhausted as scarcely yet initiated. We have only sounded the ground thus far. We have done nothing more. We are all satisfied that neither sentiment nor principle will sway the European Governments in these matters, and that their policy is purely a selfish one. Let us, therefore, appeal to that selfishness and make it a fulcrum for our lever. You have heretofore regarded England as your great point, basing that belief on her supposed necessity for your cotton. She can, and will, do without it, as the two great oracles on that subject, Messrs. Cobden and Bright, have declared; and these two have gone yet further and declared that the speediest way to secure that cotton will be the triumph of the North.

In my judgment, France is the point at which our diplomacy should chiefly be directed. The Empire, founded by Napoleon III, has been built upon a surer basis than his uncle's. He has made France a commercial and industrial nation, and his great ambition is to make her rival and excel, if possible, her traditionary foe, perfide Albion, whom she loves less than ever. Let our diplomacy be directed to that point. Let us offer to France, who has evinced a more friendly feeling towards us than England, exclusive advantages—a treaty offensive and defensive, with discriminations as to the purchase and carrying out of our great staples and her own imports—such as will bind her to the Confederacy by ties of interest. Let it once be seen that France has made such an arrangement, and that we have secured so powerful an ally, and the North will make peace with us; for she cannot ally herself with England, her rival in everything, in manufactures in shipping, in commerce, whose greatness grows with her decadence.

The great stumbling block in the way of our foreign alliance is the perpetuation of the institution of slavery. That sentiment is stronger abroad than even considerations of interest—stronger probably in France than in England. Can we make no concessions in that direction? Can we not offer a gradual emancipation to at least a portion of our negroes—say at the expiration of twenty years—so as to give our friends abroad an answer to the cry that this is a war for the perpetuation of slavery? If these two movements could be made simultaneously, and the Commissioners already abroad could be reinforced in every capital by secret diplomatic agents—younger and more active men—with instructions and powers, only to be shown in case of actual need of them—not labeled with them in advance—I think something might be done. Added to this, public opinion abroad is influenced by the press, infinitely more than in this country. Hitherto your diplomacy has been confined to the Cabinets and Legislators of Europe. Let us strike at the people. Send ambassadors to public opinion in Europe to act on the matter, so that every man may imbibe correct information on the real merits of our quarrel, and the real progress of the struggle, every morning, when he reads his newspaper at breakfast. More also can be done in France than in England, in this; owing to the peculiar position of the press in that country, and to the great deference paid to public opinion, as expressed through it by the Emperor's Government. How this can be done you will see by the programme proposed, which is based on my intimate knowledge of that press and its managers. Believe me, the Emperor will march on with a firmer step, if the ground can thus be made solid beneath his feet.

Such was substantially the programme submitted to the heads of the Confederate Government; who, while they approved of it, treated it much as the ancient Jupiter is stated to have treated the prayer of Martels—a part they granted, the rest they dismissed into empty air. With regard to the matter of emancipation, or of slavery generally, they regarded it as impossible to make any concessions, in the then temper of our people—and evidently thought I was overstating the feeling in Europe, and the necessity of any action upon it.

With regard to the infusion of fresh blood into the diplomatic representation abroad, they narrowed it down to insisting on my own return there, to cooperate with the agents already sent; considering the reinforcement of Messrs. Mason, Slidell, and myself as all sufficient in the actual position of affairs, of which they were far more hopeful than I, but suggesting they might send others in course of time. I pressed this point as hard as I could, but did not succeed in securing the supply of fresher and younger blood imperatively needed. The old traditions, and the circumlocution lessons of Washington, were repeated in Richmond, and we had to travel *super antiques vias*.[7]

My political programme for enlisting French intervention was adopted; and very tempting inducements were held out to the Emperor as the reward of prompt and active intervention in our behalf.

With all the lights of past experience and events to guide me now, I still think the policy proposed was the best and most efficient one that could have

7. According to old custom. Literally "on ancient roads."

been adopted under the circumstances. In fact, it was the only one that could be dignified with that name, the others consisting of temporary expedients and petty intrigues only.

I do not hold myself responsible for its failure.

Firstly—Because my plan was but partially adopted, and the great stumbling block of slavery never removed an inch out of its pathway; but erected as an impassable barrier by our astute adversary.

And secondly, because very incompetent hands on the other side intermeddled with and damaged it.

And thirdly, because just at the moment the Confederate proposal was formally made to the Emperor, the renewal of Garibaldi's movement "On to Rome!" distracted his attention, and tied his hands, European interests and complications demanding all his thoughts and cares.

And so the golden moment slipped away, the *entente cordiale* between England and France was drawn closer; and no French fleet came to cut the Gordian knot of the blockade, and reinstate "King Cotton" on a newer and stronger throne than ever.

Be this as it may, however, by authority of the President, I was named as confidential agent of the Department of State abroad.[8] With a delicacy, which was not reciprocated in some quarters afterwards, I had avoided even the appearance of superseding or interfering with the agents already appointed; regarding them as good figure-heads for the Confederate Government, and useful in their particular sphere. That which I selected, was private and confidential in its very essence; and based on a careful avoidance of avowed diplomatic position, which would only debar me from free intercourse with the foreign statesmen, through whom I designed initiating the policy proposed.

When the proposal was made to me to return to Europe, of course I could not refuse to take charge of my own bantling in its perilous passage across the seas, through the blockade, and keeping watch over its health after

8. The precise date of De Leon's appointment is uncertain, but it was on or before April 12, 1862, when Benjamin made reference to it in a letter to James Mason, U.S. Navy Department, *Official Records of the Union and Confederate Navies in the War of the Rebellion* (Washington, DC, 1894–1922), Series 2, vol. 3, p. 385 (hereafter cited as *ORN*). In fact, Benjamin's letter to John Slidell of that same date suggests that Benjamin learned of the appointment while writing the letter, meaning it was almost certainly April 12 (Benjamin to Slidell, April 12, 1862, *ORN*, p. 390). In his 1890 memoir, De Leon says he first asked Davis for a commission in the army, but the president asked him to take a diplomatic post instead (*Thirty Years of My Life on Three Continents* [London, 1890], vol. 2, p. 2).

arrival. So when asked, when I could be ready to start, my reply was "in twenty-four hours."

"What title, credentials or commission I desired?" None, except that of confidential agent, with a few lines from the Department, authenticating my position. To the third query, as to what salary I would wish, my reply was, "None; I propose paying my own expenses."[9]

The necessary papers were drawn up and submitted to me, including dispatches to Messrs. Mason and Slidell, and immediately after receiving the documents, I left Richmond for Wilmington, North Carolina, where the fast blockade runner Theodora, Capt. Maffit, was awaiting me, to break the blockade to Nassau.[10]

The Washington Government understood thoroughly the importance of secret missions, such as mine, and the most useful part of its work was done through them.

In verification of this, I need only name Bishop Hughes, General Scott, Thurlow Weed, Robert J. Walker,—all of whom, as well as Henry Ward Beecher—were believed to speak authoritatively, though unofficially, the views and wishes of the North, and who were made the means of communicating facts which could not be conveyed through openly accredited ambassadors.[11]

And here, an interesting little episode relating to Gen. Lee, whom I have never since seen, may not be out of place.

Immediately after receiving my appointment I was with the President, in his private cabinet, when Gen. Lee came in with a telegraphic dispatch in his hand, and calmly addressing Mr. Davis, said: "I have some news from Savannah, Mr. President." Mr. Davis looked up quickly, a shade of anxiety on his face, and replied: "I hope it is good news." "I regret to say that it is not," calmly replied Gen. Lee; "Fort Pulaski is taken." A flash of vexation passed over the worn face of the President. "Should this have been, Gen. Lee? You know that Fort, and examined its defences a short time since." "In my judg-

9. Benjamin did, however, give De Leon $25,000 as a "secret-service fund" to finance his efforts to influence European public opinion. Benjamin to Mason, April 12, 1862, *ORN*, p. 385.

10. The dispatches Benjamin gave De Leon for transport are in *ORN*, pp. 385–397, dated April 12–14, 1862. Captain John N. Maffitt commanded *Theodora*.

11. In addition to General Scott and Thurlow Weed, Robert J. Walker, Henry Ward Beecher, and Archbishop John Hughes of New York all played minor roles in Union efforts to keep England and France neutral. For more on their efforts see Lynn M. Case and Warren F. Spencer, *The United States and France: Civil War Diplomacy* (Philadelphia, 1970).

ment it was impregnable," said Gen. Lee; and he then went on to state what those defences were, adding, with his habitual fairness, "Our information, as yet, is too scanty to allow us to judge of the merits of the case. This thing only is certain: the fort has surrendered." What struck me most in this interview was the manner in which these two leaders took this reverse—the unshaken fortitude, the almost Indian stoicism displayed by Gen. Lee, and the absence of all petulant complaint on the part of the President. It was a lesson in self-command and dignity, for both doubtless felt more than they cared to show or to confess to each other.[12]

At that time Gen. Lee, unworn by the anxieties and privations which afterwards aged him so rapidly in appearance, was, I think, one of the handsomest men I had ever seen. The white head, which now gives a patriarchal dignity to his appearance, he did not then wear. His face was closely shaven, and a small dark moustache shaded his upper lip. Both in face and form he looked a young man, while the stately figure, carried with military erectness, induced one who passed him by to turn and look again.

The next day I left Richmond, and while waiting at Wilmington to run out, received the tidings of the fall of New Orleans, and received a notice of the visit of the French Ambassador, Mr. Mercier, to Richmond—two events which, in our opinion at the time, counter valued each other.[13] The "Theodora" ran the blockade successfully, after being watched by the blockaders outside for several nights, eluding their vigilance by the happy audacity of dashing out at sunset, when they did not expect her, and their fires were banked; thus getting a start, and afterwards running into such shallow water, near the Frying Pan Shoals, (with which Capt. Maffit, having been on the Coast Survey, was familiar,) that our pursuers dared not follow.

Chased over, all the way to Nassau, we outstripped pursuit, and thence I sailed via Havana to Southampton, to accomplish my mission in Europe.[14]

12. This episode further confirms April 12, 1862, as the probable date of De Leon's appointment, for Benjamin to Mason, April 14, 1862, *ORN*, p. 392, states that telegrams that same morning brought Richmond news of Fort Pulaski's fall, thus dating Lee's meeting with Davis to April 14, a date that is confirmed by De Leon's subsequent statement that he left Richmond the day after the meeting with Davis and Lee. Benjamin told Mason on April 14 that De Leon was to leave the next day.

13. De Leon reached Wilmington on April 17 and waited some time for the *Theodora* to sail (Benjamin to Samuel G. French, April 21, 1862, *ORN*, p. 397). Henri Mercier was the French minister to Washington.

14. De Leon provides an extended account of this voyage and his time in Nassau in *Thirty Years*, vol. 2, pp. 3–17. He was detained in Nassau three weeks. De Leon to Judah P. Benjamin, July 30,

NOTE:—As confirmatory of the views expressed above, I would cite the following exposition of the practice of the State Department from the pen of Mr. Seward:

FOREIGN SECRET SERVICE

Letter recently sent to the Senate, remonstrating against the proposed abolition of Secret Service Agents of Department of State:

Department of State

Washington, Jan. 28, 1867.

It is to be hoped that the bill, which it is understood has been introduced into the Senate, prohibiting the appointment of Special Agents, and terminating the functions of such agents as may now be employed, is not intended to apply to agents of that character in connection with Foreign Affairs. If it were to embrace them it would not only create great embarrassment in the management of those affairs, but would often make the transaction of important public business impracticable. Special Agents for Foreign Affairs have been more or less employed by every Administration from that of Washington to the present time. Washington himself sent Gouverneur Morris to London as a Special Agent. The occasion for such agents' cannot be anticipated; they often depend on emergencies which may suddenly arise and require an appointment, and the name of the person appointed, must not, if success is to be expected, be made public.

Special Agents, in connection with Foreign Affairs, are usually regarded as officers, under the law of nations. They are employed by all governments. Though not expressly authorized by any act of Congress, that employment has always been indirectly sanctioned. From the formation of the Government there has been an annual appropriation for the contingent expenses of foreign intercourse—from which appropriations the compensation and expenses of such agents are paid, without, it is believed, material objection.

There is special legislation by Congress on the subject of accounts for this appropriation, evidently in contemplation of the employment of Special Agents.

1862, U.S. War Department, *War of the Rebellion: Official Records of the Union and Confederate Armies* (Washington, DC 1880–1901), Series 4, vol. 2, pp. 23–24.

Some of the most important treaties of the United States have been concluded by Special Agents, and could not easily have been negotiated by any other officer.

I have the honor to be, &c

Wm. H. Seward

CHAPTER 14
MY INTERVIEW WITH LORD PALMERSTON—HIS PUBLIC AND
PRIVATE OPINIONS OF NORTH AND SOUTH

———•·•·•———

I reached London the end of June, 1862, and took a survey of the situation.[1]

Mr. Mason had then been residing there about six months, his mission being to England, while Mr. Slidell's knowledge of the French language and character, from his long residence in Louisiana, had procured him the mission to Paris. Each of the Commissioners had his secretary—salaried officers—Mr. McFarland, of Richmond, in London, and Mr. Geo. Eustis, of New Orleans, at Paris.

I found that Mr. Mason had made a favorable impression on the public and private men with whom he had come in contact. His social success was considerable, and at the Clubs, and in private circles, he was well received and much respected. His political success, however, had not been as gratifying.

The very *eclat* of the Trent affair had reacted unfavorably on the Commissioners, to whom it had given so wide spread a notoriety, and the British Government, well pleased with the escape it had made from a dangerous conflict, was disposed to avoid any future cause of rupture with the North.

This recoiled on Mr. Mason and his mission the causes of the peril so narrowly escaped. The Ministry, too, "a thing of shreds and patches," agreeing on no other principle or measure, concurred in the policy of "masterly inactivity."[2]

Lord Palmerston's private sympathies were supposed to be with the Southerners, to whom his aristocratic affinities led him, but he was growing

1. He reached London June 29, 1862 (De Leon to Benjamin, July 30, 1862, Records of the Confederate States of America, 1854–1889, Consular and Other Missions, 1861–1865, Library of Congress, Washington, DC). De Leon established himself at the Burlington Hotel on Cork Street, just off Piccadilly (De Leon, *Thirty Years of My Life on Three Continents* [London, 1890], vol. 2, p. 22).

2. This appraisal matches the sentiment expressed by De Leon in his July 30, 1862, letter to Benjamin, in which he reported that European sentiments for the Confederacy seemed to be deteriorating. U.S. War Department, *War of the Rebellion: Official Records of the Union and Confederate Armies* (Washington, DC, 1880–1901), Series 4, vol. 2, p. 24 (hereafter cited as *OR*).

old, and the fire and energy which had characterized his earlier career were giving way to the conservative tendencies of advanced age. He was more cautious and less disposed to move in new things, and *"Laissez faire"* was the policy now of his public as it ever had been of his private life.

Lord John Russell, his life-long rival—but now coupled in harness with him, which galled and fretted—the sweetness of whose temper has never been proverbial, seemed disposed to resent on the whole human race the wrongs inflicted on his vaulting ambition. He was, at that time, recognized as an incarnate contradiction, and would have "disagreed with the man that eat him" in the Cannibal Islands. He was, nevertheless, the most active member of the Cabinet, and as Secretary for Foreign Affairs had the most control over the management of the American question. So he treated both sides with impertinence, and succeeded admirably in alienating and irritating both—making British policy essentially a no-policy; and even when he inclined the balance to one side or the other, doing it so grudgingly and with such apparent ill will as to neutralize the effects of it, and induce the recipient to feel indignant at the favor. As an abolitionist in principle, and an aristocratic radical, in his sympathies he inclined to the Northern side—thus neutralizing the personal sympathies of the Premier.

Mr. Gladstone, with his usual brilliant inconsistency, was on both sides or neither alternately; first inclining Southward, and uttering sentiments highly encouraging to the Confederates, and then so glossing over or explaining away those utterances as to make them tell in the opposite direction. He continued on this intellectual see-saw from the commencement to the close of the struggle, although in several of his public addresses he gave great encouragement to the Confederates.

As early as January, 1862, he had declared his opinion at Leith, that "if the Southern States were in earnest, the struggle on the part of the Northern States was hopeless," and was considered a Southern sympathizer. Sir Geo. Cornewall Lewis, a ripe scholar, and more thoroughly read in international law than any of his colleagues, and who was supposed to inspire his son-in-law, "Historicus," of the *Times*, in upholding the paper blockade established by the North, was anti-Southern.[3]

The radical element in this coalition Cabinet, headed by Milner Gibson, and aided by Mr. Stansfeld, the alleged accomplice of Mazzini in the Orsini

3. George Cornewall Lewis was secretary of war in Palmerston's cabinet.

plot, was violently Northern.[4] So the Cabinet was kept in equipoise, and preserved its equilibrium like a boy standing midway on a see-saw, putting down his foot first on one side and then on the other, an attitude not very dignified for a great power to maintain, and which subjected it to severe buffeting from both sides alternately.

Mr. Mason was alone in London, Mr. Mann having been transferred to Belgium—his son, William Mann, a gentleman of cultivated mind and pleasing address, accompanying his father as his secretary.[5]

I found him neither sanguine nor depressed, but preserving an unruffled equanimity, which the scanty courtesy accorded him by Lord Russell, the most ungracious of private as of public men, could not disturb.

Shortly after his arrival, early in the month of February, Mr. Mason had had an interview with Lord Russell, who, without accepting his credentials as Commissioner, had received and conversed with him.

His reception on this occasion was so little encouraging that he only renewed his proposal for another interview five months later, which Lord Russell declined to grant him.

He had never had any interview with Lord Palmerston, and naturally did not like to incur the risk of a refusal. In fact, as I had anticipated, his avowed official position was a barrier.

As I was probably the only person connected with the Confederate cause abroad, who could obtain access to Lord Palmerston through my personal relations with some of his intimate friends, I thought it best to see him before going to Paris. As a matter of courtesy to Mr. Mason I informed him of my intention, and he cordially concurred with me in the utility of such an interview, if it could be managed.

Through the medium of some of my English friends who were intimate with Lord Palmerston, I caused the intimation to be given him that I had just arrived from the Confederacy, and could give him late and reliable information as to the actual condition and prospects of things there.[6] Although I knew it was impossible to blind a man of his practiced astuteness to the real

4. Thomas Milner-Gibson. James Stansfeld was a junior lord in the Admiralty Office, reputed to be Mazzini's link to British funding for his dreams of an independent Italy, thanks to Stansfeld personally providing money.

5. William Mann was later a distinguished jurist in Chicago and custodian of his father's unpublished memoirs, which seem to have been lost around the turn of the century.

6. In *Thirty Years*, vol. 2, pp. 24–25, De Leon says that years earlier he became acquainted with a grandson of Palmerston's wife, and through that agency gained the interview.

objects of my visit, I practiced no deception either on himself or his friends, but only kept my own counsel. The result was that Lord Palmerston affected a convenient blindness in the matter, and expressed a strong desire to see and converse with me. He went further, and sent me a written invitation to call upon him at his house in Piccadilly the next day, at twelve o'clock.

I did not fail to keep the appointment, and repaired to his house at the hour named in his note.

LORD PALMERSTON AT HOME[7]

I was ushered into the library, where he was awaiting me, and he rose to meet me as I entered, limping slightly as he came forward and took my hand. I observed that one foot was swathed in a large list slipper, as he was suffering from a twinge of the gout—the old foe of all "fine old English gentlemen" who live at ease—"not wisely but too well."

All the incidents connected with this interview, as well as the conversation which took place, still continue fresh in my memory; but immediately on my return to my hotel I wrote them down in extenso, and can therefore now confidently reproduce them.

His greeting was frank, unaffected and cordial, and I immediately felt the charm of his manner, devoid of all affectation; manly and simple without being rough or unpolished. No one could come into his presence and talk with him without immediately feeling as much at ease as though he were not in the company of a great man—so offhand and apparently frank were his manner and utterances. He impressed me more on close inspection than when viewed at a distance, which is the true test of a superior man; and in the careless abandon of conversation made a more favorable impression than when listened to on public occasion.

He was a man a little above the medium height, compactly and strongly built, with an ease of movement and gesture which amounted almost to grace. His face did not indicate the talent he undoubtedly possessed; being unaccountably commonplace, with no marked feature. In fact, he resembled the majority of educated English country gentlemen, and in a crowd no one would have sought him out of the mass as a man of mark. His eye was his best feature; clear, quick and penetrating, with a sly twinkle of humor ever lurking in

7. De Leon's account of the interview is based in part on his July 30, 1862, letter to Benjamin. Records of the Confederate States of America, Library of Congress.

it, which alone indicated his Irish origin, and the quick apprehension of the salient points in men and in public questions, which characterized him.

Looking at his alert, active figure, his quick movements, and the vigor both of mind and body he evinced, one would never have guessed his age, save from the narrow wrinkles about his eyes, and the slight filmy appearance of their pupils. He was at that time nearly eighty years of age, but I never have seen so old a man in such a perfect state of preservation, as no one would have judged him more than fifty or sixty at the utmost. He still preserved his hair, which was now grey.

He commenced the conversation by expressing his pleasure in seeing one of whom his friends (naming them) had spoken to him so favorably, and added that, although reasons of policy had prevented and would still prevent his seeing and talking freely to any Southern man who came accredited in a diplomatic capacity from the new government, he yet was much gratified at having the opportunity of conversing with a private individual from that very interesting part of the world, and desired that I should express my views and opinions to him with perfect unreserve.

I replied that it afforded me much greater pleasure than it possibly could to him to be allowed the privilege of seeing him, and of freely expressing to him my own views and the hopes, wishes and feelings of the Southern country, of which I was a member; for we all knew how potential his voice and opinion were with the Cabinet of which he was the head, and with the English people who placed such great faith in his judgment.

He smiled, and replied quickly and sharply, with a keen glance of his eye:

"You must remember in talking to me you are not talking to the Secretary of Foreign Affairs; that is Lord John Russell's field; and also, that I am only speaking to a private Southern gentleman, and that the expression of our opinions is personal entirely. Now, tell me, what do your people think England ought to do, and what they expect?"

I told him the Southern people thought that England ought to recognize the Confederacy as a government *de facto*, at least; that all the precedents were in their favor, and that the usage of the British Government also was.

He said: "Briefly cite some of these precedents to which you refer."

I did so, quoting the cases of Belgium, Greece and the South American Republics, of course, briefly.

He replied: "Your argument is plausible; but you seem to forget that as yet you have not established your right to recognition, and are in the first stage only—that of revolutionists. We recognize you as belligerents, and you must sustain yourselves in that position before we recognize that revolution as successful. At the present moment your great city of New Orleans is in the hands of the Federals; your other cities are all blockaded, and your capital itself is in a state of siege. The Federal Secretary of State and the British Minister, whom we recognize as the representatives of that country, both assure us that they can and will crush this rebellion very shortly. I do not think your people have yet done enough to prove the falsity of this or establish their right to recognition. Besides," he added, with a sly twinkle in his eyes, "you Southerners, as well as Northerners, have always insisted that European Governments must not interfere in affairs on the American Continent. We are adopting your Monroe doctrine in our non-intervention."

"But," I said, "Mr. Canning recognized the revolted provinces of Spain on our continent, when their situation without it would have been hopeless, and both Greece and Belgium were recognized, without doing or being able to do a tithe as much as we have done. We have a regularly organized government, whose authority is recognized by twelve States and twelve millions of people.[8] We have in the field an army of—men. We have been accorded all the rights of belligerents by the Federal Government, your own and that of France. Is not this enough to establish our claim?"

"I think not," he replied; "you must do much more to establish it. We always have recognized, and still do recognize the Government in Washington, and its representative to-day represents the people of the United States to us."

"Well," said I, "the Confederate forces to-day menace the city of Washington, and it is not impossible they may compel Mr. Lincoln and his Cabinet to evacuate that city and transfer the seat of government to Philadelphia or some other Northern city. If it is the 'Government of Washington' which you alone recognize, would you recognize its representative in the person of one who brought his commission from that place, only bearing the sign manual of Jefferson Davis instead of Abraham Lincoln?"

"No," said he, "I do not say that; that is not what I mean. You must break through the blockade that makes you prisoners within your limits, and

8. De Leon is in error citing twelve states and 12 million people. Only eleven states seceded, and though Missouri and Kentucky had representatives in the Confederate Congress, they had no legitimate standing as such from conventions or legislatures of those states. The white population of the actual eleven Confederate States was also not 12 million, but really 5.5 million. De Leon has somewhat deceptively included the total population, including slaves, of those states as well as Kentucky and Missouri, and even that came to 11.4 million. Prime Minister George Canning supported independence for Spanish colonies in the New World.

makes all communication with you contracted. You must strike some decisive blows to free yourselves, and to compel the recognition of foreign nations, and of the old Government."

"But," I said, "we only ask fair play to do this. We insist that European neutrality is not the real thing; that it is one-sided, and interpreted in such a way as always to injure us and aid our adversary. For example, the acknowledgment of the validity of this paper blockade, which is defied with impunity by the blockade runners, who earn millions of money by breaking through its paper meshes."

"We have considered that question of blockade," replied Lord Palmerston, "and accepted the existing one as sufficient. Tell me," he added, with a laughing twinkle in his eye, "did you find the blockade such an imaginary thing when you went into and came out of the Confederacy? My friends tell me not?"

This was rather a hard hit, and bringing the matter home with a vengeance for I had found it rather a hard road to travel in both instances, but I replied that "what might occasion inconvenience or difficulty to individuals was not sufficient to shut up the ports of a whole country, and that the Law of Nations—"

"Well, well," said he, interrupting me, "It's useless to dwell on that point, for we have recognized the validity of the blockade, and there is an end of it; but the same complaint your people make about our neutrality your Yankee neighbors make too; so, as both sides abuse us, we think we must be pretty impartial. It is the fate of neutrals to be complained of by both parties."

"Lord Palmerston must admit," I replied, "that his name hitherto has not been regarded in Europe as a synonym of neutrality, but rather the reverse."

"Well, well!" said he, laughing outright, as though the idea tickled his fancy that he, the great bugbear of Europe, should now be named in a cautious neutral tint. "Live and learn, I suppose; it is high time that I should prove myself a man of peace and quietness, and not a stirrer up of strife, as they have long considered me on the Continent; but, as I said before, Lord Russell is Foreign Secretary, not I, and the consideration of this matter is more in his province than mine."

"But," I responded, "Lord Palmerston is the head of this Administration, and he knows it is a rule in boxing always to strike at that point. We wish to make no 'foul blows' by striking lower, and believe that he will see that we have fair play in this fight." "Oh, certainly, certainly," said he, hastily; "you have a right to demand and to expect even-handed justice at the hands of the

English Government; but both your people and the Northerners ask more. Each of you wants us to take your side, and as we had no hand in getting up this quarrel, we really do not see why we should meddle in it."

"Simply, for the reason that, by persevering in her so-called neutral policy, England will make two enemies, instead of securing one friend, as she would by taking either side," was my reply.

"No, no" said Lord Palmerston, "this is an exceptional case; it is a family quarrel—like interfering between man and wife—both would combine to assail the intermeddler. Besides, we are no more bound to your aide than to the other. Suppose we were to take the Northern, what then?"

"We should consider it as very disinterested as it is against your interest," I responded; "but that we do not fear. We think that both the precedents and the interests of England are in our favor, and we only complain that the same neutrality which openly furnishes the North with all the supplies she needs, under Lord John Russell's construction of it, makes us, and everything intended for us, contraband of war."

"Dr. John has great reputation as a constitutional lawyer," said Lord Palmerston, "and can have no particular reason to construe the law more harshly in your case than in the other. It is the misfortune of your position at the start. Break through this blockade, get some decisive advantage, and no country will recognize you more cheerfully when you have earned your right to it, than England will."

"You know," he said laughing, "that I am accused of having strong Confederate sympathies, and you are a gallant people. Yes, a very gallant people; nobody can gainsay that. But our talk to-day satisfies me, that whatever my personal feelings or wishes may be, I have not given any grounds in my public course for the accusation of partiality.

"Now tell me about some matters and some people in your part of the world which I am curious to know." He then catechized me very minutely as to the actual state of things in the Confederacy, especially as regarded its military resources, the spirit and temper of the people, and their capacity for carrying on the war. He questioned me also closely as to the personal characteristics of the President, Jefferson Davis, whose messages he said were very strong and able, and other leading men, especially Stonewall Jackson, whose military reputation in Europe was at that moment very high. He said frankly: "The common idea of England is that the Southern people are more like us in character than the Yankees, who have too much of the old Puritan leaven in them to suit us. You Southerners we consider only as transplanted

Englishmen of the old stock. Probably the truest reflection of real English feeling is to be found in *Punch,* and you will observe the Yankee is generally caricatured very freely there."

The interview having now been prolonged for a period I thought reasonable, before rising to leave, I thought I would take a parting shot, so I returned to say: "Has it not occurred to your lordship, that in the desperation of obtaining aid and countenance here in our mother country, we may turn towards France, the traditional rival of England, and more so now than ever before, practically, and offer her such tempting inducements as may secure her intervention, to the great detriment of English interests."

He looked keenly and scrutinizingly at me, and paused, before he replied. "Yes," he said, "we have considered that point, and I will not pretend to mistake your meaning, but I tell you candidly, your hopes are in vain. You will not succeed in detaching France from England on this question, nor in breaking the *entente cordiale* which is stronger than you suppose. French and English interests are identical in these matters, and not conflicting as your people think; and you will fail to divide them. There was a time when such a thing was feasible, but not now, not now. Do not deceive yourselves with that idea. Whatever action may be taken, will be joint action, not separate. Our understanding with France is perfect."

Of course, to so positive an assertion, I could only bow my assent, though secretly unconvinced. Yet I was satisfied that Lord Palmerston was sincere, and that the sharpest arrow I had kept in reserve in my quiver was pointless for him. So I rose to go. He rose also, and in his frank, off-handed manner, put this question to me: "Now tell me frankly, what do your people think and say of us, and how do they regard the attitude of England? Speak freely, for I am curious to know?"

"Then," I replied, "if your lordship really wishes to know the whole unvarnished truth, I must answer, that the Southern people generally think and say precisely what your lordship's conversation with me to-day confirms, viz., that the Government and people of England, entertaining the most sympathetic feelings possible towards them, will intervene in this quarrel, and give them the aid of their countenance and assistance, precisely at the moment they are convinced the Southern States stand in no need of either."

"That is—hum! ha!—putting it rather strongly, is it not?" asked Lord Palmerston, slightly staggered by this unexpected answer, but not at all offended.

"I think not," was my answer, "but believe such to be the sentiment, which, I fear, the frank admissions your lordship makes of the future as well as the past policy of the Government, will confirm."

"I am sorry for that," he said, "they do not do us justice. Our embarrassments and the difficulties of taking another course are greater than they dream of. But I hope time will set it all right. Your people are fine fellows—very fine fellows."

"One word more," I said, "if your lordship will permit. Am I to consider myself at liberty to repeat to those most interested, the views and opinions you have expressed to me in this private conversation? If your lordship considers it as confidential my lips are sealed; otherwise I should greatly desire to impart them to my friends at home, whom they most concern—at the same time stating the circumstances and the conditions under which those remarks were made."

Lord Palmerston paused for a moment, bent his head, as if reflecting, and then raised it, with a gesture full of resolve and pride. "I see no good reason, "he said, gravely and deliberately, "why I should conceal my personal opinions on this, as I never have done on any other matter, either of private or public interest. I am a public man, it is true; but I have a right to my opinions, and to the expression of them, when they cannot interfere with the public interest. I have no objection—in fact, I should prefer my sentiments being known, and you have my full consent to make known to your friends here and elsewhere the substance of our conversation—which I assure you has been a most interesting one to me."

He then added, in his most cordial manner, while taking leave of me, that he would be happy to see me again at his house socially—naming Lady Palmerston's reception evenings—and inquiring particularly the probable length of my stay in London.

These courtesies were more agreeable to me from the proof they gave of his not having been offended by the frankness of my last remarks.[9]

9. De Leon gave a brief account of the meeting with Palmerston in his July 30, 1862, letter to Benjamin (Records of the Confederate States of America, Library of Congress, and *OR*, p. 24), which agrees substantially with this fuller version. De Leon also provided substantially this same account, embellished and with some variations, in *Thirty Years*, vol. 2, pp. 28–38.

PERSONAL CHARACTERISTICS

Lord Palmerston's name, then so potential in England, is now seldom mentioned, in the rush and whirl of new men and new measures, which his death
made room for.

With him perished his party, and fell also some of the strongest props of
the English throne, altar, and aristocracy. As his personal characteristics,
even more than his intellect, gave him this great power, a brief sketch of his
salient peculiarities may not be here out of place—for in him the private and
the public man were intimately blended.

Taking Lord Bacon's classification of the different orders of men, Lord
Palmerston was a ready rather than a full man—a man of action rather than of
thought; who, while Mr. Gladstone was poring over metaphysics, was playing
billiards at some country house; and while the Earl of Derby was translating
Homer, was galloping across the country after the hounds—or, even as an oc-
togenarian, devoting himself to the fair sex, and not untouched by the
tongue of scandal; yet, as a practical statesman, the superior of all, and dying
as he had lived, the incarnation of success.

His great characteristic, like the Duke of Wellington's, was wonderful
common sense, (the most uncommon kind of sense, in its highest meaning,
as applied to great affairs,) and even more than the Iron Duke he was a genuine sample of an Englishman—in his weakness as in his strength.

Although of Irish descent—springing from the famous Temple family, and
taking his only title from that country—he was the very type of the English
gentleman, and shared in all those peculiarities of manner, speech and
habits which most strike the stranger as essentially English. Thus in his
speech he had that peculiar hesitation of utterance, slightly marked in private conversation, very strongly marked in public speaking. His hum-ing
and haa-ing, especially when rising to reply to some sudden home-thrust—
after the peculiar British fashion—between each sentence, was very national.

His manner I have already described.

His habits were of the most manly kind, and although a free liver, relish-
ing the pleasures of the table and of society with a keen zest, he had so little
suffered from excess in these that he thought nothing at eighty years of age of
a ten mile gallop across the country, and habitually took his daily exercise in
the open air.

Most thoroughly characteristic of the man was the boldness with which he
defended "the noble art of self-defense" in Parliament, when some puritan-

ical remarks were made there apropos to the Heenan and Sayers fight for the belt, by Lord Shaftesbury, or some other of that Boston-British school.[10] He stood up and vindicated it as a good old manly English sport when properly conducted—and insisted that muscle and morals might go together; that the world wanted not saints or sinners to people it, but healthy men and women—wholesome in body as well as in mind—not rickety, strong-minded women, nor spasmodic, spindle-shanked men, such as now assume on both sides of the Atlantic to be the salt of the earth.

I left Lord Palmerston, most favorably impressed by his manliness and candor, but hopeless of any immediate aid from him or from the British Government, and determined to proceed immediately to Paris, as the only field of action left us.

10. John C. Heenan of Boston and Thomas Sayers of England fought the first great international boxing championship heavyweight fight April 17, 1860. It ended in a draw.

CHAPTER 15
THE CONFEDERATE OFFER MADE TO THE EMPEROR—
HOW HE RECEIVED IT—A MONTH AT VICHY

————◦•◦————

Convinced by my interview with Lord Palmerston, that British policy was too firmly fixed to be shaken by any diplomacy of ours, and that our only hope was in enlisting French aid, irrespective of English, I immediately proceeded to Paris and delivered to Mr. Slidell the dispatches I had brought over.[1] I found that another movement for obtaining English recognition was on the tapis, and that Mr. Lindsay, the member for Sunderland, was the chief mover in it.

Mr. Lindsay's relations with the Emperor were of a peculiar and intimate kind. His thorough practical acquaintance with all matters connected with the shipping and commercial interests of England, and of the Continent, had caused the Emperor to seek his counsel in the framing of his great commercial treaty with England; and, next to Mr. Cobden, there was no one whose opinions that astute ruler prized so highly. Availing himself of that intimacy, Mr. Lindsay had seen the Emperor, and was evidently much encouraged to persevere in his motion, from the sympathy he supposed was manifested by the Emperor in that regard. I saw Mr. Lindsay on my arrival at Paris, and conversed very freely with him, explaining to him the results of my conversation with Lord Palmerston, which he did not consider as conclusive as I did. Of course, while his movement was pending, it would not have been either courteous or politic, in any way, to have interfered with it. So we awaited the result.

Mr. Lindsay returned to London, and brought up his motion in Parliament on the 18th of July, where it gave rise to a long and animated debate, by far the most interesting and most thorough yet had in that body. It ended in his withdrawal of his motion, at the suggestion of Lord Palmerston, who demanded that it should be left to the responsible Government to judge "what

1. De Leon said that he established himself at the Hôtel du Rhin on the Place Vendôme. *Thirty Years of My Life on Three Continents* (London, 1890), vol. 2, p. 47.

could be done, when it could be done, and how it could be done." Mr. Lindsay's proposition was twofold: Firstly, as to acknowledgement of the Southern Confederacy as an established Government; secondly, proposing mediation. The failure was as signal as on the previous occasion, one year before, and it was made plain that the non-intervention policy of the Ministry was in conformity with the views and wishes of the great majority in Parliament.

With the collapse of this effort, the field was again open to us to try our new policy. It was impossible to obtain any conjoint action. Was it possible to secure separate action from the French Emperor? That was now the vital question, and it was determined to give it an early and speedy solution.

THE EMPEROR AT VICHY

Among the Emperor's fixed habits, he has that of passing every year a month at Vichy, the waters and baths of which he regards as very beneficial to his health. The time he chooses for making the season there embraces from the 15th of July to the 15th of August, during which period it becomes quite a fashionable resort, not for the gayer part of the Parisian world, who prefer Ironville and Deanville, but for a more respectable and steady class. Vichy is about eight hours' ride, by the Orleans railway, from Paris.

Mr. Slidell sought an interview with the Emperor, and was requested to go down to Vichy where an audience would be accorded him. He, therefore, went to Vichy and was received by the Emperor, and unfolded the views and wishes of his Government, and the propositions which I had brought over.[2] The interview was satisfactory, as far as it went, and encouraged high hopes; but the Emperor did not commit himself. He took the matter into consideration, neither accepting nor declining the tempting offers made him. Nor, to the best of my knowledge and belief, did he ever give a definite and positive answer in regard to them. The temptation was very great, but then the risks were great also. So he took the matter under serious advisement.

Mr. Slidell, after his interview, returned immediately to Paris, and awaited the result of this bold stroke. I went down to Vichy, ostensibly to pass the season there with my family, having procured letters of introduction from influential French friends to some of the Emperor's immediate

2. Slidell's account of the interview is in Slidell to Benjamin, July 25, 1862, U.S. Navy Department, *Official Records of the Union and Confederate Navies in the War of the Rebellion* (Washington, DC, 1894–1922), Series 2, vol. 3, pp. 479–489.

household, in which letters my affinities and connections were mentioned, as well as my very recent return from the Confederate States.[3] These letters insured me much attention from the gentlemen to whom I brought them, and, as I had anticipated, I was very soon undergoing a very thorough pumping process as to the resources, prospects and actual condition of the Southern States. In this way, I believed I could accomplish more good to the cause, than by any direct means; for, of course, I suspected the origin and source of those queries, although I never intimated any such suspicion. I confess that in the commencement of the affair, I was quite sanguine as to the success of the movement; but when days passed into weeks, and no sign was made, I began to be distrustful.

From the indications and from all the information I gathered at the time, I still believe that the Emperor's first wish was to avail himself of the golden opportunity thus presented him of advancing the material interests of France at the expense of her rival, England, and taking, as he loves to do, the initiative in the solution of a great political problem. I further believe that he would have taken some decisive steps in this matter, even had he not ventured to accept the proposal made him, but for the new European complication just then created by Garibaldi.[4]

The Emperor's life at Vichy—so different from his ordinary one—favored my plans, for he had there the leisure and the absence from distracting cares which he never found elsewhere. It was as easy there, and it would have been impossible elsewhere, for him to devote much time and attention to any single subject, and I hoped to keep his attention on this all-important one of ours, and to give any information he might need through my French acquaintances who had access to him.

The month at Vichy is really the Emperor's holiday vacation. For the time, he relieves himself of the burden of ceremonials and etiquette which are the taxes of royal position, and enjoys the repose of a private gentleman. With public affairs he seems there to occupy himself but little, although his Ministers come down occasionally to consult him. He lives in a small house with a few chosen friends, without state; walks or drives out, and goes hunting or

3. De Leon and his wife rented rooms in a hotel overlooking the villa belonging to Johann Strauss, Jr., the composer, which was occupied by the emperor at the time. *Thirty Years*, vol. 2, p. 64. He wrote an article about this episode titled "An Emperor's Vacation at Vichy" for *Scribner's Magazine* in 1873.

4. Garibaldi's army was then threatening to capture Rome and evict the regime officially recognized by Napoleon.

fishing like any private person. Printed placards warn the people at large not to make any demonstrations on his appearance among them in the public grounds, and beyond removing their hats as he passes, none are made.

The pomp and pageantry which he affects at Paris he dismisses here.

The Empress does not accompany him on his annual visits to Vichy; therefore, the gay butterflies of the court buzz and flutter around her in her summer retreat at St. Cloud or elsewhere and the Emperor can rough it as he likes.

The natural beauties of the situation are not great—the most attractive feature of this famous bathing-place being the open square in the centre of the town, where, sitting or promenading under large shady trees, and listening to the music of a fine band stationed there morning and evening, the visitors congregate, and idle away the intervals between meals, drinking the mineral waters and bathing.

The days are very long, the sun very hot, the drives in the neighborhood dusty and uninteresting. There are no gambling tables there, as at Baden. The Emperor passes his time like others, and seems to like it, as he may constantly be seen walking or driving about, and attending the balls and theatres—it being his only annual rest for busy body and busier brain.

DEMAND FOR ENGLISH RECOGNITION

About the time we were instituting these movements of secret diplomacy in France, Mr. Mason was making a direct and vigorous effort to obtain recognition of the Confederacy from Lord Russell. The report which I had given him of my interview with Lord Palmerston had not fully convinced him of the hopelessness of the effort; and, at any rate, he deemed it expedient to renew formally the demand he had made for recognition at his interview on the preceding February.

He, therefore, on the 24th of July, sent a dispatch to Lord Russell, recapitulating the arguments he had previously made, ending with a formal demand.[5] He also, in another dispatch, asked for a personal interview.

Lord Russell promptly declined the proposed interview, and, with less promptitude, responded to the request for recognition in a decided negative, stating that "the time for recognition, in the opinion of her Majesty's Government, had not yet arrived."

---

5. De Leon notes "the new demand" in the margin, suggesting he intended to include the text of the demand in a subsequent edition.

Mr. Mason then attempted to convince Lord Russell of the invalidity of the blockade under the convention of Paris, but did not succeed in convincing him on that point.

Still unconvinced by Lord Russell's reply that he truly represented the feeling of Parliament, the friends of the South determined again to press the matter of recognition on Parliament.

On the 4th of August, in the House of Lords, Lord Campbell and Stratheden, the son of the famous Lord Chancellor, brought in a motion for the production of the correspondence, basing upon it a demand for Southern recognition, which he sustained in an elaborate speech.[6]

Earl Russell refused to produce the correspondence, declaring it was unofficial, as the envoy of the Confederate States had never been officially recognized. He added:

> We remained as we were a few months ago; we have not altered our position, and there is little more than that fact contained in the dispatch. In the event of adopting any new line of policy, I should think it necessary to communicate with the maritime powers of Europe before taking any steps.

In a dispatch addressed to Mr. Benjamin, dated July 30, from Vichy, I thus summed up the situation as it presented itself to my judgment at that time:[7]

> I found public opinion in England in very much the same condition as when I left that place in January, with a tendency to depreciation, in consequence of the series of reverses our arms have experienced.[8]

After relating and commenting on my interview with Lord Palmerston, the dispatch went on thus:

> The fixed conviction of my mind was and is, that England will insist on a masterly inactivity as she regards it, and will restrain France from acting also, as long as possible. Her reasons for so doing you can comprehend as well as I can explain them.

6. John, Lord Campbell and Stratheden.

7. The original of this letter is in Records of the Confederate States of America, 1854–1889, Consular and Other Missions, 1861–1865, Library of Congress, Washington, DC. It is printed in its entirety in U.S. War Department, *War of the Rebellion: Official Records of the Union and Confederate Armies* (Washington, DC, 1880–1901), Series 4, vol. 2, pp. 23–26 (hereafter cited as *OR*). De Leon's excerpts here are substantially *verbatim*.

8. The original of De Leon's July 30, 1862, letter to Benjamin is in Records of the Confederate States of America.

The pretext is "fair play."

It is but just to add that the popular sentiment in England, before, and especially since the tidings of our late victories, as far as I can judge, is decidedly in our favor. But they are not willing to pay the price of war, to indulge the sentiment, and the course taken by the Tory (opposition) party proves this.

* * *

At Paris I immediately put myself in communication with the press and with gentlemen of influence and position who are friendly to us—one of whom is related to the Emperor, and wields great influence at court and elsewhere.[9]

The journals I found very accessible and amenable to reason.

We have the *Patrie,* the *Constitutionnel,* and the *Pays*—all three semi-official papers. Against us are the radical journals and the Orleans; but since the return of the young Princes from America, I think we can secure the latter.[10]

The effort is now being made.

Although the Emperor is absolute master of the situation, he yet desires that public opinion should march with him, and the only difficulty we have to contend with is the slavery question.

We are trying to change this issue by proving that not to be the matter in dispute.

The Emperor is here in the house next to my hotel. I have made the acquaintance of some, and am intimate with one, of his personal suite, and been enabled to throw much light on the question.

* * *

Should anything important transpire soon I shall find or make a way to give you sure information.

Mr. Slidell has doubtless given you the details of his interview with the Emperor. I therefore refrain from touching on that subject. It was the *premier pas* to which I am desirous of adding another. That the Emperor is most anxious to intervene all his people here tell me.

M. Baroche, Chief of the Council of State, and M. Thouvenel, have just left Vichy.[11]

The immense moral gain to us from our late victories and the present attitude of the two sections, you cannot overrate.

Whether it is sufficient to enforce recognition, the utterances of the Sphinx who rules Europe will not permit us to judge.

9. In this last sentence De Leon strays from the actual text of his original dispatch in order to conceal the identity of the relative of the emperor who was so friendly. It was Ferdinand de Lesseps, cousin of the empress, and later engineer of the Suez Canal.

10. He refers to the princes who were with McClellan.

11. Jules Baroche.

As to the fate of the proposition brought over by me, I am yet in ignorance. Upon the whole, I think the prospect of an early recognition (which will involve intervention) to be most probable and, in fact, most imminent.

A week hence I hope to be able to give you exact information on this subject.

The establishment of credits abroad is essential. This can be done in Paris with ease, by the Government sending cotton to parties here, who will immediately advance several millions upon it. If the Government will authorize me to make such an arrangement, one of the great capitalists here will do it forthwith—the Government delivering the cotton in the Confederate States to agents sent or named by the capitalist here.

* * *

Confederate credit has not risen on the ruins of the Federal—now far below par.

* * *

Our friends here are now as unreasonably sanguine as they were unduly depressed on my first arrival, before our victories had brightened the Southern sky. I do not share in their illusions, and see the long road we still have to travel before reaching our resting place.

* * *

I have discovered that Bishop Hughes is busily beating up recruits in Ireland and haranguing for the North. I have taken active and, I believe, efficient measures to counteract his labors. He boasts he can bring 20,000 men to the rescue of the North. We shall see.

Such were the material portions of my dispatch from Vichy, and such was the actual condition of Confederate diplomacy at that hour. I remained two weeks longer at Vichy, but saw the flood tide of our hopes receding rapidly and turning to the ebb, even before I left.[12]

---

12. In De Leon to Benjamin, July 30, 1862 (*OR*, p. 25), De Leon states that he is awaiting a response to a request for an interview with the emperor. However, discouraged by news from elsewhere, De Leon withdrew the request soon thereafter and did not actually have the audience with Napoleon (De Leon to Benjamin, September 30, 1862, Records of the Confederate States of America; also in *OR*, p. 100). He did, however, submit observations and suggestions that France break the blockade, recognize the Confederacy, and receive in turn a European monopoly on Southern cotton, through intermediaries at Vichy, and in *Thirty Years*, vol. 2, pp. 68–69, he maintained that he received encouraging replies, but for the difficulty of slavery. De Leon asked if a gradual emancipation in the South might relieve the emperor's concern on that score and wrote to Richmond to see if such a move would be possible. The response from the Confederate government was an emphatic "no."

Garibaldi's "Rome or Death" had disturbed the repose of Europe, and the busy brain at the Tuileries had nearer interests to occupy it than the American conflict.[13]

Yet the Emperor gave us no cause to despair. The matter was postponed by the pressure of other and more immediate interests—that was all. So we had to possess our souls in patience and wait until European skies grew more serene.

If no words of encouragement were given to us, neither were there of discouragement. So I returned to Paris less hopeful than when I left it, but not discouraged, and turned my attention toward the manipulation of public opinion through the press, while waiting the slow march of diplomacy.

How I fared in this work, and the peculiar characteristics of French journalism, shall be explained in a subsequent chapter, especially devoted to this theme.

13. The Italian revolutionary Garibaldi had led a march on Rome seeking to depose King Victor Emmanuel, under the cry "Rome or Death." It failed and Garibaldi almost lost his life, but meanwhile it so upset the equilibrium of European politics that the Confederacy became a secondary concern for Napoleon.

CHAPTER 16
HOW OUR SECRET NEGOTIATIONS PROGRESSED—
WHAT IMPEDED AND FINALLY FRUSTRATED IT

———•◆•———

Two months later I again wrote a dispatch to Richmond, explaining the progress we had made in the negotiation, and the leading causes which impeded it. As this was a full and fair picture of the situation at the time, I here reproduce the principal portions of that dispatch. It was dated at Paris, Sept. 3oth:[1]

In my dispatch of July 3o, from Vichy, I had the honor of submitting to the Department a hurried sketch of the position and prospects of our affairs. Imperfect as it was, the rapid tide of events at home and abroad, has since drifted us so far away from those landmarks, that I deem it unnecessary to recapitulate, and now propose to exhibit the actual condition in which we find ourselves to-day, on the stage of European politics.

It is my duty to submit to the consideration of the Departments several proposals of a public character, which have been made to me, as Diplomatic Agent by responsible parties here, and which may possibly be worthy of the serious consideration of our Government.

But, firstly—As regards our present prospects of formal recognition.

"When my last dispatch was written there was good reason to believe that France, or its ruler, had not yet positively decided upon the line of conduct to be pursued, and that the temptation to act independently of England was very great, from motives both of policy and pride.

While England promptly and publicly refused recognition in response to Mr. Mason's formal demand, the simultaneous movement of Mr. Slidell here did not meet with a similar reception from the French Government, and officially the same suspension of judgment has been kept up to this day.

No formal announcement of the refusal of France to recognize the Confeder-

1. The original of De Leon's September 3o, 1862, letter to Benjamin is in Records of the Confederate States of America, 1854–1889, Consular and Other Missions, 1861–1865, Library of Congress, Washington, DC, and printed in U.S. War Department, *War of the Rebellion: Official Records of the Union and Confederate Armies* (Washington, 1880–1901), Series 4, vol. 2, pp. 99–105. Again, his quotations here are substantially *verbatim*.

ate Government has ever appeared in the official or semi-official journals here—which contrasts strongly with English action—nor (as far as my information goes,) has any such formal answer ever been given Mr. Slidell.

The tide which was setting in so strongly towards our recognition, when my last communication was made, was turned by the frantic folly of Garibaldi in Italy, which created a serious crisis in Europe, and rendered it evident that France could not and would not act alone in the American question, while so grave a complication continued. That complication, far from having ceased with the capture of Garibaldi, (sustained, as he is, in prison, by the active sympathy of England, and the revolutionary party of France,) is, on the contrary, daily becoming more grave. It has forced out an unwilling utterance, even from the Emperor himself, on the Italian question, in the publication of his instructions to his Minister of State, &c. (Enclosed)

Opposed, therefore, as he is to the policy of Victor Emanuel, sustained by England and the Liberal party on the Continent, as well as to the policy of the parti Pretre who clamor for the restitution of the whole of the patronage of St. Peter to the hands of the Pope—and also to the Red Republicans, who raise the cry of "Rome or Death"—the role of the Emperor is most delicate and difficult at this moment.[2]

It was knowledge of these things, and the assurances of those very near him, at Vichy, that his mind was entirely preoccupied with these new and alarming questions, which induced me to withdraw from his Secretary my proposal for an informal audience, on the plea of sudden and pressing business at Paris. As such an interview would only have been a ceremonial one, and without results, I deemed it best to keep that pleasure in reserve.

That the Emperor himself is friendly to us, and our cause, there can be no doubt. That he regrets having been overpersuaded by the Russell Cabinet into the recognition of the blockade, when it was only a paper one, is equally certain—for he says so himself, and he has recently declared, in private conversations with members of the British Parliament, that England has kept and continues to keep him back from intervention in American affairs.

His Cabinet concur with him in opinion, but differ as to joint or separate action.

Mr. Thouvenel rigidly adheres to the English alliance, and is less friendly to us than either the Count de Morny and the Count de Persigny, who carry the majority of the Cabinet with them.

* * *

With the tide of public opinion in England running so strongly in our favor that even Lord Shaftesbury and Exeter Hall now abandon their Yankee sympathizers as

2. Napoleon and the Italian question.

unsound on the Abolition question, with but two presses in London favorable to the North, (the *News* and *Star*,) both uninfluential, and with the strong pressure put upon them by the Emperor, it may be asked why the British Cabinet delay recognition? As far as we can judge they act from mixed motives. They believe that recognition of the South would lead to war with the North, and regard the Northern marine as a standing menace to their commerce, which offers such rich spoils.

Moreover, the cotton famine—strange as it seems—pays the manufacturers handsomely, as recent statistics prove. The glut of the manufactured article, and consequent depreciation of price, has been prevented by our civil war, and the stoppage of the cotton supply. Hence the ardor of Mr. Bright and the Manchester men for non-intervention in our quarrel. Add to this the enormous cost of a war with an adversary so powerful and so reckless, and England's policy can be understood, if it cannot be justified by the law of nations, or the impulses of humanity.

Europe professes to be sickened by the sight of useless slaughter, across the Atlantic, but upraises no voice and lifts no finger to arrest it. Our sole reliance must be on God and ourselves, and happy am I to know that such, too, has become the rooted sentiment of our people, upon whose heroic efforts and sufferings all Europe now looks with wondering admiration. I believe our recognition to depend more on the events now transpiring in Maryland than on any other early cause. We, on this side, can only hope to reap the fruits which the sweat and blood of our brethren have been poured out to produce.[3]

It may be necessary to add that the recognition talked of by the British and French Governments, and which our continue successes would hasten, does not formally involve mediation or intervention, but is supposed to lead to both. The other European powers have left the solution of this question, by common consent, to France and England.

* * *

There are, however, two disturbing causes to the long patience of France. One is the breach daily widening between the continental policy of England and her own, especially in Italy. The other is the pressure put upon the Government by the industrial class, whose sufferings have been, and continue to be, great; and the French workmen will not suffer like dumb cattle, as the English operatives do.

From the Councils General of several of the French Departments, petitions for relief have been sent up to the Emperor, and published in the journals,

3. He refers to Lee's invasion of Maryland, which by this time had already ended in failure at the Battle of Antietam, September 17, 1862. Prior to receipt of news of the defeat, Lord Russell in England was ready to propose in cabinet that England ask for a cease fire and offer to mediate between Union and Confederacy, which some believed would be a first step to recognition and eventual European aid to the South. Even after learning of the defeat Russell still wanted to try, but found no support in the cabinet. Anthony Cooper, Lord Shaftesbury, was a prominent reformer.

blended with complaints that the cause (the American war) should be permitted to continue, and warning the Government of the consequences of an increase in that suffering and discontent. At Rouen, Lyons, and in the Northern departments, both public and private charity have been ineffectually resorted to, and immense public workshops established to give employment. But every day the evil increases, and with it the inquietude of the Government.

Then follow specimens of these petitions, and comparative estimates of the cotton consumed in France before and during the war.

It is supposed that the Emperor, in view of these complications, has sent to Mexico a force more than adequate to settle that question, as more than 40,000 men, independently of the naval force, have been dispatched. The intrigues of Mr. Corwin with the Mexican Government are well known here, and properly appreciated.[4] If, therefore, the *entente cordiale* between France and England should be broken, or the crisis in the manufacturing districts become too threatening to be allowed to go on, the Emperor has prepared himself for that active interposition which alone could be effectual.

I may add that the very serious state of things in Russia does not tend to reassure us as to the continued tranquility of Europe, which seems now in a condition very similar to that which preceded the convulsions of 1848.[5]

Such was the actual condition of our negotiation with the French Emperor two months after it had been submitted to him, and the extracts given from my dispatch indicate my fears of its failure at that time. I knew well that this was one of those cases in which delay, proverbially dangerous, was apt to be fatal, and that unless the seductions of the proffer were sufficient at once to enlist the imagination as well as the judgment of the Emperor, that the longer he deliberated upon it, the smaller would be the chance of its acceptance.

The unexpected complications in European politics which arose in consequence of Garibaldi's movement, had also altered the situation, so as to shake greatly my confidence in the success of the scheme, of which I was sanguine immediately after my arrival, and upon its first presentation. The

4. Thomas Corwin was sent by Lincoln as a minister to the insurgent government of Benito Juárez in Mexico in April 1861, his mission being to combat Confederate efforts to obtain recognition from Juárez.

5. De Leon misquotes himself, and in the process either he or the compositor included a typographical error. In his original letter De Leon wrote of his concern that "the very serious differences between the King of Prussia [not Russia] and his Parliament do not tend to reassure us . . . ." Records of the Confederate States of America. A civil revolt in Poland brought down a heavy response from Russia, and the king of Prussia broke with his parliament in supporting the czar.

elder Disraeli has written a series of remarkable papers on "events which might have happened," showing what infinite changes might have been made in the world's history had certain events transpired; yet among them all there is not one which is more worthy of a place in that record than the abortive, though important, negotiation now for the first time revealed in its complete proportions.

It is hard to say what the consequences of the Emperor's acceptance of that proposition might have been; but it is more than probable that the issue—both for the Confederate States and for France, as well as for the United States—would have been far different. I believed then—I believe now—that it would have terminated the struggle favorably for the Confederacy, and have made France, instead of England, the great centre and controller of the cotton trade, and that the North, though not so powerful politically as she is to-day, would be more prosperous, more happy, and with as bright a future before her. For the war once terminated, contiguity and mutual interests would have bound the two confederacies together by treaties, offensive and defensive, against foreign powers, and reciprocally advantageous as to commercial affairs, constituting a reunion in everything but in name, and finally resolving itself back again into that bond with newer and stronger guaranties. The vexed and ever-disturbing question of slavery would have found its solution, for the time at least, in such a shape as to permit both the policy and the pride of the South to consent to its peaceful abolition by gradual emancipation, the only sure and safe method to avoid the miseries under which the South is slowly dying by painful extinction now.[6]

6. Marginally De Leon notes the "error" and "gradual emancipation," though the context of the paragraph suggests that after the fact he regarded the idea of gradual emancipation as anything but an error.

CHAPTER 17
PRESS WORK IN PARIS AND THE PROVINCES—SECRET SERVICE
AND ITS RESULTS—FRENCH JOURNALISM

———•◦•———

Leaving Vichy about the middle of August, I returned to Paris, and commenced organizing a regular system of communication and correspondence with the city and country press.

Both classes are very numerous, for journalism is a very great power in France, as the severity of the restrictions put upon it proves.

The Emperor is not a man to waste his thunderbolts, and he deals with the press as with a first class power.

Every time he has endeavored to give more freedom to the French press, by removing some of the restraints and some of the censorship over it—the liberty thus given has been used so strongly against him that he has had to put still stronger restrictions upon it, through fear of revolution and the overturn of his empire.

For it is a curious fact, that the French press generally, as well as the most able and vigorous of the young and rising writers of France, such as Prevost Paradol, Pelletan, and others, are anti-Napoleonists, liberal to the point of being almost if not quite Republican.[1]

In order to counteract these hostile tendencies on the part of the press, it is submitted to the severest restrictions possible, and its existence depends to a great extent on the will of the Chief of the Bureau of the Press. The pains and penalties he can inflict at his discretion are sufficient to cripple, if not destroy any journal he wishes to break down.

This Bureau of the Press, is a branch of the Ministry of the Interior, though the Chief of this particular Bureau is practically independent of that minister, who however, is held responsible for his acts.

No journal can be established in France without special permission of the Government, and a considerable sum of caution money has to be deposited,

---

1. The journalist L. A. Prevost-Paradol and the deputy Eugene Pelletan were among the leading republicans, along with Victor Hugo and others among the literati.

which is forfeited if the conditions of the concession are not complied with. Besides this, the journal is published under rigid censorship as to all political matters, or all personal ones connected with the dynasty, and three "avertissements" or warning from the Bureau of the Press are sufficient to suspend the publication of the paper and suppress it. The law of the press is so elastic that the "avertissements" can be stretched to cover an infinity of cases; and when once open war is proclaimed by the Government against any doomed journal, its fate is sealed. It has required all the influence and powerful backing of Emile Girardin, together with his own wealth and that of his friends, which is very great—to sustain this warfare, which he has recently been doing—but to my knowledge his is the only instance in which it has been attempted without immediate ruin to the rash journalist who braved the unequal fight.[2]

This circumstance has given a peculiar character to French journalism, a character of indirectness, of subtle and concealed sarcasm, of ironic insincerity. The smouldering fire nourishes a hidden heat, and only throws out sparks, but it glows all the hotter for its suppression.

Every weapon of covert attack and bitter innuendo that ingenuity can devise is employed against the Government, which must give some ostensible and plausible reason for suppressing a journal, and thus the Director of the Press has no sinecure, but takes his daily walk over hot ashes, with fires scarcely concealed under them.

There is a division into official, semi-official, partisan and independent journals.

Thus the *Moniteur* is the great official journal of the Empire. Whatever is announced under its official head is "By Authority." It is purely the mouthpiece of the Government.

In each of the Departments of France there is also a small official organ, which reproduces from the *Moniteur*, or echoes the orders and the views of the Prefect of that Department.

Next in order come the semi-official journals, such as the *Constitutionnel* (morning,) and the *Pays* (evening paper,) and the *Patrie* also semi-official, yet liberal in its tendencies.

Each of the parties has its organ also. The Partie prêtre (or Church party,) had Mr. Vevillot in the *Univers*; the Orleanists and Legitimists, the *Journal des*

---

2. Émile Girardin was publisher of *La Presse*, one of France's most influential magazines.

Debats; the Radicals, the *Siecle* and *Opinion Nationale*, the organ of Prince Napoleon.[3]

As one of the most important functions I had assumed was that of ambassador to public opinion, and the press was the only medium reached, I immediately occupied myself in making the personal acquaintance, and where I thought it agreeable or advisable, established social relations with the editors of the leading Paris journals and their chief contributors.

I carefully selected and organized a corps of writers, who drew their facts and their inspirations from me on stated days of the week, and whose duty it was carefully to collate and comment on the items of American news, by each successive mail, giving them of course the construction most favorable to the South.

Further than this, I secured the admission of three carefully prepared digests of news, and of arguments into what are termed the "correspondences" of the provincial press, which control the entire public opinion of France, outside of Paris. As this is an invention peculiarly French, a description of it may not be out of place in this connection.

These "correspondences" are not, as might be supposed, simply the letters from the correspondents of the journals respectively, nor does each journal have its separate correspondent. On the contrary, they are printed sheets to make up the inside of the country papers, with the exception of the local advertisements, carefully made up from the Paris and foreign papers by competent editors, containing items of news, editorials on current topics of interest, discussions of questions agitating the public mind, &c. which are prepared at Paris, and forwarded to the country journals in a form ready to be transferred to their columns bodily.

They are made up once a week, as most of these journals are weekly and furnish the residents of the Departments all their information on such topics; few Frenchmen living in the country going to the expense of taking a daily journal.

Hence the leverage obtained by access to these "correspondences," and the filtration of facts and opinions through their agency was very great, and soon told on French public opinion in the country, reacting thence on the capital and the Government.[4]

3. Luis Vevillot.

4. De Leon owed his access with these "correspondences" to Paul Pecquet du Bellet, which he acknowledged in *Thirty Years of My Life on Three Continents* (London, 1890), vol. 2, p. 48, when he

For the support of Napoleonism comes from the country, not the city, strange as it may seem when the immense flood of patronage and array of office-holders and people dependent on the Government in Paris are considered. Moreover, Napoleon has done more to beautify Paris and enrich its inhabitants than any previous ruler, and has attracted a perfect flood tide of foreign gold into it annually, by making it the chosen resort of all the wealthy strangers from every other country.

Yet, in spite of all this, the representation of Paris in the Corps Legislatif always had an overwhelming majority of its members in opposition to the Government, and at the present time, I believe, has all.

In the rural districts lies the strength of the Government; from thence comes its majorities, and their views and wishes therefore must seriously affect the action of the Administration.

Therefore, the echoes of their correspondences coming back to Paris were considered as indicating the tone of popular feeling.

Even in the city, the French journals, irrespective of the censorship, are conducted on very different principles and under a very different management from either the English or the American newspapers.

Not to mention the editorials, double leaded, in the semi-official journals, which are always knows to have been "inspired"—that is, to have emanated from some Minister or high official in the confidence of the Government, the whole internal management of the paper is different in many respects.

Each leading journal, it is true, has its "Redacteur en chef," or chief editor, who controls the politics and policy of the paper; but there is seldom any corps of regularly salaried assistants.

There are ever a large number of recognized writers for the journal, who compete for the admission of their articles, and are only paid for such as are accepted and inserted. Hence it is a most precarious dependence, and the majority of writers for the French press are poorly paid and not overburdened with means.

Making it a profession, they are willing to lend their pens and their talents to any cause which is not directly at variance with their principles; and on all foreign questions Frenchmen usually are so profoundly indifferent that they are apt to espouse that side which enlists their services.

---

referred to him as "one connected with this press bureau who, being himself descended from a Louisiana family . . . was avowedly a sympathiser with the Confederate cause."

There is a very large quantity of intelligent ability and cultivated talent seeking employment in this way at Paris, and many of these writers, like the "free lances" of the middle ages, will enlist in any cause and contend faithfully for it, just so long as the contract lasts, and no longer.

The office of a French journal, therefore, is a theatre of eager and anxious competition among the contributors daily, each striving to get his own contributions in, to secure his "bread and circus"—the two wants of the modern Frenchman, as of the ancient Roman. Articles on any subject of interest furnished to these writers are gladly accepted and adopted, as they reap the benefits of their publication. Through these avenues, and by this means, it was easy to indoctrinate the French press on a topic like the American struggle, of which in the beginning they knew little, and probably cared less, as did the majority of their country men.

Yet early in 1862, the curiosity which first animated them begun to deepen into interest, and by keeping the theme constantly before the public mind, a strong sentiment in favor of the South began to exhibit itself toward the close of the year.

In order to develop and give form to that sentiment, I prepared and published through Dentre, the famous publisher of political pamphlets (*brochures*), in the Palais Royal, a pamphlet entitled, "La Verité Sur Les Etats Conféderés," which was intended as a brief resume of the merits and actual condition of the struggle, and an exhibit of the resources and condition of the South.[5]

This pamphlet, extensively circulated, produced some impression, and was even brought to the attention of Mr. Dayton by M. Drouyn de Lhuys, then Minister of Foreign Affairs, in one of his interviews with that gentleman, and is referred to by Mr. Dayton in his dispatches to Mr. Seward. I procured also the publication of other brochures of a similar character from time to time, and the insertion of more elaborate articles in the weekly and quarterly reviews, which are very able, and greatly control educated public opinion in France.

It was confidently asserted, and generally believed at the time, that both

---

5. De Leon misspells his publisher's name. It was E. Dentu of 13–17 Palais-Royal in Paris. See appendix 3 for a translation of this pamphlet. According to De Leon to Benjamin, September 30, 1862, the pamphlet was published in early August, 1862 (Records of the Confederate States of America, 1854–1889, Consular and Other Missions, 1861–1865, Library of Congress, Washington, DC). De Leon took particular care with the portrait of Davis that appeared as frontispiece, expressing the belief that the portrait encouraged the pamphlet's wide circulation.

the Washington and Richmond Governments resorted to the system of sub-sidies, usually employed by all governments to strengthen the hands and in-crease the circulation of foreign journals favorable to their respective causes, and there can be no doubt such was actually the case. A continental journal—not a French one—had the candor to admit the fact to me, coupled with an intimation that, as it was purely a business transaction, like an ad-vertisement, that at the expiration of the stipulated time of its contract, a higher subsidy would secure its support on our side. The figure named was a very large one, for its support really was valuable; but, for many reasons I did not make the little arrangement proposed. This was a game which two could play at, and in this, as in most other matters, the superior financial re-sources and credit of the North gave it great advantages over its rival, which had comparatively little cash and less credit, until the successful launching of the Confederate cotton loan in Europe temporarily supplied both.

Never in the history of mankind was such a struggle, on so large a scale, commenced and continued with such utterly inadequate resources, and the only wonder now is that it was protracted so long. The work of diplomacy abroad was crippled by the same want of means, which made the commis-sariat and equipment of the Southern armies insufficient; and the foreign agents, like the generals at home, had to substitute their personal efforts and energies for the more persuasive inducements of hard cash.

It is but just, however, to the foreign press to say that much of the support accorded to the Confederate cause was unbought, either by direct or indirect subsidies. Much came from conviction and personal good will; and one edi-tor of a leading French journal having been asked by me what return the Government or myself could make him for his powerful aid, replied that as he had seen through one of my intercepted despatches that some presses had been subsidized, the only return I could make him would be to inform the Department, that he never had, or never would accept anything for his advocacy. This, of course, I did, to his great satisfaction.

This gentleman was M. Delamarre, *redacteur en chef* for the *Patrie*, which journal was in great part his own property.[6] Apart from mere bribery, there is no good reason why the laborer on the press should not be considered as "worthy of his hire" as any other laborer who works with his hands alone—though, of course, it is as infamous for a man to sell his convictions as for a woman to sell her virtue.

6. M. Delamarre was a banker who also owned and sometimes edited *La Patrie*.

My own theory always was that the man or the press that could be purchased, for "a consideration," to advocate doctrines or measures in which they had no real faith, were rarely worth the purchase of money.[7]

Yet, on the other hand, it could not be expected that professional writers could afford to give their time and labor for nothing to a cause and a people with whom they were in no way identified.

When I reached Paris and commenced my work, there were but three journals in that city, and about half a dozen in the province, supporting the Confederate side. Six months later we had obtained the advocacy of all but five of the Paris journals, and my "correspondences" were inserted in six hundred and twenty of the provincial presses.[8]

It was the habit of the Emperor, at that time, to keep himself informed as to the tone of the provincial press on the American question, and the Directors of the Bureau of the Press had orders, at stated intervals, to report to him a list of the journals supporting or opposing the Confederacy.

The rapid and great change of tone in these journals attracted his attention at this period, and he sent for and catechised closely one of the officials connected with that Bureau, as to the probable cause of these sudden changes, as I afterwards learned from that gentleman.

When the fact is stated that the "correspondences" referred to reached every nook and corner of France, and without being actually partisan gave a Confederate color to the news transmitted, the great power of this machinery will at once be seen.

It reached not less than six hundred journals of every shade of politics.

I do not think the agents of the Federals, active and industrious as they were, ever thought of utilizing this machinery.

The net results of my labors were briefly summed up in a despatch written to Richmond the commencement of October, from which a few extracts are taken:[9]

Finding that nothing could be effected for the moment in the field of diplomacy, and that the Emperor was most cautious in moving with public opinion, instead

---

7. Yet, in his October 1, 1863, letter to Davis, cited above, De Leon clearly asked for money, saying "we must buy golden opinions" in the French press.

8. Du Bellet in his memoir put the number of newspapers carrying Confederate propaganda at 200. William Stanley Hoole, ed., *The Diplomacy of the Confederate Cabinet of Richmond and Its Agents Abroad* (Tuscaloosa, AL, 1963), p. 66.

9. In fact, these extracts come from the same September 30, 1862, dispatch already cited. Records of the Confederate States of America.

of striding in advance of it, as is generally supposed, I have turned my attention to the manufacture and improvement of that article, through the agency of the press—still a great power in France.

Very erroneous ideas prevail as to the actual restrictions on the liberty of speech and writing here. With the exception of criticising the royal person and Government acts, or of reviving dynastic differences, great license of political discussion is allowed to the French press.

The *polemiques* of the different journals are most widely and eagerly read in the restaurants, cafés and reading rooms, where much of Parisian life is passed. I found both our friends and foes in the French press lamentably ignorant and terribly prejudiced as to the real merits of the question, and as to the actual condition of the two parties in the struggle.

To my surprise, the slavery question, which has been dropped in England, was made the great bugbear in France, and our advocates were pleading piteously in extenuation of our sins in that respect, and shuddering at the epithet *esclavagiste,* with which the partisans of the North were pelting them.

Strange as it may seem, there is really more feeling for the black on this side of the channel than on the other, as the sentimental side of the French character has been enlisted by the supposed sufferings of that race.

The North, from the commencement of the struggle, has spent money freely in the manufacture of public opinion, especially at Paris, at Brussels, and on the Continent generally. To counteract these influences I have been compelled to use extraordinary exertions, which I am happy to say, have wrought great results within the last two months.

Without descending too much to particulars, it is only necessary to say that the Southern cause is now ardently and efficiently supported by all the semi-official journals in Paris and the provinces—a network covering France, by some of the clerical journals before hostile to us, by the organs of the manufacturers and industrial classes at Lyons, Bordeaux, Rouen, &c.; while at the same time the fire of the opposition has slackened, and from an offensive they have been driven into a defensive attitude.

To correct the numerous misrepresentations current abroad, I have published a brochure under my own name, entitled "La Verité Sur les Etats Conféderés," to serve as a brief and text book for our friends in the press.

You will observe that in this publication the ground is broadly taken that the South is able to vindicate her independence without foreign assistance, and is rapidly doing so; that her resources are ample for her needs; that she has nothing to apologize for in her peculiar institution but has ever been the best friend of the black race. It is further stated that the question of slavery is not at the bottom of this quarrel, and that the negroes at the South sympathize with their Southern friends, and hate and distrust the Northerner, as they have good right to do.

These novel ideas have been taken up and reechoed in the French press in every variety of shape and language, and have put the question in an entirely new aspect. It has been necessary to employ a corps of writers to keep the subject before the public, as amateurs cannot be relied on for more than occasional labors, and I have secured some very efficient ones. The South owes much to the writers who have labored so diligently in the French and English press, without reward or even recognition of their services. I have found them pursuing their thankless task under great disadvantages, and fitting acknowledgments should be made them. I, therefore, tender their names to the Department.[10]

* * *

By a perusal of the files of English papers sent, you will see why my labors have chiefly been confined to France.

The real merits of the question, and the relative position of the belligerents, are as well understood at London as at Richmond, and there are few points on which we can give them any information, except such matters of detail as are touched on in my letter to the English press, a copy of which has been forwarded.

By special request of Mr. Thackeray, I have prepared a narrative of my personal experiences in "breaking the blockade," which greatly interested him, and may attract the attention of the British public to the matter of the blockade, and the high hand carried by Northern cruisers on the ocean towards the English flag. It will appear in the October number of the *Cornhill Magazine*.[11]

A biographical sketch of President Davis, with strong political bias, appeared in the September number of *Blackwood's Magazine*, the tory organ.

All these publications tend to concentrate public attention on the men of our revolution and its incidents. The recent exploits of Stonewall Jackson and Gen. Lee have made their names historic here.[12]

10. The names that De Leon omitted from his newspaper article appear in the original letter to Benjamin, and include: Paul Pecquet du Bellet, Edward Gaulhac, and Charles Girard in Paris and George McHenry and Henry Hotze in London.

11. De Leon and the writer William Makepeace Thackeray had been friends for some years before the war. *Thirty Years*, vol. 2, pp. 84–85. The *Cornhill Magazine* article appears as appendix 2.

12. De Leon refers to the victories by Lee and Jackson at Cedar Mountain on August 9, and the Second Battle of Manassas August 29–30. Word of the September 17 defeat at Antietam would not have reached him yet.

CHAPTER 18
THE ENGLISH PRESS AND ITS INFLUENCE ON DIPLOMACY—
ITS LEADING WAR CORRESPONDENTS IN AMERICA—
HENRY WARD BEECHER'S TESTIMONY

———•◦•———

It will be remarked, that in my dispatches, as in my narrative, little is said of the English press, and that my labors in the secret service were directed chiefly to France. This is easy of explanation.

There was neither the opportunity nor the necessity for such labors as mine on the English press, for two reasons. In the first place, the real merits and actual condition of the struggle were understood as thoroughly at London as at New York; and secondly, every leading London journal had its special correspondents on the spot, whose descriptions and estimate of affairs were received with undoubting faith, and whose letters gave to the British public the estimate on which it relied.

Besides which, the great English journals resemble more the American, in respect to their being strictly party journals,—representatives of party organizations, whose policy they adopt and sustain—than the French, whose party lines are not so strictly drawn; and each of them, therefore, relying on its correspondents for news, shapes its policy according to the exigencies of its party.

All that could be done in England, therefore, was to give such aid and comfort to the journals which sustained our cause, as could be derived from an increase of their circulation; subsidizing them was out of the question, as no English journal could live which was known to be subsidized—and these things always are known finally—one of the oldest and most respectable English papers having perished, in consequence of having accepted a subsidy from the French Government, a short time before.

Hence the only avenue to the English public was through the medium of separate publications, chiefly in pamphlet form, though one large book, that of George McHenry on the cotton trade, was also published.[1] But we shelled

---

1. George McHenry was a Pennsylvanian supporter of the Confederate cause, who had outlined his position in his 1862 "Why Pennsylvania Should Become One of the Confederate States of

our adversary with pamphlets, some of which had a wide circulation, and with communications to the newspapers, whenever any topic of interest arose—the paternity of many of which was never suspected by the papers which established them. There are gentlemen now in the North, who, as a mater of future interest, have made collections of Confederate documents of this kind, and they can testify how very numerous and diversified those contributions to the current literature of the day really were.

At one period a specific proposition was made to me by a gentleman connected with the Conservative or Tory party, and who professed to represent important members of that party, for the establishment of a press which should represent those two interests conjointly. The *Herald*, the acknowledged organ of the Tory party, was not at that moment supposed to represent the whole organization, and the feuds and factions which then crippled the Conservatives under Mr. Disraeli's leadership, were supposed to favor the creation of such a new organ.

I thought favorably of the proposition, and made two visits to London to try and manage the matter, but it fell through for want of sufficient encouragement from the Conservative leaders, and of sufficient means to float it successfully.

This was the only active step taken by me in that direction, and its failure did not encourage me to renew the attempt.

All the leading English journals took their positions on the American question long before the French or Continental presses comprehended the real nature or actual issues of the conflict, and as before stated, the sympathies of almost the entire London and country press were on the Southern side.

It has been truly said by the Liverpool *Post*, one of the few English journals which espoused the Northern side, that "nearly all the aristocracy and a large portion of the middle classes were adverse to the North and in favor of the South—always with a protest against slavery. Out of four or five hundred English newspapers, only five were bold enough openly to support the North. Even Reynolds, the editor par excellence of the lower class in London, was against them." The only staunch and strong supporter of the unpopular side in London, was the *Daily News*, organ of the Radical party, and its evening satellite, the *Star*, which does the dirty work for its more dignified morning brother, of which it is the evening edition. All the other leading London

---

America." De Leon here refers to McHenry's book, *The Cotton Trade: Its Bearing upon the Prosperity of Great Britain and Commerce of the American Republics, Considered in Connection with the System of Negro Slavery in the Confederate States*, published in London in 1863.

journals, whether ministerial or anti-ministerial, leaned to, if they did not openly support, the South.

Rev. Henry Ward Beecher, who made his observations on the spot, summed up his experiences of British sentiment in a pithy manner. His summary was in the main correct, and the same state of feeling prevailed up to the close of the struggle. The press was but the echo of this popular sentiment.

"The great commercial class," said Mr. Beecher, "is against us. The influential clergymen and laymen, both of the Established Church and of the Dissenters, are, as a class, against us. Parliament, in sympathy and wishes, is five to one against us. The conservative intelligence of Great Britain is against us. All there is on the surface of society representing its dignities, its power, its intelligence, is anti-American." He comforts himself, however, "with the assumed fact that the laboring classes are in favor of the North," which was at that time a fallacy, though it has since become an established fact, for democracy has made giant strides in England since the close of the American war.[2]

As parallels are ever instructive, it may not be amiss to give the London press opinion of Mr. Beecher, which may have aided in forming his opinion.

The *Saturday Review*, the ablest weekly journal in England, thus prefaced its criticism of one of Mr. Beecher's sensation lectures at Exeter Hall:

> As the first year of the American civil war is to the third, so is Bishop McIlvaine to Henry Beecher.[3] The clerical emissaries who have been sent to advocate the Northern cause in England have deteriorated. The Evangelical Bishop's mission was, at the worst, but a silent failure; it simply collapsed from inanity. But the blazing preacher's lectures, though equally failing to address the British mind by argument while they surpass in vulgarity and impudence the bishop's milk-and-water apologies, perhaps more faithfully reflect the present aspect of the contest. The war has become more embittered, more bloody, more wicked and Mr. Beecher is quite worthy of the latter stage of his cause.

ENGLISH LETTER WRITERS

The American correspondents of the London press—notably Mr. Russell, Dr. Charles Mackay, Mr. Sala, and the eccentric New York correspondent of

---

2. Henry Ward Beecher, Congregationalist minister, and noted anti-slavery advocate and pamphleteer.

3. Charles Pettit McIlvaine, Episcopal Bishop of Ohio.

the *Standard*, "Manhattan," from the North, with Mr. Lawley from the South—gave the most reliable information obtainable from the other side, in English opinion.[4]

Their letters, recopied into all the English journals and largely copied from in the Continental ones, did more to form and fix public opinion abroad than all the voluminous dispatches of diplomats, or messages of Presidents. As to the Congressional debates, no one paid any attention to them.

All the state papers on either side, and arguments of writers, were regarded as special pleadings by interested advocates, while these correspondents of the journals were supposed to be impartial observers, and their statements accepted as the correct version of the facts and incidents passing before their eyes.

Thus Russell's graphic account of the flight at the first Manassas, which was all he saw of that conflict and of which he could truly say "pars fui," having evidently partaken of the panic he so vividly describes, led the foreign public to share in the Southern delusion that "the North would not fight."

When he retired from a post which his unpopularity at the North would not permit him to retain, his successor, Dr. Charles Mackay, viewing all men and things on this side from an European standpoint, and contrasting the peaceful scenes he had left with the weltering tumult of those into which he was suddenly plunged, produced an unfavorable impression on the minds of his countrymen, both as to the *morale* and *materiel* of the Northern people.

Like George Augustus Sala, whose talent for caricature exceeded his, he reversed the example of Balaam, and coming to bless, remained to curse.

These three correspondents, photographing as they did the scenes passing before their eyes, and coolly analyzing thought, speech and action in the midst of a population breathing the heated atmosphere of civil war, naturally gave great offence.

But the pictures they drew, and the facts they recorded, have outlived the passions which gave them birth, and the muse of history hereafter will find much of her material in the record they made while the events were transpiring.

Widely different in character and culture as these three men were, their letters are all the more valuable from that very diversity.

4. De Leon refers to some of the best-known London correspondents in America: George A. Sala, Charles Mackay, William "Bull Run" Russell, Francis Lawley, and "Manhattan" for the London *Standard*.

Dr. Russell certainly wields the pen of the ready writer. He has that fluency of expression and quickness of perception which seem the birthright of the educated Irishman, and a wide experience of many climes and many people, from her Russian snows to Italian sunsets and Indian jungles, had made him a cosmopolitan observer. On his return to England, though sore at the treatment he had received, he announced his private belief that the North would win, and adhered to the idea throughout.

Dr. Mackay was personally as different a man from Dr. Russell as could possibly be conceived. The one was a man of action, the other of sentiment; the former a man of theories, the latter intensely practical. A thoughtful, serious student, who had passed more time with books than with men—burning the midnight oil in the study, never in the camp—a pleasing poet whose verses will live, he saw things here with a poet's eye, and his sympathies soon attracted him to the weaker side. His criticisms upon New York and Washington gave scarcely less offence to our thin-skinned countrymen than the rougher pleasantries and harder hits of his predecessor, and reacted abroad.

In the case of George Augustus Sala, the rebound was even greater; for he came over an avowed supporter of the Northern side, having been a sympathizer from that early period of the struggle when he figured at London as the guest of that eccentric genius George Francis Train, at a breakfast intended to counteract Confederate intrigues, and the dignified reserve of the United States Minister.[5] As a demonstration the breakfast was certainly a success, owing possibly to the excellence of the champagne, or the fast Train conveying it down the thirsty and sympathetic throats of the literary men there assembled.

Whether the thirst of George Augustus Sala was not entirely quenched on that occasion, or the enthusiasm evaporated with the champagne, certain it is, the most biting sarcasms on the Northern people, politically and socially, came from his prolific pen. Having made New York too hot to hold him, he returned to London, and published a bulky volume of his impressions of "America in the Midst of War," which confirmed English prejudices against the American people.

To the apprehension of most educated Englishmen, the true history of the civil war in America was to be found in the correspondence of these three men, to whom must be added Francis Lawley, the most graphic and eloquent

5. George Francis Train was a wealthy shipping magnate known for his eccentricity, including three balloon trips around the globe that may have made him the prototype for Jules Verne's Phileas Fogg in *Around the World in Eighty Days*.

chronicler of the Southern side—whose letters to the *Times* from Richmond and the battle fields were looked for and read with an avidity which is difficult to describe. This was partly owing to the difficulty of obtaining any authentic information from the blockade-bound South, partly from the high literary merit of the letters themselves—for both in style and substance they are most admirable models of that class of composition.

Mr. Lawley had enjoyed rare advantages both in culture and position, was a ripe scholar, a polished writer, and trained to diplomacy as private secretary to Mr. Gladstone.

Such a man in such a situation, whose charms were heightened by the mystery surrounding it, could not fail to make the men and things connected with the Confederacy intensely interesting, and he threw around both a halo which has not even yet faded away from the English mind and heart, but hovers yet over the dim ghosts of those once breathing and living things.[6]

These four men, then, were among the most powerful, though involuntary, assistants in my mission of influencing public opinion. They really controlled the sympathies of the English people and the English press, leaving us little to do but reproduce their utterances.

In this connection it is impossible to pass over without mention a writer for the *Times*, who exerted a powerful influence on public opinion—Mr. James Spence, of Liverpool, whose letters were ably and vigorously written, with a strong Confederate bias.[7]

He wrote from Liverpool on the arrival of each steamer a resume of the intelligence, political and military, and the beauty of his style and language enhanced the effect of his arguments.

His book on the American struggle was by far the ablest produced in England, and will survive the occasion which gave it birth, as a philosophical analysis of the origin and causes of the war.[8]

George McHenry, also, a Philadelphian, contributed many articles and wrote a book on the cotton trade, which powerfully affected the opinion of the commercial community, being a vigorous writer and thinker devoted to the Southern side.

But, in default of any active operations on the daily and weekly press, we

6. Lawley's dispatches from the Confederacy have been published as *Lawley Covers the Confederacy*, edited by William S. Hoole (Tuscaloosa, AL, 1964).

7. Mason introduced De Leon to Spence soon after his arrival in London that summer. Mason to Benjamin, July 30, 1862, U.S. Navy Department, *Official Records of the Union and Confederate Navies in the War of the Rebellion* (Washington, DC, 1894–1922), Series 2, vol. 3, pp. 492–493.

8. *The American Union* (Liverpool, 1862).

published and circulated pamphlets, addresses, reports of public meetings, and some few more bulky volumes.

In one instance I revived a plan of the famous Wilkes, by issuing a reply to one of Mr. Bright's speeches in the shape of a broad-sheet, sold by the news-boys for a penny.[9] The success of this plan was great, as the following extract from a dispatch will show:

> Enclosed you will find copy of a reply written by me in response to a violent as-sault on the Confederacy by Mr. Bright, at Birmingham, ten thousand five hun-dred copies of which were sold in London, Birmingham and Liverpool in two days. Had I published five times as many I believe they would have circulated too. Mr. Bright has since addressed his constituents, but has not repeated either his slanders or his invectives, but has adopted a very mild tone in his allusions to American difficulties.
>
> I invented and adopted this form of publication to avoid the modifications and suppressions inevitable in its publication in a newspaper in England—the circulation of Mr. Hotze's paper, the *Index*, being too small to give the requisite circulation.
>
> I am in communication with correspondents and contributors to London pa-pers here, and in that way occasionally try to act on English opinion. My chief labors, however, have been directed to the formation and improvement of public opinion in France.[10]

I caused, also, the messages of President Davis to be reprinted and widely circulated throughout England, besides having them translated into French, German and Italian, and circulated among the leading statesmen and thinkers of those countries.

By these means I sought to neutralize the inactivity of the politicians by a direct appeal to the people; and in England, as in France, the success of this appeal was very great. The masses of the people in both countries were for the South. Political prudence alone kept the governments in equipoise.

9. De Leon's copy of his reply to Bright's speech is in the Edwin De Leon Papers, South Car-oliniana Library, University of South Carolina, Columbia.

10. The extract is from De Leon to Benjamin, January 28, 1863, Records of the Confederate States of America, 1854–1889, Consular and Other Missions, 1861–1865, Library of Congress, Washington, DC.

CHAPTER 19
THE MEXICAN INTRIGUE IN ITS EARLY STAGES—
CONFEDERATE CONNECTION WITH IT—THE EMPEROR'S
PROPOSALS FOR AN ARMISTICE AND FOR MEDIATION

It has already been explained that by the middle of October it became evident that the Emperor entertained no serious intention of accepting the proposal which I had brought over, although he continued to roll it, like a sweet morsel, under this tongue, and would not definitively reject it. One of his most remarkable characteristics is his patience; and the pertinacity with which he adheres to an idea, and the persistency with which he follows it up, long after all probabilities of its adoption have ceased, is probably one of the chief secrets of his success. I knew that the proposition was one at once flattering to his vanity and seductive to his imagination, that we had gained much and lost nothing by making him the proffer, and that his friendly feeling towards the South would be increased by the proposed alliance, almost protectorate, we had so freely tendered. Besides which, the changed tone of the French press was calculated to strengthen any resolve he might mature, so without over confidence, yet without despondency, I watched and waited for the final result of my proposition, trusting that some event in the chapter of accidents might yet make it successful.

But those chances never came, and the European complication thickened instead of clearing away. The Italian question—the Greek question—the Polish question—all successively clouded the horizon—and France herself began to smoke and glow like a volcano nursing an eruption.[1]

Then, too, the Mexican complication, unfortunate in its conception, and still more unfortunate in its conclusion for France, occupied much of the Emperor's time and thoughts.

It has frequently been supposed that this Mexican intervention owed, if

1. In the margin De Leon notes these questions as "three barriers." The "Italian question," of course, was the threat to the recognized regime from Mazzini and Garibaldi. The Polish matter was the uprising against its rulers, while in Greece King Otho was deposed in the fall of 1862, presenting France and other powers with the dilemma of deciding on a successor to support.

not its origin, at least its active prosecution, to Confederate intrigues and Confederate diplomacy.[2] But this is not the case. The credit or discredit of this sanguinary episode, ending with the death of the gallant Austrian Archduke, who was at once its pretext and its victim, and whose heroic death redeemed any errors of judgment he may have committed, was begun, continued and ended, without the direct complicity or aid of the Confederate agents abroad, or the Government at home.

Mexican intervention (as is well known) originated in a joint effort on the part of the Spanish, English and French Governments, to compel Mexico to pay debts due to the subjects of those three powers. When it became evident to two of them that the third had ulterior political designs, and mediated carrying out the favorite Napoleonic idea of reestablishing the Latin race and monarchical institutions across the Atlantic, they precipitately withdrew from the enterprise, and left the Emperor unaided to carry out his own plans. He found his ally in the Austrian Archduke, and although he knew well he could and would obtain Confederate support, had he or the Archduke sought it, yet he deemed such support, or rather any alliance with that struggling people, as more dangerous than useful. He thought, and thought truly, that a common enmity was as sure and as strong a tie as a friendly understanding, and that they could always count on having a friendly neighbor so long as the Confederates were on the Mexican frontier. So no negotiations, no understanding, no *entente cordiale* ever was proposed or established between France and the Confederate Government, or its accredited agents abroad, though officious volunteers did annoy Prince Maximilian in Austria and elsewhere, and were snubbed for their pains. In Paris we were more prudent, and finding out very soon that the high contracting parties were too cautious to commit themselves to any entangling alliances with a people, whose success was yet uncertain, and whose sympathies and aid they were sure of in any event, we discreetly kept in the background.[3]

I had early opportunities of ascertaining this policy, for the Chevalier de

2. De Leon in the margin clarifies "Mexican intervention" as what he calls the "Maximilian scheme."

3. Briefly, monarchists in Mexico opposed to the reforming government of Benito Juárez appealed to Napoleon to oust Juárez and create a new monarchy in Mexico by invading and installing a ruler of his choice, backed by French might. In 1863 French troops did invade, and the following year Napoleon installed Archduke Maximilian of Austria on a newly created throne. The adventure was doomed from the start, in part by Napoleon's cynical pursuit of French self-interest and by Maximilian's ineptitude as a ruler. In 1867 French troops were withdrawn and Napoleon abandoned Maximilian, who was soon overwhelmed and taken by Juárez and executed. The episode provided

Soldapina, who was the personal friend of Maximilian and his most trusted agent and counselor at Paris, was very intimate with me, and our social intercourse was frequent and most friendly. He established the *Memorial Diplomatique*, as the organ of the future Emperor of Mexico, to whom and to whose fortunes he was warmly devoted, even to and after the bitter end, and through him I soon learned what the policy and wishes of his chief were in this regard, which I promptly communicated to the head of the Confederate Government.[4]

Therefore, when the Archduke arrived at Paris, to hold high carnival with the Emperor and his agents, although I had known him personally at Egypt, where on the occasion of his visit a few years before, as Admiral of the Austrian fleet, I had seen and conversed frequently with him, having been charged by the Diplomatic Corps, as "dozen" or chief of that corps, to welcome and dispense their courtesies to him, I yet forbore intruding upon him.[5]

Through M. Debranz I intimated my reasons for such reticence, and received his courteous acknowledgments for my discretion, which satisfied me I was right.

Mr. Slidell, more zealous, and possibly not so well informed as myself, sent to request an audience, (as I was informed,) and his meditated civilities were declined—the Prince intimating that his position was too delicate to admit of his manifesting any affiliation with the Confederate cause or its agents.[6]

On the contrary, the future Emperor indulged the hope that he could conciliate the Northern Government, and many and various were the overtures made in that direction—and several times with apparent prospects of success—as both M. Elorio, Maximilian's private secretary, and Mr. Seward, know better than most people, and which diplomacy remains secret still, in

---

some encouragement to Confederates, who thought that with France on the other side of the Rio Grande from Texas, the European nation would soon become an ally.

4. Debranz V. Saldapenna.

5. Maximilian arrived in Paris March 5, 1864, for his final meeting with Napoleon before going to Mexico. De Leon is unclear as to whether this is the arrival he mentions.

6. In fact, Slidell had expected an invitation to meet with Maximilian in Paris on his visit in March 1864. When that did not come, Slidell asked for an interview but was denied, and he attributed that to Napoleon's influence since, by this time, Napoleon had decided to distance himself from anything tending toward diplomatic recognition of the Confederacy. U.S. Navy Department, *Official Records of the Union and Confederate Navies in the War of the Rebellion* (Washington, DC, 1894–1922), Series 2, vol. 3, pp. 968–970.

spite of the numerous publications already made about Maximilian and his Empire.

The later project, also, of establishing a separate colony in Sonora, under the auspices of ex-Senator Gwin, which was, and is still, imagined to have been a Confederate intrigue—was only a joint project of the Emperor Napoleon and Dr. Gwin—in which the Confederate Government were neither asked, allowed, or expected to take any part, beyond the fact of the belief of its promoter that his personal affinities and influences might attract Southern emigrants to his new principality.[7]

So far from aiding or assisting Dr. Gwin's project, we looked with some apprehension to its development, for our chief and most pressing want was for men to fight our battles, and we feared the drain on our young men, which the temptations of the gold fields of Sonora, under French patronage, might hold out to our people.

I have anticipated the regular march of events in dwelling on these topics, because I deem it best at once to dispose of these fallacies, and to show that the whole Mexican affair, from first to last, was devised and carried on without any more aid and comfort from us, than that which was derived from our expressed sympathy with a movement, which was disagreeable to our opponents, and which promised us a friendly ally on our Southern border in the event of our ultimate success.

THE ARMISTICE AND MEDIATION PROPOSALS

On the 4th of November the Emperor gave Mr. Slidell another audience, informally, at St. Cloud, which set all the *quid nuncs* agape, for the fact was indiscreetly promulgated and published in the newspapers.

The object of that interview, however, very soon transpired, as the suggestion for a joint proposal for the armistices shortly after excited public attention.

The very fact, however, of the Emperor's seeing the Commissioner, gave birth to hopes never destined to be realized, and fostered at home the delu-

---

7. William Gwin was a dynamic, if sometimes foolish, character who strode across much of mid-century America's history. A pro-slave Democrat who served in Congress first from Mississippi, then as senator from California, he went to France in 1863 hoping to persuade Napoleon to settle slave-owners in Mexico. There is no evidence that the Confederate government was a party to his plan to create a "dukedom" of Sonora, with himself as duke. Eventually Napoleon and Maximilian both repudiated the plan.

sion that the Foreign Agents of the Government were doing, or about to do, important things abroad, and that Mr. Slidell's relations with the Emperor were improving. Some fanciful letter writers expatiated largely on the topics, and produced very false impressions on the minds of the Confederate President and people in this respect.

The Confederacy and its agents were simply in the hands of the most scientific of political players—the Emperor—from first to last.

It will be seen from the date of the dispatch making the propositions to Russia and England, that this interview took place just one week after the proposal had been made to those powers; though not yet made public.

MEXICAN REVELATIONS

Recent revelations made in France through the *Revue Cotemporaine*, by the Count de Keratry, and the documents and correspondence published by him, have thrown a flood of light on that page of secret history.[8]

While he in no way implicates the Confederates in these intrigues, he directly charges on Mr. Lincoln, and his Government, direct correspondence and promises of assistance to Juarez—and even quotes letters which he himself saw in the Mexican archives, while Maximilian was in the City of Mexico.[9]

M. de Keratry states that he saw with his own eyes, among the captured baggage of Gen. Comonfort, proofs of the correspondence passing between the Mexican and American authorities, and among others a letter from President Lincoln to Juarez, in which the following passage occurred: "We are not at open war with France, but you can count on us for money, cannon and volunteers—which we shall assist."[10]

If this letter be genuine, it is a curious commentary on Mr. Seward's virtuous indignation against England, for her violation of the strict duties of a neutral.[11]

8. Count Auguste-Hilarion de Kératry.

9. As with the supposed quote from a Lincoln letter to Comonfort, this is hearsay and came to De Leon from a biased source. No Lincoln-Juárez correspondence has to date come to light.

10. Ignacio Comonfort was president of Mexico until forced out of office by Juárez in 1858. Comonfort fled to the United States, but by 1863 he was back and serving as a general and secretary of war in Juárez's cabinet.

11. De Leon puts his finger on the salient point here. The letter almost certainly was not genuine. Amid the thousands of items of surviving Lincoln correspondence, there is not one between him and Comonfort or Juárez, and the content here does not represent the Union position in Mexican affairs.

As this question was seriously occupying the Emperor's mind when our proposition was submitted to him, I would recur to the fact that about two weeks before the Vichy interview, the Emperor had developed his purposes and policy in Mexico, in a letter to Marshal Forey, in command of the new expedition.[12]

This letter, dated at Fontainbleau, 3d July, contains this remarkable passage, embodying one of the "Napoleonic ideas:" "If, on the contrary, Mexico preserves its independence, and maintains the integrity of its territory, if a stable government can be maintained with the assistance of France, then we have restored to the Latin race on the other side of the ocean, its force and its prestige."

This public revelation of the Emperor's secret thoughts, viz: that he designed restraining the encroaching steps of the Anglo-Saxon, as opposed to the Latin race on this continent, struck Europe with surprise—but its echo was far louder in the United States, and these words gave Juarez a new and powerful ally in the so-called Anglo-Saxons of the Northern States—to whom he certainly owes his final success.

But as subsidiary to his Mexican project the Emperor found it expedient to keep the Confederates in good humor, for any combination of the Northern and Southern people on this question would tend to frustrate utterly his plans, which the existing division aided. But for the civil war in the United States he never would have made the attempt to violate so openly and boldly the Monroe doctrine. The moment the war ceased the enterprise would be as hopeless. His policy therefore was, without committing himself too far, to conciliate the Confederates.

He, therefore, struck on the happy thought of proposing an armistice in conjunction with the English and Russian Governments, knowing well, as he must have done at the time, either that those governments would not join with him in that action, or that the Northern Government could not accept it without virtually abandoning all hope of subjugating the South.[13]

An armistice meant peace, and it was now obvious that peace, under the then aspect of things, meant separation of the two sections.

12. Major General Elie Frédéric Forey led the French army invading Mexico and established the provisional government for Maximilian to take over.

13. Napoleon raised this armistice proposal with Slidell in a meeting on October 28, 1862, and then suggested it to England and Russia two days later. De Leon is mistaken in thinking that Napoleon wanted it to fail, however. France needed Southern cotton, and Napoleon needed to quiet dissident voices in his country that objected to his neutral policy.

For no sane man believed that the North could consent to open the Southern ports and allow the South to recruit her exhausted energies, with the intention of resuming the conflict with an enemy thus strengthened and refreshed.

In every alternative, therefore, the proposal would benefit the French Emperor, and would also give him the great moral sanction of European opinion; so he not only proposed this qualified intervention, but made that proposal public through an authoritative publication of it in the *Moniteur*, placing both Russia and England in a very awkward position.

When that new move was made, my hopes of obtaining French intervention on our own account faded away, although I still deemed it possible that the Mexican complication might indirectly bring about that result.

It may be that the construction we placed at the time on this proposal of the Emperor was unjust to him, and that he was really actuated by the high and honorable considerations so strongly urged in that circular. He is a man inspired by a most lofty ambition, and capable of great thoughts as well as great acts. But a sentimental regard of the welfare of the human race on grounds of pure humanity has not generally been regarded as one of his attributes, and he has not, therefore, received full credit for the act.

This renewal of efforts on the part of the French Government to intervene in American affairs was probably due in great part to the change of Ministry.

In the month of October, Monsier Thouvenel was replaced in the Foreign Office by Drouyn de Lhuys, who was understood to entertain different views, both on the Italian and American questions, from his predecessors.

Monsieur Thouvenel, as before stated, was a strong advocate both for the English and Northern alliance, and had persistently shaped his policy so as to conciliate both.[14] Drouyn de Lhuys advocated a policy more decidedly French, and was disposed to seize any opportunity which would promote French interests, either at Rome or in America, which might arise, independently of his views or wishes of either of the Cabinet above named. The substitution of this statesman for M. Thouvenel was, therefore, regarded by us as a most happy augury, and as a proof of the intention of the Emperor to take some steps in advance, without waiting for the slow cooperation of England.[15]

14. In the margin De Leon notes of Thouvenel, "French minister too," the meaning of which is cloudy.

15. Drouyn de Lhuys came to power when Thouvenel was dismissed over handling of French interests in the Italian revolt of Garibaldi. De Lhuys would exert considerable authority and influence,

We knew that we had staunch friends always near the Emperor in the Count de Persigny and in the Duc De Morny, and with the removal of Monsieur Thouvenel, thought the chief obstacle to action removed.

One curious step taken by the French Government gave rise to distrust as to its real motives, and also gave great dissatisfaction to the English Government, formal complaint having been made of it by the Ministry. After sending the proposition to the two governments, before a reply was received the text of M. Drouyn de Lhuys' despatch was published in the *Moniteur*—a most unprecedented proceeding, and which looked like forestalling public opinion and the action of the governments appealed to. No explanation was ever given as to why this was done.[16]

This overture was made on the 30th of October, 1862, and was promptly rejected both by England and Russia, on the ground of its inexpediency and certain rejection by the Northern Government.

The rejection by Russia was made without many phrases; that of England was more cautiously worded, expressing the desire of the British Government to act in concurrence with France on the American question, and basing it on the conduct of France in the Trent affair, thus gratuitously insulting the North by the reference, while alienating the South by refusing to intervene.

These were Lord Russell's words:

> Neither her Majesty the Queen, nor the British nation, will ever forget the noble and emphatic manner in which the Emperor of the French vindicated the law of nations and assisted the cause of peace, in the instance of the seizure of the Confederate Commissioners on board of the Trent.

The *Moniteur* declared of these responses that they "did not constitute a refusal, but only an adjournment," adding, "but if our information be correct, the hesitations of the Cabinets of London and St. Petersburg are apt soon to terminate. A feeling prevails in America, North as well as South, favorable to peace, and that feeling gains ground daily."

The meaning of these utterances was made plain two months later, when the Emperor again took the initiative, and without asking any cooperation, intervened singly in the American quarrel.

---

even on the emperor, though in the end Napoleon made his own decisions. He was a master of verbal camouflage, often leaving listeners mystified as to what he actually said—not a bad trait in a diplomat.

16. Drouyn de Lhuys published his letter in the *Moniteur* on November 13, chiefly to inform the people of their government's action in seeking peace in America.

EXTRACTS FROM DESPATCHES TO STATE DEPARTMENT,
FEBRUARY 28, 1863

Enclosed I send for use of the Department the expression of the views of the most influential members of the French and English press on the Emperor's last move. England appears still to echo Lord Russell's "not yet." A significant assurance was given in the Chambers that the 5,000,000 loan "would be all that was necessary." One thing is sure, that the Emperor cannot long sustain the prolongation of the cotton famine, and would not if he could.

With regard to the approaching session of the British Parliament, the Tories are in a position to make capital out of the question, if so disposed. But, in my judgment, the "masterly inactivity" of the Palmerston Cabinet is accepted by the English people as their proper policy, and I do not think it will be varied unless the rapid march of events compels a change.

Why England should be afraid to provoke the enmity of the North, with the rich prizes she could offer their cupidity in the spoils of her merchant marine, which covers every sea, is obvious; besides which the recently published trade returns show the very profitable business she has substituted for her exports of cotton goods in furnishing warlike stores to the North alone. The unpublished lists of similar export to the South would greatly swell the sum total, and British industry is still profiting most largely by our expenditures in various shapes, that shall be nameless. The distress in the manufacturing districts has been tided over successfully by the grandest display of national energy and public charity witnessed in modern times, and England can now afford to be a calm spectator of our war.

Not so with France, where the same resources and the same public spirit do not exist, or have not been found available, and where the distress of the manufacturing operatives has increased and is increasing, and with it the popular discontent. Government has been obliged to come directly to the aid of the manufacturing districts, and the subsidy voted by the Corps Legislatif is only a partial relief.

The industry has been diverted into other channels; but the trade of France is suffering fearfully from the interruption of relations with the Northern and Southern States, not having found the same compensations as their more energetic neighbors across the channel.

The proportion of ventures made from France for the supply of our wants has hitherto been very small, but is now increasing; and as her trade with the North was in articles of luxury and taste, the revolution has checked it almost entirely in addition to the depreciation of currency now ruling in New York. But the present condition of Europe with the unfortunate expedition to Mexico (the proportions of which are rapidly expanding and developing) gives rise to grave disquietudes to all thinking men here, and must add heavily to the load of cares which press heavily on the head of the Emperor. He looks worn and wearied, and well he may; for complications are thickening around him and his empire, which must feel every disturbance in the equipoise of Europe.

Had we but been blessed with a clear sky in Europe during our civil war, we should have seen its end long since, through foreign intervention; but with each lull in our storm, there come heavy clouds on the European horizon, obscuring our sunshine.

The Bourse, that touchstone of war or peace, has been much agitated since the news of these national combinations, and the speculators seem to snuff war. The intimate connection known to exist here between financial and political combinations renders this susceptibility suspicious.

From this sketch of the actual condition of the continent, it must be evident to your perception and that of the President, that the rulers of Europe, at this moment, have sufficient occupation at home, without venturing into the whirlpool of American intervention. But the conviction is now beginning to be universal that the resources, the energies, and the heart of the North, are all failing, and that the war of weapons and armies are well nigh over.

The European view is, that so soon as the war of sections ceases, the conflict between State and federal authorities, which is the basis of secession, will further dissever the confederacies.

CHAPTER 20
THE EMPEROR'S LAST EFFORT AT MEDIATION—
WHAT WE HOPED TO GAIN BY IT—SIMULTANEOUS SNUBBING
OF FRANCE BY MR. SEWARD AND MR. BENJAMIN—
FRENCH INTRIGUES IN TEXAS

We were greatly disappointed at the result of the Emperor's proposition, but it did not seem to affect him much, for he had matured, or at least projected other plans, of which we were soon to hear.

Shortly after the failure of his armistice proposal, he sounded both the Northern and Southern agents in relation to his new plan, and to the best of my knowledge and belief received encouragement from both sides to present it.

His new plan was to approach the Northern Government directly through his ambassador at Washington, and propose to them, without suspending hostile operations, to name commissioners who should confer with other commissioners appointed by the Confederate Government as to terms of peace.

Mr. Dayton, in communicating the intention of the Emperor to make this proposal, makes the suggestion that "this overture answered what were supposed to be the objections to the previous proposition for armistice or mediation.

Firstly: It proposed no intervention of any kind on the part of foreign powers.

Secondly: Did not involve any suspension of hostilities.["]

For us, the adoption of this proposal would have been a step in advance, for it would have amounted to a quasi recognition of the South by the North. Moreover, we believed that the North, wearied by the war and its want of success, was ready to allow "the erring sisters to depart in peace," and only wanted a decent pretext in foreign pressure to do so.

So much if the proposition was adopted. In the event of its refusal by the North we thought the pride of the Emperor would be wounded, and that his sympathies would be reenlisted on our side. Besides which, we greatly miscalculated the necessity of France to terminate the struggle and open our ports.[1]

The conference at Hampton Roads at a later period of the war was probably the offspring of this Napoleonic idea.[2]

We all saw how fatally it failed in its end, although at that time it seemed little short of insanity for the South to demand all it could have gained, if victorious in the strife. We can therefore judge what the fate of the Emperor's expedient would have been, even had it been adopted.

The peremptory rejection of this proposition by Mr. Seward, and the language in which it was made, gave offence to the susceptibilities of the French people, as an extract from my despatches written at the time will prove.[3]

But he was sagacious in his refusal, in a diplomatic point of view, since his consent would have been construed abroad as an admission of Northern despondency if not of despair.

We were encouraged by this demonstration of the Emperor's, for it gave the Confederacy the moral support derived from the expression of his opinion so distinctly implied, viz: that the North could not subdue the South by force of arms, and that the hour for the voluntary reconciliation of the combatants had arrived.

Just after this proposition was made by the Emperor in favor of the South, a captured blockade runner brought to light the fact of an apparent collision between the Confederate and French authorities, based on a supposed or suspected plot to detach Texas from the Southern Confederacy, by which the web we sought to weave was nearly broken.

---

1. Napoleon's proposal of a six-month armistice and European mediation was a case of the Emperor having nothing to lose. If it worked, he was a hero in the eyes of his people, French mills would once again have cotton, and the opening of Confederate ports would stimulate moribund French trade. If it failed, it would be because of British, Russian, Union, and/or Confederate refusal, and Napoleon still would have gained credit with his people for trying something to their benefit.

2. The so-called Hampton Roads Peace Conference took place February 3, 1865, when Lincoln and Seward met with Stephens, Hunter, and John Campbell representing the Confederacy. They discussed armistice, but it was clear from the first that there was no ground for compromise between Lincoln's insistence on recognition of supremacy of the Union and reunification and Confederate insistence on independence.

3. Seward's rejection was not insulting, but brisk, maintaining that since Napoleon had not approached the United States directly with his suggestion, there was no need for the United States to respond to an uninvited French intrusion into American affairs.

THE FRENCH PLOT IN TEXAS

Mr. Benjamin's intercepted despatches revealed the fact of his having dismissed the French Consul from Texas, on the ground of his having instituted intrigues to detach that State from the Confederacy, with the view of making it a French colony![4] The despatches conveyed the impression resting on the Secretary that the French Government was not ignorant of, even if it had not directly sanctioned this intrigue, which was at once cowardly and perfidious under the circumstances. The publication of these despatches made it necessary to counteract their bad effect—so I immediately took steps to accomplish that object—by causing it to be intimated in the proper quarters, that although we had no doubt of the honor and good faith of France, compromised in this matter by an overzealous and injudicious representative, yet it was due to her, as well as to us, that a formal contradiction should set the slander at rest forever. The steps taken are thus briefly summed up in the following extracts from my despatches of that date:[5]

> On the receipt of New York journals containing the intercepted despatches taken from Reid Sanders, off Charleston, I thought it best some formal contradiction should be made by the French Government, through the public press, to its alleged complicity in the Texas intrigue.[6]
>
> I therefore caused the paper containing the correspondence to be laid before M. Mocquard, private secretary to the Emperor, by the hands of a friend of mine, who is a member of the Emperor's private Cabinet.
>
> M. Mocquard declared to him that they were not aware of the publicity given to the correspondence through the Northern press; and in the *Moniteur* of two days after appeared the formal contradiction, which you will find herewith enclosed, (marked B.)

4. In the margin De Leon has written "Benjamin's Plan," most likely a reminder to include Benjamin's correspondence in the affair in his revised memoir. More on this apparent plot will be found in U.S. Navy Department, *Official Records of the Union and Confederate Navies in the War of the Rebellion* (Washington, DC, 1894–1922), Series 2, vol. 3, pp. 556–559 (hereafter cited as *ORN*), and in Alfred Jackson and Katherine Abbey Hanna, *Napoleon III and Mexico: American Triumph over Monarchy* (Chapel Hill, NC, 1971), p. 118.

5. De Leon to Benjamin, February 23, 1863, Records of the Confederate States of America, 1854–1889, Consular and Other Missions, 1861–1865, Library of Congress, Washington, DC. A December 13, 1862, dispatch from Benjamin to De Leon had been captured and published in the New York press.

6. In the margin De Leon notes "see letter," suggesting he intended to quote the actual correspondence in a later version. Reid Sanders was the son of George N. Sanders, who went from Charleston to London to try to expedite construction of ironclad warships for the Confederacy being built on contract by his father. His blockade runner was captured and his correspondence taken from him and published in the Northern press. *ORN*, p. 627.

* * *

The ship-building and cotton bond negotiations were already whispered about all over Europe, and frequently alluded to in English papers. The only revelation was that of the Texas imbroglio, which we have turned to good account.

The real facts connected with this imbroglio were simply these: The French Consular Agent in Texas conceived the idea of making that State a French province, and not only broached the idea on the spot, but even had the temerity to make the proposition to one of her Senators in Congress, who revealed it to Mr. Benjamin and the President.[7] The very absurdity of his choice of confidants, should have proved the farcical character of the affair, but Mr. Benjamin's imagination saw more than met the eye in their wild attempt, and he treated it as a serious plot to dismember the Confederacy, and came near alienating our only and last hope in Europe, by the gravity he attached to it.

This incident, trivial as it seemed, may have had something to do with cooling the interest the Emperor had manifested for the Confederacy, for he never afterwards renewed any of the extraordinary attempts he had previously made in our behalf.[8] Thus Mr. Seward's and Mr. Benjamin's despatches, curiously enough, came much at the same time to convince the Emperor that non-intervention in the American quarrel was the safest and most dignified course.

HOW NEAR RECOGNITION

From my despatches of that date will be seen what the progress of our diplomacy was, and how high the flood-tide, which soon after began rapidly to ebb. At this moment we were really nearer recognition than ever before or after.

Jan. 28.—The departure of the mail connecting with Nassau compels me to forward the very important despatch of Monsieur Drouyn de Lhuys without commentary—although the document needs none.

This second overture of the Emperor, while it proves his anxiety to put an end to the war, both in the interests of France and of humanity, does not, to my mind, indicate his intention of intervention, should his proposal be refused by the Lincoln Government.

---

7. De Leon notes in the margin that he should include "more of Benjamin."

8. In fact, there is little evidence that Napoleon was even aware of the Texas imbroglio, nor that it influenced his policy toward the Confederacy.

I am not even thoroughly persuaded that in that event he would even adopt the milder expedient of recognition—which many of our friends here suppose.

With this despatch of the French Minister I send you the commentary in the shape of the vote of 5,000,000 francs, by the Corps Legislatif, for the relief of the distressed operatives whose sufferings and whose impatience both progress with dangerous rapidity. But speculations from any one, as to the designs or motives of the one mind now ruling France, are idle, for he keeps his own counsel more closely, and mystifies the world more successfully with each successive year.

His own Ministers are not permitted to do much more than register his decrees, and he has no confidants; we can, therefore, only scrutinize as "through a glass darkly," the movements of his policy, and the workings of a mind fertile in plans and wonderfully patient in their execution.

I may safely say, however, that we owe much of the sympathy now felt and expressed for us, both here and in England, to the conviction that we have won our cause, and that the North, staggering under a succession of disasters on the battle field, and crushed under her colossal debt, must shortly abandon the struggle.

This very conviction, however, now retards our immediate recognition, or the intervention of foreign powers; who, regarding the Northern States now with mingled distrust and aversion, yet believe in their power of inflicting injury, as men will view with some apprehension the death struggle of some desperately wounded wild beast.[9]

A MONTH LATER

On the 28th of February, 1863, an elaborate despatch, surveying the whole situation, was sent by me to Richmond, the salient points of which are herewith presented:[10]

Through the unsolicited courtesy of the New York journals, I have had the pleasure of reading your despatch addressed to me, and await with much interest the promised despatch which is to unfold more fully your views and wishes in relation to our future operations.

In the meantime, in conformity with your instructions, I shall continue to keep the Department informed of the events transpiring in Europe, as bearing on the probable action of the European powers.

* * *

9. De Leon's original January 28, 1863, letter is in Records of the Confederate States of America.

10. De Leon's original February 28, 1863, dispatch is in Records of the Confederate States of America.

The record of events subsequent to date of my last despatch, will not be an eventful one, with regard to our question.

It can only chronicle the fixed determination of the European powers to allow us to settle our internal differences in our own way, and in our own time—the policy of non-intervention ostentatiously proclaimed by England, and with politic professions practically adopted by France, still giving the key to the situation here. Since my last communication the American question has been brought up in the British Parliament and Corps Legislatif, in both bodies with the same result, viz: the strict observance of the *statu quo*—as the enclosed extracts and synopsis will show.

* * *

No one who understood the matter here, ever believed that the Emperor's supplementary proposal to the North to enter into negotiations with the South would be accepted or entertained by the Lincoln Cabinet, although the *Tribune's* adroit suggestion of throwing the onus of refusal on the South somewhat staggered opinion on that point. Yet it is looked on as a good stroke of policy on the part of the Emperor, as contrasted with the icy and callous egotism of England, who waits and watches, but makes no sign.

A distinction certainly must be drawn between the conduct of the man who calmly contemplates a fellow-being in the agonies of drowning, without either aiding him by act or voice, and of another, who, under similar circumstances, rushes off in hot haste to summon the aid and the life boats of the Humane Society! Such I conceive to be the substantial difference in the attitude of the two nations, and although, like the individual in deep water, we would prefer active, personal interposition, we yet cannot afford to despise the proffered sympathy which may result in final rescue. The discussions in the two Parliaments—or rather the absence of them—give the most conclusive evidence of the understanding existing between the two nations on this point.

Mr. Seward's reply to the Emperor's last proposition has just been published in the English papers, and has excited some surprise and self-felicitation on the English side of the Channel, and much smothered anger and mortification on this. Not because any one supposed this proposition would be accepted has this effect been produced, but because of the arrogant and defiant tone which breathes through this answer.

That this unexpected tone and attitude of the Lincoln Cabinet may greatly alter the position of things is evident, but it is as yet too early to judge how far the reaction in favor of the South may go—whether it may lead to speedy recognition, or some shape of intervention. The debate in the English Parliament, expected next Monday, may develop something.

I send you the first echoes to Mr. Seward's thunder from French and English journals.

CHAPTER 21
THE CONFEDERATE COTTON LOAN—WHO ORIGINATED AND WHO WORKED IT—ITS INFLUENCE ON CONFEDERATE CREDIT AND DIPLOMACY IN EUROPE

———•◦•———

There is no subject which has given ground to more fabulous and more scandalous stories, than the Confederate Cotton Loan. Both its origin and its history have been enveloped in romance, and the romance of business, in our day, exceeds that of fiction. The wildest and most improbable stories, relative to this transaction, have been circulated on both sides of the Atlantic, and to this moment the origin of the Confederate loan is as mythical as the parentage of Homer's heroes.

As I happen to know the secret history of this transaction, as well as its influence on our foreign relations, I propose, in this chapter, briefly to chronicle its birth, life, and burial.

In my earliest dispatches from Europe I impressed upon the Richmond Government the importance and necessity of establishing credits abroad, and indicated how it could be done. The proposals submitted to me by various foreign capitalists, as accredited diplomatic agent of the Government, were transmitted by me, but were never seriously considered, as far as I could learn.

The uncertain and shiftless system of remitting bills of exchange on London, purchased at high rates, or even of sending over gold, was the expedient adopted, after it was found that supplies could not be obtained on credit, or for payment in Confederate money.

But private enterprise anticipated the tardy action of Cabinet and Congress in this matter.

In the Autumn of 1862, there arrived in Paris a well known Southern politician, equally well known in the Washington lobby as a very adroit manager of contracts. He brought with him contracts for supplies of all kinds, to a very large amount—payable on delivery of the articles at some stipulated point in the Confederacy, either in Confederate money or in cotton, at a fixed price, at the option of the seller. He was promised a commission of almost one hundred per cent profit in the event of success, with which very large margin it was supposed he could tempt some bold English or French speculators to take the risks incident to the operation.[1]

I had known this gentleman in Washington years before, and he called upon me at Paris, shortly after his arrival, and opened his budget; and I was much surprised to learn the magnitude and value of the privileges he had obtained from the new government.

He proposed to me to cooperate with him, and offered a liberal interest in the operation, if I would consent to aid him in putting it through.

This I declined, informing him that it was not in my line and that I could not spare my time from the very different labors in which I was engaged; but that any assistance I could give incidentally to the furtherance of so useful a work, should be cheerfully accorded.

About a month after our interview he called again, and stated to me that his chief difficulty arose from the fear of contractors that Confederate money might depreciate, and that they would lose in that way.

He requested me to give him a letter expressing my belief that no such advantage would be taken, and that the payments would be made *bona fide,* according to the spirit, not the letter, of the contract.

As I did not doubt the perfect good faith of the Confederate Government, the letter was written, for I supposed that it would have proved sufficient to satisfy the speculators, who were tempted by the large profits. It proved, however, that the bait was not sufficient, and the negotiation could not be perfected.

It was while these efforts were making that the idea of the Confederate Cotton Loan suggested itself to the brain of a speculative Frenchman, well known in Paris, but not at all known in America. And it happened in this wise.

Failing in enlisting regular business houses in his speculation, the gentleman who held these contracts, looked around him to find some adventurous capitalist, or speculator, who could be tempted to undertake the affair. He could do nothing in London, so he returned to Paris.

In the latter place, through the medium of an English house agent, he was

1. In the margin De Leon has identified this man as "G.M.S.," an inadvertent error, since the man he refers to is clearly George Nicholas Sanders. A ubiquitous troublemaker, Sanders was a Kentuckian who promoted the "Young America" movement of Stephen A. Douglas in the 1850s and then became a Confederate sympathizer. In 1862 he secured a contract from Secretary of the Navy Stephen M. Mallory to arrange for building ironclads in Europe in return for Confederate cotton.

introduced to Monsieur Carteret, who had organized the omnibus system of Paris, and was interested in various other large speculative operations.[2]

This gentleman seriously inclined his ear to the tempting propositions, and when our compatriot appealed to him for assistance, applied himself sedulously to this matter.

He said he knew a young and energetic banker, who might cooperate, and proposed a conference, which was accordingly held.[3]

The result was that the banker asked a guarantee, or at least an endorsement of the validity of the contract from the Confederate Commissioner at Paris, Mr. Slidell, whom he did not then know.

If the Commissioner said the thing was good and valid, why then he would see what he could do to assist his friend Carteret (with whom he had other affairs,) in pushing it through. If not, the affair had better be left alone.

The young banker was Monsieur Erlanger, and through the good offices of the English house agent once more he was duly presented to Mr. Slidell in company with M. Carteret, who spoke no English, and our compatriot, who spoke no French.

The tripartite conversation which took place led to no practical result.

The Commissioner threw cold water on the sanguine contractor, by intimating his doubts as to the paying nature of the job, under the conditions and restrictions which limited it—besides which the date of the contract was long anterior—the limit of time given had expired—and various other reasons—the issue of which was, that the contractor and his job received a death blow where they anticipated a support.

But the introduction of the French gentleman led to new negotiations on a different basis. Before commissioner and bankers parted, the intimation was somehow thrown out, that although that particular negotiation would not do, yet there was ample space and verge enough for a new one, on a different line. For example, there was Capt. ——, now in Paris, fully accredited to purchase arms and supplies, and ready with the sanction of the Commissioners to issue cotton bonds for them.[4] This was an opening.

---

2. In the margin De Leon wrote what appears to be "Beginning of loan." The man referred to is Nicholas Carteret.

3. In the margin De Leon identifies the banker as "Erlanger." That is Émile Erlanger of Erlanger and Company.

4. In the margin De Leon identified this man as "Caleb Huse." Huse, of Alabama, was sent to Europe by the Confederate War Department as a special purchasing agent and remained there throughout the war.

The astute Frenchman who had organized the omnibus system, and the equally astute banker, who was watching to make his *coup,* saw something feasible in this. So the contractor who had introduced them was thrown overboard, and had conferences with the new parties proposed, and carried out.

Monsieur Cartaret, (who spoke no English,) in a law suit he afterwards instituted to recover his share of the commissions on the negotiation of the loan, but a small part of which he alleged had been paid him by his colleagues—swore that he originated the idea of the Confederate Cotton Loan on the basis finally adopted and carried out by Monsieur Erlanger.

His suit, however, was compromised the evening before the trial was to have taken place, but what he compromised for was never divulged to a curious and inquiring public. Let us, however, hope that the inventor in this case did not meet the usual fate of those who have originated most new discoveries for the benefit of communities.

The banker laid the foundations of his fortune, and of signal ultimate success in this negotiation.

From M. Carteret's antecedents it is reasonable to suppose he did not abandon his suit without a valuable consideration.

As to the unfortunate contractor and compatriot—who was the medium of contract between these opposite poles—the electric sparks only passed through him—but no light or heat remained with him. His contracts fell through, and he received none of the commissions so liberally lavished on the projectors of the loan, as was apparent on the preliminary investigations to the suit referred to—a full report of which was published in the *Gazette des Tribunals,* or law reporter of Paris.

As before stated, Monsieur Carteret claims the paternity of the Confederate Cotton Loan, which Monsieur Erlanger undertook to carry into practical operation, with the sanction and support of Mr. Slidell, who sent and recommended the project to his Government.

Mr. Erlanger displayed great energy and skill in his management of the matter in its earlier stages. He sent several agents by different routes to Richmond, fortified by Mr. Slidell's recommendation, and furnished with drafts of the terms on which the proposed loan was to be given to him and his associates, and negotiated with the public. Some of the messengers went by the blockade, others through the North.

The proposition of M. Erlanger & Co. was submitted by these agents to the

Confederate authorities at Richmond, and after some modifications was sent into the Confederate Congress for its sanction.[5]

Some discussion took place in secret session in regard to it, and some diversity of opinion prevailed—but it was finally endorsed, and the agents came back to have it carried out.

The loan was launched shortly afterwards, and proved at first a great success. The contract was all to the advantage of the banker and his associates.

They obtained the loan at 74, with power to issue the stock at 90, in the foreign market; and obtained besides a commission on the gross sum of one and a half per cent, for introducing and manipulating it.[6]

They had, besides, the privilege conceded them of waiving the execution of the contract, if within three months time from the arrival of the proposition in Europe the banker found he could not place it.

That such remarkable advantages were given may be accounted for by the fact that it was legislated upon by a Congress blindfold, and ignorant of such matters, and negotiated by a Commissioner who was more favorably known in the field of diplomacy than of finance.[7]

The nominal sum to be raised was £3,000,000 sterling, but of this sum either a third or a fourth part was reserved by the Confederate Government for its own use.

When it is further seen what opportunities the European bankers had of manipulating the loan over which they had such absolute control, and of "bulling" or "bearing" the stock, it can easily be understood how dear the Confederate States and people had to pay for their whistle.

Still, when the loan was first launched, it seemed a great success, financially and politically.[8]

5. De Leon notes in the margin that the Erlanger proposition was discussed in the Congress in "Secret Sessions." Secret sessions were a political bugbear to the Davis opposition, which argued throughout the war that debates ought to be in the open and publicized. Congressional leaders, however, realized the lack of unanimity in their ranks and wisely kept public knowledge of their arguments to a minimum by closing the doors to much of their debate.

6. De Leon noted in the margin that the loan was at "16 1/2%." In fact, De Leon's figures are a bit off. The loan contract provided that Erlanger got a 5 percent commission for disposing of the bonds, plus everything realized in sales above 70 percent of the face value of the bonds, as well as other commissions. U.S. Navy Department, *Official Records of the Union and Confederate Navies in the War of the Rebellion* (Washington, DC, 1894–1922), Series 2, vol. 3, pp. 568–572 (hereafter cited as *ORN*).

7. De Leon identified the commissioner spoken of as "Slidell."

8. De Leon wrote "5" in the margin, meaning 5 million.

It was announced in the *Times* and other papers that 15,000,000 had been subscribed for instead of 3,000,000, and the stock was quoted at from 2 to 3 premium. It was issued at 90, the bankers making their great *coup* at once, and the subscriptions in England were *bona fide*, and very large—though I believe very little indeed was ever taken in France.

Contrary to the prevailing impression, and even to the statements published under authority of the Washington State Department, the subscription had little political significance, and the names of no prominent members of Parliament figured then or afterwards on the lists. Neither Mr. Gladstone, Mr. Gregory, Mr. Roebuck, nor any of the prominent sympathizers of the South in Parliament, ever owned a dollar of that stock—the published lists to the contrary notwithstanding.[9]

The largest holder was Sir Henry de Houghton, one of the richest baronets in England, and descended from one of the oldest families.[10]

From the commencement to the close of the controversy, he ardently espoused the Southern side, and subscribed £200,000 for the loan. Each drawing and payment of interest he reinvested—so that at the close he probably held one-tenth of the entire loan—and I believe holds it still, his great fortune enabling him to sustain a loss sufficient to ruin most men.

Many other private gentlemen, merchants and military men, subscribed sums of £10 or £5,000, and a great swarm of cotton speculators went into it to secure a control of the cotton which it pledged; but I sincerely believe that no portion of that loan was given away in subsidies to influential men to secure influence—as was charged at the time, and is still credited in many quarters. I can frankly say that if such were the case I never was able to get any inkling of it. It was a gigantic and a costly job, of which the projectors reaped the sole benefit—and the Confederates only got the contingent remainder.

I never assisted in or approved of this job, for many reasons—on the contrary, was opposed to it from its incubation up to its chipping the shell. When, however, it was a fixed fact, in common with many others I thought it a duty to take some of the stock, and was one of the sufferers at the end.

The chief attraction it presented to the English mind was the control it gave, or was supposed to give, of Southern cotton.

It soon became a gambling stock, and its fluctuations were wonderfully

9. De Leon wrote in the margin that these men "did not subsc[ribe]."
10. Sir Henry Bold Houghton, later Lord Houghton.

rapid—varying with each steamer's news—and sometimes in the course of a week rising or falling 12 per cent.

Viewed from a political standpoint, there can be no question that the successful placing of this loan, with the attendant circumstances, produced a powerful influence in favor of the Confederacy, apart from the material interests it enlisted. But it is equally clear that this influence was but temporary, and that the reaction from the same cause was greater than the advance.

The names of prominent Southern agents were mixed up with its negotiations and its rich spoils, in a way seriously to damage whatever prestige or influence they may have carried before; and the proof of the shock given to public confidence by its management was to be witnessed by the fact that this first loan was the last the Confederate Government ever could negotiate on any terms abroad.[11]

Monsieur Erlanger at this time had neither the capital nor the connection necessary to put the loan on the market. He merely exploited it; and, through the agency of two powerful English houses, after obtaining the concession, succeeded in floating it. These were the houses of Schroder & Co., of London, and Fraser, Trenholm & Co., of Liverpool, who took the matter in hand and did it—the originators of the project giving a slice only of their enormous concessions of £3,500,000 as a bonus, and taking neither risk nor responsibility.[12]

I do not suppose that a neater financial operation was ever made than that which sprung out of the tripartite conversations to which I have already alluded.

This brief history of the Confederate loan will show that the financial ability displayed by the Confederate authorities at home was not very remarkable. As it was the only successful negotiation initiated or conducted by Mr. Slidell, he is certainly entitled to a full share of any merit that may attach to it, or any benefits which may have accrued from it, to Confederate interests abroad.

The loan when first issued commanded a premium of two or three per cent; but it soon fell to par, where it continued for some time, then slowly fell, with occasional fluctuations, as the Confederate cause brightened or darkened, until it finally sunk among the ruins and rubbish of the lost Confederacy.

11. In the margin De Leon notes "so was___," but his intent is unclear.

12. J. H. Schroeder & Co. were Erlanger's London agents, and Fraser, Trenholm & Co., were the Confederacy's financial agents in England, connected with George Trenholm, the last Confederate secretary of the treasury.

It was probably for a long time the most speculative stock ever floated on the London Stock Exchange.

Immediately after the loan had been negotiated, Mr. McRea, of Mississippi, was sent over, as financial agent, to take charge of its disbursement, which function he performed to the end.[13]

As I had no agency in the matter of getting up this loan, so I had no interest or knowledge as to its distribution or disbursement, neither of which matters fell within my province, and, therefore, cannot say how or where it was expended, and whether, as was charged, a contingent remainder of it survived the Confederacy.

After the grand finale of the Confederacy there was no one, either in Europe or in America, empowered to investigate such matters; and several propositions which were made by some of the ex-agents in Europe to appoint a board from their number to receive the reports of all disbursing agents so as to wind up all Confederate affairs in order, failed to be carried out.

So I presume that mystery—if mystery it be—will never be solved satisfactorily, although the agents of the Federal Government abroad have made as great exertions to find Confederate funds as were ever displayed in search of the lost treasures of Captain Kidd, and generally with about the same success.

The very few persons who knew anything about this subject kept their own counsel; and, as they are outside the reach of questioning, will probably preserve the same discreet silence to the end.

As the Confederate loan was born in mystery, so did it live and die, and where its remains were deposited is utterly unknown to the writer.

When the financial history of the Confederacy comes to be written—if ever that task shall be attempted—it will not compare with the military, or even with the diplomatic, ineffectual as all the efforts in the two latter proved. Both in arms and in diplomacy the Confederacy had some successes and gained some triumphs. Its financial record is but a series of mistakes in its earlier history, when something might have been effected, and its management passed into abler hands too late to redeem the errors of the system which had made Confederate money valueless abroad and depreciated at home, and stabbed fatally its credit in Europe, by the only petty loan ever negotiated there. As wars in our day are fought as much with gold as with steel, one of the great causes of the Confederate failure may doubtless be

13. Colin J. McRae was from Alabama, not Mississippi, and served as a delegate to the first congress at Montgomery, and from 1863 onward was the Confederacy's chief financial agent in Europe.

traced to the financial mismanagement of resources amply sufficient to have established larger credits (if properly administered) than were required.

But the Confederate loan, whose history has been briefly sketched, did little temporary good and much permanent injury to Confederate credit, and never could be repeated. It serves now as a sad memento of the Confederacy to the unlucky holders who still retain it.[14]

Curious as it seems, it still preserves a small nominal value, and orders for its purchase are frequently given, even now. A committee of bondholders, comprising a number of influential and respectable Englishmen, hold regular sessions, and have obtained legal opinions from eminent jurists as to the lien which attaches to the relics of Confederate property from those bonds, issued as they were by a government acknowledged as a belligerent both by the Northern and European Governments. And there are sensible business men in London to-day who believe that at some future time that stock will represent value again, as it stands on a totally different basis from any other Confederate obligation issued during the war.

So, of all the creations of the Confederacy, the last spark yet left glimmering is to be found in these Confederate cotton bonds.

The argument briefly is this: While the Richmond Government had possession of the cotton in the South, and the control of Southern resources, it pledged them for the payment of these bonds, which are in the hands of *bona fide* holders, unconnected with the Confederacy, and, therefore, unaffected by any action of Congress. They simply made a contract, for the fulfillment of which Confederate cotton and property, into whatever hands they have passed, are responsible. The Washington Government takes that property subject to that lien.

Such is the argument of the bondholders, and the bonds in England are regarded by many persons as a good offset to the Alabama claims, which point, when those claims are adjudicated or submitted to arbitration, will probably be pressed.[15]

With regard to the original value of these bonds, no two opinions were entertained by the great majority of English business men. The only distrust

14. The Erlanger cotton loan was a disaster financially. The Confederacy gave up a third of the potential income in the share set aside for Erlanger and even more in commissions. Moreover, when the value of the bonds soon began to fall and then collapsed after the summer of 1863, agents were forced to buy back many of the bonds to keep the price up artificially, costing the South more revenue.

15. De Leon refers to the "Alabama claims," suits for damages filed on behalf of American shippers who suffered losses as a result of the depredations of Confederate commerce raiders like the

ever excited was through the attacks made on Southern credit by Robert J. Walker, who, as a secret agent of the Washington Government, indefatigably employed his pen and tongue for the double purpose of breaking down Confederate, and raising Federal, credit in Europe; for the latter's bonds fell twenty per cent below those of the former when he commenced his labors.

Harping strongly on the string of Mississippi repudiation, with which he sought to identify President Davis, Mr.Walker strewed his pamphlets "thick as the leaves in Vallambrosa," and did produce more effect than any other agent abroad.[16] He not only attempted to spike our guns, but to inspire faith in Northern securities, and it is but just to him to say that he succeeded in this work. The restoration of confidence in those securities abroad, especially in Germany, was in my judgment more due to his indefatigable efforts and plausible explanations than to any other cause, and the "sinews of war" were supplied from those sources, without which the strong right arm of the North would have been stiffened, if not paralyzed. I believe Mr. Walker has received small thanks from the North for these services. I know he incurred the fiercest indignation from the South, which was proportionate to the mischief he was effecting.

In "The Familiar Epistle to Robert J. Walker, from Jonathan Shipsby, of Screamerville," every weapon of ridicule and denunciation was used against him, and every inconsistency in his long public life used to diminish his influence and weaken his statements.

This testimony to the services of Mr. Walker can be more relied upon from the fact of its proceeding from the same pen which wrote the epistle.[17]

Federal credit abroad may be said to have dated its revival from the time of his secret mission; and Mr. Chase showed his judgment in the selection of

CSS *Alabama* that were fitted out in England. In 1868, as De Leon was writing, the claims were being adjudicated without success, and not until 1872 would a tribunal finally direct that Britain pay some damages to settle the issue.

16. Robert J. Walker was a Pennsylvanian who moved to Mississippi and achieved political success as a senator, becoming secretary of the treasury for President Polk. When the Civil War came, he remained a staunch Unionist. De Leon's reference to "repudiation" refers to accusations that as a senator from Mississippi before the war, Jefferson Davis had advocated the state repudiating its debts owed on bonds. Walker tried to frighten European investors away from Confederate bonds and loans by implying that after the war Davis would repudiate those debts, too.

17. De Leon wrote the pamphlet, whose actual title was *A Familiar Epistle to Robert J. Walker, Formerly of Pennsylvania, Later of Mississippi, More Recently of Washington, and Last Heard of in Mr. Coxwell's Balloon, from an Old Acquaintance, to which Is Prefixed a Biographical Sketch* (London, 1863). De Leon published it under the pseudonym of Jonathan Slingsby of Screamersville. It is misidentified in Cullop as *A Familiar Epistle from an Old Acquaintance*, perhaps because it was referred to as

his predecessor in the Treasury, for the very fact of his having previously filled that post gave weight and authority to his statements.

In my earliest dispatches from Europe I urged upon the authorities at Richmond the necessity of establishing credits abroad on a firm basis, and submitted to them several propositions from parties of undoubted responsibility, on fair terms. But none of these were ever considered possible, because no private interests were enlisted, and nothing in the nature of a job presented. As early as January, 1863, I wrote as follows:

> In my previous dispatches I have taken the liberty of suggesting the vital importance of establishing banking credits in Europe to avoid the ruinous "difference of exchange" demanded and exacted by mercantile houses for Confederate funds.
>
> We learn that one of the several overtures made our Government is on the eve of accomplishment, and unless some arrangement be made for sufficient funds for purchase abroad, are satisfied that the Government might as well cease sending over agents with contracts they find impossible to execute.
>
> The hawking about of these orders has produced an unfavorable impression abroad as to the financial management of our affairs. Many of the contracts entered into by the Confederate Government have remained unexecuted, in whole or in part, from the inability or refusal of the agents of the Government to meet the accruing liabilities. Enclosed you will find a letter addressed to me by Mr.—, which speaks for itself.[18]

To this proposition from a responsible French capitalist, to advance funds on the security of cotton pledged to him, and to be shipped to cover his advances, I never even received a reply.

---

such in the *Index*. It has sometimes been mistaken as the work of George McHenry, but De Leon clearly acknowledges his own authorship, as does Hotze, who calls it "a very clever pamphlet" in *ORN*, p. 966. De Leon's brother Thomas Cooper De Leon also identified his brother as author in his letter to Jefferson Davis of December 1863, in which he sends Davis a copy of the pamphlet (Lynda Lasswell Crist, Kenneth H. Williams, and Peggy L. Dillard, *The Papers of Jefferson Davis*, vol. 10, *October 1863–August 1864* [Baton Rouge, LA, 1999], p. 141). De Leon noted a printer's error with his nom-de-plume, and in the margin corrected it by adding "Slingsby." He also added in the margin that the pamphlet was "from the pen of Edwin De Leon [and] several editions [were] published [of the] pamphlet of [57] pp." At least eight editions of 1,000 copies are known to have been printed, and De Leon was very proud of its popularity. "It has had an immense success, and has silenced that very versatile gentleman effectually," De Leon said of the attack on Walker. "The Publishers inform me that it has been noticed by almost every Journal in the British Dominions, and has been circulated very extensively." De Leon to Benjamin, December 23, 1863, Records of the Confederate States of America, Consular and Other Missions, 1861–1865, Library of Congress, Washington, DC.

18. This comes from De Leon to Benjamin, January 28, 1863, Records of the Confederate States of America, Library of Congress.

Several months after the successful negotiation of the Erlanger loan, in view of its inadequacy to fulfill all the objects desired, and from the fact that it was looked upon from the first as a mere speculative operation, the chief benefit of which ensued to the lucky originators, I made the following practical suggestions to the Department, which shared the fate of its predecessor, after which I interfered in that matter no more. In August, 1863, the subject was thus referred to:

> Another topic may claim at least passing notice, on which practical suggestions have frequently been made before.
>
> I refer to the confusion which prevails in our financial affairs on this side, and the want of a proper business head to control them, the authority and powers given to Mr. McRea being inadequate for the exigencies of the case. British capital and interests are now so heavily involved in our success that a proper financial agent, and properly accredited, armed with securities of the Confederate Government and with power to control disbursements, with some large banking house of the first class, for an amount equal to all our wants while this war lasts.
>
> I still regard the Erlanger loan as an unfortunate experiment, which has done more damage to Confederate credit than can easily be remedied, and such is the opinion of much better business heads than mine.
>
> Sometime since Mr.—— (whose name and reputation are familiar to you) promised me to digest and send a plan by which the whole matter could be simplified and arranged. Should that plan prove acceptable there is no man on either side of the water more capable of carrying it out than he, although I do not know whether he would accept so onerous and thankless a task.[19]

But no further effort was made in this direction, nor opportunities improved. Agents of the War and Navy Departments worked at cross-purposes with each other and the financial agent, and made separate contracts with the French and English contractors much at their own discretion.

The skein had become so tangled that probably the shortest mode of untying it was the forcible clipping of the threads by the failure of the Confederacy, which absolved forever all the relations of debtor and creditor, which Federal investigations recently have failed to ascertain.

In the almost expiring hours of the Confederacy, in February, 1865, an intimate personal friend of Mr. Benjamin and Mr. Slidell was sent over, nominally to negotiate another loan, the bare possibility of which at that time could scarcely have entered into any one's imagination on either side.

19. This comes from De Leon to Benjamin, August 3, 1863, ibid. In it he clearly identifies "Mr ——" as James T. Soutter of Fredericksburg, Virginia.

He only succeeded in inflicting loss on the truest friends of the South—the original holders of the Erlanger stock—who were induced to hold on to their ventures in it by the hopeful pictures of things inside the Confederacy, of which the outside world then had no more knowledge than of the interior of China.[20]

So, when the loan bubble broke, the chief damage was inflicted on those credulous persons—the early manipulators of it having pocketed their profits and retired long before. Its latter phases were worthy of its first. *Requiescat!*

The following short extracts from the legal proceedings in the suit brought by Mr. Carteret against Mr. Erlanger to recover his share of its immense profits throw some light upon the darkness that has hitherto enveloped that mysterious job.

That suit, commenced in the English and afterwards continued in the French Courts, gave the public the first glimpse it had behind the scenes of the pantomime. But just as the whole machinery that produced its "startling effects," was about to be opened to the gaze of the public, lo, the curtain fell! and Mr. Carteret compromised with the banker and his friends.

Let us hope that in the final scene of this pantomime, virtue was rewarded—a result not always so entirely certain on the political as on the scenic stage:

[*Translation.*]
Court Imperial
Audience of Tuesday, April 20, 1864
DECLARATION OF NICHOLAS CARTERET.

It will be remembered that during the course of the past year the house of Emile Erlanger, of Paris, put forth through a house at London, (Schroder & Co.) a loan of 75,000,000 francs for the Confederate States of America, guaranteeing the payment thereof by its cotton.

The first idea of this loan originated with Mr. Carteret, (former advocate of the Council of State,) who had submitted it to Mr. Slidell, the Commissioner of the Southern States at Paris, as well as to several bankers—among others to Mr. Erlanger, who adopted the proposal and was put into communication with Mr. Slidell, by M. Carteret, for the discussion and conclusion of an arrangement to that end.

20. De Leon speaks of Duncan F. Kenner, who, like Benjamin and Slidell, hailed from Louisiana. In February 1865 he did arrive in Europe, not to negotiate a loan, but to sound British and French leaders on whether or not slavery was the obstacle that kept them from recognizing the Confederacy; he was empowered to hint that the South might agree to some form of emancipation in return for recognition of Confederate independence. His mission got nowhere.

At the time of that presentation Mr. Carteret explained to these two his idea, which before that time had not occurred to either of them. He also took care to stipulate that a share of the profits on the operation should be reserved for him, which was twenty times promised him—by Mr. Erlanger—to himself personally, and to several of his friends.

But Mr. Erlanger always eluded and deferred signing a regular engagement for services which could not have been useless, especially as regarded the cooperation of the Minister of Foreign Affairs and of Mr. Mocquard, Secretary to the Emperor; for, on the departure of his two agents for the States, Mr. Carteret obtained for them (through Mocquard) a dispatch from the Cabinet of the Emperor, to the French Consul at Richmond.

While this was in progress—and before the result of Erlanger's application was known—Mr. Carteret had occasion to submit to the house of Rothschild the project of a large operation in Southern cotton, and was invited to prepare the means of carrying it out. He thought it due to Mr. Erlanger to inform him of this circumstance, and Mr. Erlanger protested against it, saying it would destroy his project, reproaching Mr. Carteret with destroying his own work and a certain fortune which the loan would give him (Carteret). Yielding to these urgent prayers Mr. Carteret abandoned the Rothschild project.

A short time after this, and before the return of Erlanger's agents, Mr. Carteret again insisted on obtaining a written acknowledgement of his interest in the affair from Mr. Erlanger, who then offered to advance 10,000 francs on account, which Mr. Carteret took. But, being presented a receipt to sign payable on demand, he observed that this would seem to disavow his interest; but, upon Mr. Erlanger's demanding whether he doubted his good faith and loyalty, he signed it.

But after the loan had been concluded, emitted and received, with a clear benefit for the bankers of 19 per cent on 75,000,000—that is to say, a gain of 14,000,000 francs, (near $3,000,000)—Mr. Erlanger offered him 10,000 francs more. This Mr. Carteret refused, and with the Englishmen, his associates in the origin of the affair, instituted suit against Erlanger at London, where the loan was actually issued, for 2 1/2 per cent commission—fixed by his counsel, the first advocates at the English bar—or viz., 1,875,000 francs.

On his side Mr. Erlanger demanded payment on the receipt for 10,000 francs given by Mr. Carteret; and the French tribunal before whom the parties appeared, after examination and cross-examination of all the parties, rendered its judgment in favor of Mr. Carteret.

Mr. Erlanger having said and repeated that Mr. Carteret could not be of any use to him in this business, Mr. Carteret produced before the English tribunal (Court of Queen's Bench) an engagement signed by the first banking houses to pay him a commission of 5,000,000 francs for the negotiation of an Italian loan, if successful; and he is also prepared to prove that, at this movement, he conducts operations of more importance than the Erlanger loan.

(Signed) CARTERET.

Upon the foreign basis, as shown in Mr. Carteret's statement was based the PLEA OF CARTERET'S COUNSEL.

The plea of Erlanger's counsel seeks to establish that Carteret's intervention was useless, and that Mr. Slidell—according to his own testimony—would not have treated with Erlanger on Carteret's recommendation, and would have treated with him without such introduction on information he subsequently obtained.

2. This presentation (of Mr. Erlanger to Mr. Slidell) was made for another affair—the Tucker contract.

3. Since that time, Carteret never saw Slidell.

There are two replies to this argument.

The first is furnished by the contradictions contained in testimony of Mr. Slidell. (See evidence.)

The second and more general allegation merits some development.

It is very clear that the intention of Erlanger, after the introduction to Slidell, was to set aside Carteret, and to leave him no active part in the affair he had proposed.

For this reason he always conversed with Mr. Slidell in English, a language which Carteret did not understand. For the same reason, He always afterwards visited Mr. Slidell alone, giving Mr. Carteret no notice of such visits, or of the conversations that ensured. But to prevent all disquietude on Carteret's part, he declared to him and to his friends that his interest in the affair should be acknowledged and very largely remunerated. The demand now made by Erlanger is a trick of Erlanger, of which Carteret has a right to complain.

But why should Carteret have accepted this position?

1. He always did insist upon his rights; but politely and like a man of the world, who, without proof, could not tax a colleague to his face without disloyalty.

2. Transactions like this cannot be conducted with the same strictness and formality as ordinary contracts.

When a project like this has been conceived, a banker must be found to execute it. The idea is the property of the first; the business details must be arranged by the latter, and confidence must be mutually reposed during the negotiations.

This is the whole case.

The testimony of Mr. Slidell referred to as contradictory in the above pleas of Mr. Carteret's counsel, was that used in the French courts in the case of Erlanger vs. Carteret, on the 7th of February, 1864, to recover the 10,000 francs on the receipt before mentioned.

The deposition is as follows:

MR. SLIDELL'S TESTIMONY.[21]

Court of Queen's Bench, in case of Joseph John Arnold, M. D. Wilson and Nicholas Felix Carteret, plaintiffs, vs. Emile Erlanger, defendant.

Evidence taken by commission by Messrs. Mangham and Leakey, English counselors at law residing at Paris, at the office of Mr. Leakey, No. 4 rue Castellane, Paris. George Bulkey, Esq., advocate for plaintiffs. Jarvey Hosmer, Esq., advocate for defendant.

Viva voco interrogations, examination and cross-examination, 8th of January, 1864.

John Slidell, Esq., &c., &c., being duly sworn, deposed as follows:

I know Mr. Melvil Wilson, one of the plaintiffs.[22] I am on good terms with him. In the month of September, 1862, I remember seeing or having seen him several times. I do not think that the subject of my interviews with him in September was on the subject of the Confederate loan. I had two or three interviews with him in the month of September. To the best of my recollection Mr. Arnold and Mr. Wilson presented themselves to me in the month of September several times. They also presented to me Mr. Carteret, another of the plaintiffs, I think also in the month of September. Mr. Carteret and Mr. Wilson arranged an interview between Mr. Erlanger and myself. I think my first interview with Mr. Erlanger was on the 29th of September, 1862. On my first interview with Mr. Erlanger, he was accompanied by two of the plaintiffs, possibly by all of them; but I cannot distinctly recollect which. I cannot recollect by which of the three plaintiffs Mr. Erlanger was presented to me. I do not think I had any conversation with Mr. Erlanger in their presence, except of the most general character. Mr. Erlanger was presented to me as a banker, who was prepared to make advances of money to the Confederate Government. I told him I had no authority to borrow money for the Confederate Government, but that there was a regular agent for the purchase of arms for the Government, whose powers, I thought, might be sufficient to authorize him to borrow money on such conditions as he thought reasonable, having regard to the urgent need of the Government. I do not think any mention was made as to conditions at this, or any subsequent interview at which these plaintiffs assisted, or were present. These plaintiffs called to see me frequently afterwards on the subject of a loan; but I do not remember to have consulted or conferred with them upon this subject, except to mention that myself and Major Huse (the agent of whom I had spoken) were negotiating with Mr. Erlanger. These plaintiffs did speak to me on the subject of the reward they ex-

21. De Leon's copy of the original of this published testimony, dated February 7, 1864, is in the Edwin De Leon Papers, South Caroliniana Library, University of South Carolina, Columbia.

22. Melvil[le] Wilson has eluded further identification to date.

pected for their aid in the negotiation of the loan, and I subsequently communicated to Mr. Erlanger the substance of what they said. I told Mr. Erlanger it was doubtful if anything came of the affair; but if it did succeed, something ought to be given them which they had a right to, not as negotiators, but for the pains they had taken in the affair, for which I should be pleased to see them reasonably recompensed. In arranging for the loan I never made it a condition that these plaintiffs should be recompensed. After all the terms of the negotiation were finished—but certainly not before—I repeated to Mr. Erlanger what I had said to the others, or to some of them (Mr. Wilson was certainly one of them) on the subject of compensation. I told him I considered it a small matter. But as I desired to avoid even a moral obligation in this matter, I should like him to do that which I thought myself morally bound to do. I never supposed I had incurred any legal responsibility, having no authority to bind my Government in such matters, and never pretending to have any. Mr. Erlanger consented to do as I desired. The contract for the loan was signed October 28, 1863, and for this reason I think the negotiations were terminated on the 20th, or certainly two or three days before the 28th. I informed Messrs. Wilson and Arnold that Mr. Erlanger would carry out what I had promised them. This is a copy of the contract. I do not wish to deposit it here, but have no objection to a copy being made on conditions of being returned to me to-morrow.

CROSS-EXAMINATION OF MR. SLIDELL.

I made the acquaintance of Messrs. Arnold and Wilson first. They presented Mr. Carteret some weeks afterwards. Messrs. Arnold and Wilson first came together and were presented to me by Mr. John Arthur, (English house agent.) It appears to me that they first called on the matter of a certain contract which Mr. Tucker pretended to have to furnish arms for the Confederate Government. When Mr. Erlanger came to me the first time, with Messrs. Arnold and Wilson, I think he desired to know whether the contract of Mr. Tucker was a good and valid contract. I gave to Mr. Erlanger the same opinion on this contract that I had given to the others; that is to say, that I did not think it a practicable contract, both from lapse of time and from the depreciation in the value of the currency in which it was to be paid.[23] It seems to me that Mr. Erlanger then said, in the presence of those persons, that the reason for which he had come was to be satisfied as to the value of this contract. This contract of Mr. Tucker had no connection whatever with the loan afterwards negotiated, except that it was thus I sent Mr. Erlanger to Major Huse, who was charged to buy munitions of war, and with whom he might make better arrangements than with Mr. Tucker. The conversation which passed between Mr. Erlanger and myself, in presence of the plaintiffs, was of a general

23. Beverly Tucker of Virginia obtained a contract in November 1861 with the Confederate war department to purchase munitions in England. *ORN*, p. 426.

character; but after Mr. Erlanger had come alone to see me, and I had taken information from competent sources as to his character, and his capability of performing his engagements and received satisfactory answers, I treated him with confidence. The plaintiffs had nothing to do with our subsequent negotiations.* I should not have treated with Mr. Erlanger himself had not the result of my inquiries been so satisfactory. I should not have acted on the introduction of the plaintiff, being myself comparatively a stranger at Paris, with but a limited acquaintance with bankers or the commercial world here. I knew nothing of the plaintiffs except through the introduction of Mr. Arthur, except that Mr. Wilson informed me he was the son of an eminent merchant, who had large dealings with American trade at London. I know nothing of Mr. Arnold or Mr. Carteret. I had no authority, either expressed or implied, to contract any loan whatever for the Confederate States. All that I did was to transmit to my Government a copy of the contract, with a report of the respectable character of Mr. Erlanger. I am aware that contract was not finally made in the exact terms of that which I have produced; but, with modifications, it was made the base of another contract for a loan. When the plaintiff, or some of them, set up a claim for remuneration, it was to me personally they addressed themselves. They never pretended they had a right to compensation from Mr. Erlanger. It was not in the form of a reclamation; it was only an insinuation that they were entitled to something. I have never admitted any responsibility. It was only a gratification that I proposed to give them, as they had nothing to do with this affair except in introducing Mr. Erlanger. This was altogether useless, as I should have done the same thing had Mr. Erlanger come to me without any such introduction. [Mr. Bulkley, plaintiff's counsel, objected to this last remark.] I never made, and was never authorized to make any offer of remuneration to plaintiffs on the part of Mr. Erlanger. The only thing I represented to Mr. Erlanger was that, if the affair succeeded, I had promised a gratification should be given these gentlemen. This conversation took place after Mr. Erlanger and myself had definitively agreed as to terms of contract for loan.

EXAMINATION RESUMED.

Mr. Erlanger made no difficulty in agreeing to the proposition I made him, to give this gratification to the plaintiffs. Messrs. Wilson and Arnold were presented to me by Mr. Arthur; Mr. Carteret by the other two. When the first interview took place between Mr. Erlanger and myself, in presence of plaintiffs, it is my opinion that allusion was made to the contract of Mr. Tucker. Nothing was

---

*Mr. Carteret confirms this in his brief to his lawyer, complaining that in all subsequent interviews, when he was present, Messrs. Erlanger and Slidell conversed in English—a language he did not understand—of which he complained to Erlanger. Mr. Slidell spoke French with much ease and fluency. The suspicions excited in Carteret's mind by this incident were smothered by Erlanger's assurances.

said on this occasion about a Government loan. The conversation was relative only to a credit which should be opened by Mr. Erlanger to Major Huse, to purchase munitions of war. I know nothing of the base of the agreements, which were inserted at a later day into the contract between Mr. Erlanger and myself, until it was brought to me completed. Mr. Carteret never proposed to me the basis of an arrangement which was completed at a later day. I am of the opinion that there was no question of this loan on the 26th of September; there certainly was not in the form it finally assumed, and in which it was adopted. The conversation turned on general projects, relating to advances of money by Mr. Erlanger to Major Huse, to purchase munitions of war.

    (signed) JOHN SLIDELL.

    (Signed) F. S. LEAKEY.

             [Pour traduction conforme.]

    (Signed) MOURALAVY,

             Traducter en Français.

APPENDIX 1
THREE LETTERS FROM A SOUTH CAROLINIAN, RELATING TO
SECESSION, SLAVERY AND THE TRENT CASE

———————•◦•———————

By Edwin De Leon[1]

INTRODUCTORY

The writer of the Letters, now republished from the journals in which they first appeared, was one of the earliest advocates in the United States of Southern Rights, including the Right of Secession.

In order to prepare the South, and warn the North, of the inevitable issue of continued aggression and class-legislation, superadded to language of coarse insult on the part of the latter, he established a journal at Columbia, the capital of South Carolina, in1847, devoted solely to these objects.[2] From this duty he was summoned to Washington in 1849, by formal invitation of the Southern Members of Congress, to establish at the Capital (in conjunction with Ellwood Fisher, of Virginia) a "Southern Press," which, conjointly, they did establish.[3] Of that journal he and his colleague had charge until, after the nomination of Mr. Pierce for the presidency, in August, 1852, it was discontinued; when the writer addressed to his countrymen words of warning, at the time unheeded, but which subsequent events have unhappily verified, the South being suddenly awakened from its dream of false confidence, by the clutch of its "Northern Brethren" on its throat. The argument, as between North and South, has been long since exhausted, and since we have stood to our arms it will never be resumed; but "a decent respect for the opinion of mankind" urges us to explain the reasons which have compelled our separation, and the attitude we have occupied since the strangling knot of "Union" has been severed by the sword.

In the hope of contributing, however feebly, to a better comprehension of the actual circumstances connected with this revolution, the writer reproduces these

1. Published in London in 1861 by Smith, Elder and Company.

2. The Columbia *Telegraph* commenced publication in 1847 and ceased in 1851 shortly after De Leon went to Washington.

3. De Leon and Ellwood Fisher edited the *Southern Press* from 1850 to 1852.

Letters, which may enlist the attention of those whom a more pretentious work might repel.

London, Dec., 1861.

LETTER I

To the Chevalier Hippolyte de St Anthonie,
Secretary General,
African Institute, 22, Place Vendôme, Paris.
Sir,

Since the receipt of your letter of April 3o, announcing my nomination as Honorary Vice-President of the "Institut d'Afrique" of Paris, founded in 1838 by many noble and distinguished persons of all countries, for the abolition of the slave trade and slavery, I have carefully examined the statutes of that association, and am compelled to decline the proffered honour as incompatible with my principles and opinions. At the same time, I must beg you to tender the Committee of Presentation, who have paid me this unmerited compliment, the assurances of my grateful regard; and I pray you, also, sir, to accept for yourself my acknowledgements for the letter to which I now respond. In my own country my name has been much connected with this very subject, but always in opposition to a mistaken philanthropy, which, in my judgment, has assumed to be wiser than Providence—stronger than God—and which, wherever triumphant, has brought forth weeds, ashes, and blood as its only fruits; as which witness the emancipation of St. Domingo and the British West Indies and the horrors of the collie traffic in red skins to substitute for the black. It is no reproach to the eminent names that appear in your association to say that we, who live under the system, must comprehend it better than those who either draw upon their imaginations for their facts, or accept them from the poisoned lips and pens of our native traducers, themselves equally ignorant or heedless of the truth.

Let them reflect whether any large community would willingly and cheerfully live in and die for the permanence of an institution that really was at once a misfortune and a crime, and a clinging curse to themselves and their children. Even now the spectacle is presented to the world of eight millions of white freemen deliberately discussing the disruption of a beloved confederacy, as an alternative to be preferred to the abolition of slavery in the Southern States of the American Union. This alone should convince foreign philanthropists of the hopelessness of the task they have undertaken, in imitation of the benevolent ladies in *Æsop's Fables*—"to scrub the Ethiop white"—even did not all previous experience teach the same lesson. Nor are these sentiments strange as coming from an American citizen. The fathers of our Republic refused to recognize either an equal or a citizen in the negro. They left him to that condition that he has ever occupied since the hieroglyphics were engraved upon the rock tablets of Egypt—(where he figures ever as a bearer of burdens; never as a conqueror or a King)—down to the present day when France seeks "apprentices," and America retains slaves, in his descendants. With regard to the slave trade, America first declared it piracy, and at this moment her vessels are busy in suppressing the traffic. Should not an American prefer to follow in the footsteps of the sages and patriots of the Revolution, rather than in those of a faction, which in his own country has as its chief prophets an elderly female romancer, and a male "Belisarius," who have paraded their "stars" and their "stripes" over Europe for the disgrace and defamation of their native land?[4] From these reasons, which I might, but will not, multiply, you will perceive, sir, that I could not, consistently or honourably, either accept or be silent under the embarrassing circumstances in which your communication placed me. But, while responding with perfect frankness, I have sought to do so with all respect to gentlemen whose motives I do not question;—and remain with sentiments of high consideration, your obedient servant,

EDWIN DE LEON,

Agency and Consulate General of the United States of America in Egypt.
Alexandria, June 30, 1860.

LETTER II

To the Editor of "The Times."
Sir,

As you have allowed Mr. Cassius M. Clay, newly-appointed Minister to Russia by the Federal Government at Washington, to shoot a Parthian arrow at the Confederate States, allow one who has recently resigned a commission in the same service briefly to respond to the questions which he has asked and answered for himself.[5]

The good old English doctrine of "fair play" demands this, especially since Mr. Clay has drawn upon his imagination for his facts and figures and has sought alternately to cajole and bully England while calumniating the large body of his countrymen, whom he stigmatizes as "traitors."

1. "What are we fighting for?"—"We, the people of the United States of America," are construed by Mr. Clay to mean the people of the Northern States alone and the

4. The "elderly female romancer" is Harriet Beecher Stowe, author of *Uncle Tom's Cabin*. The reference to "Belisarius" is unclear. Belisarius was a 6th century A.D. Byzantine general of great skill and accomplishment. Since context shows that De Leon's "Belisarius" was a leader in the anti-slavery movement, he may be referring to John C. Frémont, who had been Republican nominee for the presidency in 1856 and was now a Union general. He might also mean Winfield Scott, though he was not identified with the antislavery movement in any significant or symbolic degree.

5. Cassius Clay's remarks in London have been touched on above.

members of the regular army, the only "fighting" thus far having been at Fort
Sumter and in the streets of Baltimore. It is a fact universally known in Europe, that
eleven Southern States have already formally seceded, and three more will certainly
do so if Federal threats of "coercion" ripen into acts, giving the Southern
Confederacy an area of territory immensely larger and more fertile than the
Northern, and a population entirely homogeneous.[6] The quarrel is a sectional one,
North against South, and slavery a mere pretext, as the history of the controversy
proves; for the Northern leaders since their accession to power, by a vote of little
more than a third of the American people, have declared their willingness to
guarantee to the South the possession of their slaves in all the States wherein
slavery now exists, and to give *additional securities* for the rendition into slavery
fugitives from the South.[7]

As to talk about "rebellion," "conspiracy," &c., addressed to intelligent
Englishmen, it is worse than idle; and in view of the deliberate action of the British
Government and the Royal proclamation, recognizing the belligerent rights of the
Confederate States, becomes simply impertinent. The analogy attempted to be
drawn from the secession of the Sovereign States of the South from the Federal
Union and the secession of Scotland or Ireland from England, is simply too absurd
to discuss. But Mr. Clay goes on to say:—

> The professed friends of the independence of nations and popular rights, have not
> only overthrown the Constitution of the United States, but the Constitutions of the
> "Confederate States" themselves, refusing in every case to refer their new usurpation
> to the votes of the people, thus making themselves doubly traitors to both the States
> and the nation.

Yet this statement is in direct contradiction to the substantial truth, since "in
every case" the people, through State Conventions, specifically called for the
purpose have initiated and adopted the ordinances of secession.[8] To have called
another Convention to ratify the proceeding of the former, could in no manner
have altered the result; and was not only useless, but would have caused a delay of
two or three months of most precious time in the organization of the Government
and army. If we look to usage, the Constitution of the United States was never

---

6. De Leon's statement that eleven states had seceded is intriguing, considering that North
Carolina, the eleventh and last state to secede, did so on May 20, just three days before the date of
De Leon's letter, which could hardly yet have been known in Paris where De Leon wrote. He has
probably edited his letter for pamphlet publication in light of later events. The three states he expected to secede are Kentucky, Missouri, and Maryland.

7. De Leon here completely avoids mentioning the actual bone of contention, the spread of
slavery into the unorganized territories of the West.

8. Again De Leon clearly avoids the issue, refusing to acknowledge that Clay meant that the people at large were not given a choice by referendum on secession. Such referenda did take place in
Texas, Tennessee, and Virginia, but nowhere else.

presented to the people, but was submitted to the Conventions in each State for ratification, precisely as the Confederate Constitution. Results have proven the wisdom and necessity of prompt action on the part of the South, when the tottering Administration at Washington props itself up with 30,000 bayonets in the Federal City, and cries out lustily for an army of 150,000 men, to enforce a Union as painful and repulsive as that of the Siamese twins, but happily not so vital to both.[9]

We do not desire to bandy epithets at our adversaries, but Mr. Clay should know that we regard as "doubly traitors" those who, born and bred on Southern soil, not only desert but defame their Southern brethren, in arms against a worse than Austrian despotism. The *ad captandum* cant about the "despotic rulers of 4,000,000 enslaved Africans," "the tide of barbarism rolling back over emancipated Europe," &c., may be adapted to the taste of North-western stump speakers, but will only cause every sensible Englishmen to smile at such a specimen of "Spread-Eagleism."

2. "But can you subdue the revolted States?"—"Of course we can," says Mr. Clay. "Of course you cannot," say those States, and have joined issue of battle thereupon. But if Mr. Clay's be a foregone conclusion, and the Federal Government can "blockade them by sea and invade them by land, and close up the rebellion in a single year, if we are let alone,"—why these pathetic and objurgatory appeals to a Power that has just formally declared its intention to be neutral? Why this perversion of facts and figures to impress the conviction on the mind of Europe? for we of the South, too, only ask to be "let alone;" and if invaded, in the stout hearts and arms of her own sons the South finds, and will continue to find, sufficient protection, the sentiment of your great poet who sang the "Lays of Rome" animating every Southern heart:—

"For how can man die better
Than facing fearful odds,
For the ashes of his fathers,
And the temples of his gods?"[10]

"If all the Southern States were to make common cause" (which they have done since the Northern sword has been thrown into the balance), they can bring into the field, according to the last census, 1,250,000 fighting men between the ages of eighteen and forty-five years, besides all those above and below those ages respectively, who would take up arms against the invaders of their hearths and homes.

9. In referring to "the Siamese twins," De Leon refers to Chang and Eng of P. T. Barnum's famous show.

10. De Leon refers to Davis's April 29, 1861, message to the special session of the Confederate Congress when he declared that "all we ask is to be let alone." The poet is Thomas Babington Macaulay, author of *Lays of Ancient Rome*, from which the quotation is taken.

The bloody battle-fields of Mexico, where the South furnished about 45,000 and the North about 20,000 men, can attest to Southern valor and discipline; and the veterans of the army and navy who have left the Federal to join the Confederate service are well capable of commanding troops who have never believed that "force was necessary" to cement fraternity, volunteering, as they have done, solely for defence, not for aggression.[11] The old watchword of the Jacobins in France's darkest days of blood and tears, *"Fraternité, ou la mort* (Be my brother, or I will kill you!)" is now the rallying cry of the "free North," not the South, who stands with drawn sword beside her own altars. Is that a watchword to enlist the sympathies or stir the pulse of free-born Englishmen, when a new reign of terror is sought to be inaugurated once more, under the desecrated name of liberty, over the smiling fields and happy homes of the South? We cannot, and we will not, believe it. England has forever been a generous foe,—she will not be a faithless friend.

The statement that the "the population of the Slave States is divided perhaps equally for and against the Union," is without a shadow of a foundation. The secession of the South now forms a part of history; and never in the annals of mankind has such a unanimity of sentiment and action been manifested by any people as in the formation, deliberations, and actions of the cotton States. Since the domestic *cóup d'état* attempted by the Northern President, the same spirit has spread like a fire on a prairie over the border States, as witness the instantaneous action of Virginia, North Carolina, and Tennessee, with Missouri and Kentucky moving in the same direction; or, more striking still, the reception of the Northern volunteers in Baltimore,—once regarded as most loyal to the Union, but now mourning, like Venice, under a foreign yoke, and powerless for the moment to avenge the blood of her children slain in resisting the profanation of their soil.

3. "But can you govern a 'subjugated' people and reconstruct the Union?" This question answers itself. The distinction between "subjugating the revolted States" and "putting down the rebel citizens" is a distinction without difference; and the necessity of "reconstruction" admits the fact of the existing dissolution of what once were the United States of America, one segment of which now arrogates the title, as it would absorb the functions, the powers, and the property, of the whole, even as in the decadence of the Roman Empire the effete descendants of the Cæsars aped the style and titles of their mighty progenitors, though all power and prestige had departed.

Truthfully did *The Times* of May 7 characterize this conflict on the part of the North when it said,—

The call for immediate blockade of the whole Southern coast has been so violent and so universal in New York, that we must assume it will be the first attempt energetically made

11. De Leon's figures are hardly unbiased here. In fact, volunteers from North and South were much more even in numbers.

by the Northern States. It is to their evident interest that it should be so. The existence of New York depends upon this war being short, sharp, and successful. The New York people are, as regards the cotton growers, masters resisting a revolt of their slaves, creditors arresting escape of their debtors, traders dreading the departure of their customers.

Of this, however, let both friend and foe rest assured, that neither to force nor fraud will the Confederate States succumb; and it is no easy task to subjugate 12,000,000 of people, who will maintain by the sword, if compelled, their independence against their former allies, now their most inveterate and unscrupulous enemies.

The questions which Mr. Clay, Minister to Russia, has thought fit to address to the English people, in anticipation of the diplomatic action of the accredited ambassador, Mr. Adams, have been so well and so thoroughly answered by *The Times* of the 20th, that it would be wrong to mar that perfect picture by one touch or tint in addition. I therefore quote this paragraph:—

Mr. Clay must really allow us to give our own version of the honour and interest of England. Our honour and interest is to stand aloof from contests which in no way concern us, to be content with our own laws and liberties, without seeking to impose them upon others, "to seek peace and ensue it," and to leave those who take to the sword to fall by the sword. In war we will be strictly neutral; in peace we will be the friends of whatever Power may emerge out of the frightful chaos through which Mr. Clay sees his way so clearly. And that neutrality, which is recommended alike by our interest and our honour, we will not violate through fear—no, not of a hundred millions of unborn men.

These are word of "truth and soberness," indicating worthily the attitude which it behoves England to take in this quarrel; and it is a position which the Confederate States will never murmur at nor gainsay, until England feels that honour and her interests demand a formal recognition of the new Confederacy.

Very respectfully,
EDWIN DE LEON,
Ex-United States Consul-General for Egypt.
Paris, Hôtel du Louvre, May 23rd, 1861.

LETTER III

To the Editor of the "Daily Telegraph."
Sir,

In common with other citizens of the Confederate States, exiled from their homes by the arbitrary and lawless acts of the Government of Washington, I have read with mingled feelings of amazement and indignation the account given in the journals of the forcible seizure of four of our citizens from the deck of a British mail steamer, in violation of the law of nations, and in contempt of that flag which the world has hitherto ever respected and feared.[12] This daring outrage has inspired in our breasts sensations of the deepest regret that anything connected with us or our cause should have indirectly occasioned annoyance, or have subjected to insult, a Government which has so faithfully and honourably preserved an unbroken neutrality between both belligerents, under circumstances of unparalleled temptation to break the paper blockade which has King Cotton bound. The people of England will do the Confederates the justice to acknowledge that no act or work of ours has at last forced this Government into an unwilling participation in our civil war. But the question now arises among us, whether we are still to consider England a safe asylum; for if our people can with impunity be torn from beneath the folds of her flag upon the open sea, under protest of her officers, with every accompaniment of insult, what guarantee of safety have we here? or how can we venture beyond the prison bounds of this island, into the very harbours of which our would-be gaolers pry to seize us. The mission of the *James Adger* to your waters is now explained. An accident only has preserved the British people from the mortification of seeing their flag insulted and defied under their very eyes.[13]

But the distance of the actual occurrence detracts nothing from the enormity of the flagrant wrong which has been perpetrated, and in every British bosom a throb of manly indignation must be felt at the mingled audacity, insolence, and cruelty which have characterized the whole proceeding.

That this act should have been perpetrated by the fragment of the nation which ever resisted "the right of visitation and search," even to the verge of actual war, and whose ablest statesmen have established reputations by contravening such right,— adds bitterness to the insult, and proves how far Mr. Seward counts on the forbearance and long-suffering of England. As against other nations, such a claim might have had some precedent in the musty records of old folios, or the incidents of almost forgotten wars; but, as between America and England, the precedents and the practice have been all the other way. That retribution will steadily and sternly be visited upon the wrong-doers, we cannot permit ourselves to doubt; but the unexampled patience which has been manifested toward the Federal Government at Washington, under repeated acts of discourtesy and illegality, must plead our apology for making this appeal to the British public, and its most powerful exponent; and a few considerations connected with it may not be entirely misplaced. Suppose, for a moment, the case reversed. Imagine the sensation to be created in England if a Confederate cruiser were to stop a British steamer from New York, and make all the Northern passengers her prisoners. Would not one cry arise throughout the land at such a proceeding? Yet, if the right be accorded to one

12. De Leon refers to the *Trent* affair.

13. The USS *James Adger* was sent to pursue the CSS *Nashville* when it was believed that Mason and Slidell were sailing to England aboard her.

belligerent, it must assuredly be accorded to the other—the mere alleged or suspected character of the individuals or the port from which they come not varying the nature of the fact. The law of nations gives no such right, which would involve the destruction of the commerce of all neutral nations, and legalise kidnapping in its most repulsive form, while it would render the flag of every nation a mere worthless rag, to be trampled on with impunity by every lawless ruffian styling himself a belligerent. Thus, too, the mightiest nations might fall victims of the quarrels of the most insignificant. The common sense of mankind repudiates so monstrous an absurdity.

Although, with a chivalrous honour rare in our days, the Southern officers of the Federal navy, among her best and bravest (as the names of Tattnall, Hollins, Ingraham, Barron, and Pegram, attest), retired from the service, leaving in the hands of the Federal Government the vessels they commanded, and with which our coasts are now being ravaged and our people murdered, we yet are not entirely powerless on the sea, and soon will be less so.[14] It is easy to anticipate the effect on British commerce (which, like Puck, puts a girdle round the Earth) if this system of legalised piracy be winked at by the British Government. But these are considerations unnecessary to be pressed upon a people justly proud of their dominion over the seas, and of that flag which "has braved the battle and the breeze" unsullied for more than a thousand years. Interest must be lost sight of when honour is at stake; and truly did the officers of the *Trent* represent their countrymen, in the words of mingled defiance and warning which they addressed to the captors, whose naked cutlasses and yawning port-holes showed the nature and spirit of their mission.

Cold, indeed, must have grown the great heart of England if it beats not responsive to the manly and truthful words of Captain Williams, which will find their echo throughout Christendom.[15] On the Pacific shore a counterpart to this outrage has also been perpetrated, in the seizure of Senator Gwin and his companions at Panama, under circumstances of equal treachery and violence, and in defiance of national comity.[16] This proves the fixed intention for Mr. Seward to be a law unto himself, and to stretch the perquisitions of the Federal Government over land and sea alike, in defiance of law and right, and of the opinion of the civilized world. If further proofs were needed of such intention, we have them in the declaration of General Scott at Paris, that, previous to his departure, this policy

14. Josiah Tattnall, George Hollins, Duncan Ingraham, Samuel Barron, and Robert Pegram all resigned from the U.S. navy to enter Confederate naval service.

15. Richard Williams was captain of the mail steamer *Trent*.

16. Gwin, an outspoken champion of slavery and Southern rights, was on his way from California to the East by way of Panama in 1861, ostensibly to take his seat in the senate, when he was arrested on suspicion of intending to aid the Confederacy and held for almost two years before being released.

had been determined upon; and the latest advices from the Northern States announce the fact, that several vessels have been sent out to establish and carry out effectually this "espionage" and kidnapping on the high seas, of which Mr. Seward can claim the paternity, and all the honours accruing from it.[17]

That the honourable men who still cling to the fallen fortunes of the Stars and Stripes will do this dirty work of police detectives, I do not believe: they will only throw it into congenial hands; and the consequences are obvious to British interests and British commerce.

You may ask, What motive can prompt Mr. Seward to so strange and mad a procedure? That question can easily be answered by those who know the man and his career. The author of the "irrepressible conflict" between North and South, which he has made his ladder to climb up to power, he has ever entertained the desire of building up a Northern empire, of which the British dominions in America should form a part.[18] This he has not only avowed in conversations, but in published speeches, over and over again. Forced into a policy of "coercion" by the frantic passions and blind arrogance of the Northern mob, inflamed by demagogues, he has reluctantly been dragged on in a direction the opposite of that he aimed at. The progress of the war—if progress can be predicated of a "movement retrograde"—has only satisfied him of its inutility, and he has exhausted every device to turn our internal strife into the channel of a foreign war, or into a foreign intervention which would result in peace.

To effect this object, he selected the only Power that would suit him. While English subjects were seized, imprisoned and harassed, on most flimsy pretexts, men of no other foreign nationality were disturbed. The remonstrances of Lord Lyons in these cases were treated with rudeness and contempt. This failing to bring on either the quarrel or the intervention sought for, the next experiment was the forcible seizure and arrest of British subjects with British passports from British steamers in the harbours of New York and Boston, the Ambassador's remonstrances being treated yet more cavalierly. This also failing to bring on the collision coveted, the audacious and piratical proceeding which has convulsed Europe was deliberately determined upon, on the testimony of General Scott and the New York journals, and has produced the long-sought consummation.[19] To

17. De Leon refers to a published letter by General Winfield Scott that appeared in the French press on December 4, 1861. In it Scott denied that he had stated, as reported, that Washington had determined to seize Mason and Slidell, even if it had to take them from a neutral nation's vessel. He did affirm, however, that the *James Adger* was on the lookout to take them from the Confederate vessel *Nashville* if it caught her, a distinction De Leon fails to recognize in his diatribe.

18. Seward's most famous remark was his declaration of there being an "irrepressible conflict" between the interests of the free states and the slave states. De Leon is hyperbolic in going on to describe Seward's supposed lust for empire.

19. De Leon writes in response to rumors and with a definite purpose to inflame anti-Union feelings in mind, and as a result misstates Union intentions and plans.

frustrate this scheme of vulpine cunning and wickedness, most characteristic of its author, the plain and proper course for England and Europe to take is clear as a sunbeam.

In my reply to the letter of Cassius Clay I ventured to say, on behalf of my fellow Southern countrymen, that we would be content to await the recognition of the Confederate States by England until her statesmen were convinced that her honour and interests demanded it. Will you pardon me for suggesting that the hour has now arrived, when both conditions will be fulfilled by that act of simple justice towards a Government which has proved itself self-sustaining and permanent? The blockade, once declared by England as void as it really has been, in view of the fact that 421 vessels have broken it, would then fetter commerce no longer; and Mr. Seward, caught in his own trap, would be compelled to submit to the arbitration of a congress of nations, whose award would avert the necessity of more bloodshed.

Such a recognition of the Southern Confederacy now would also seem due to humanity, sickened by the sight of useless slaughter in a war waged no longer for victory, or reconstruction of the shattered Union—like a broken mirror, whose fragments never can be reunited—but continued for vengeance, and from a sense of shame at repeated humiliations; which war must grow fiercer and more fell, unless England, with sword and olive branch in either hand, strides into the arena and commands peace.

I am, Sir, yours, &c.

EDWIN DE LEON.

Burlington Hotel, December 2, 1861.

APPENDIX 2
"HOW WE BROKE THE BLOCKADE"[1]

———•◆•———

[By Edwin de Leon]

It was at Karnak, among the ruins of the temple of Thebes, that the far-off echo of the secession of South Carolina reached us. A special courier had been sent up the Nile to inform us of the death of a very dear friend at Alexandria, and the messenger brought with him also the journals which announced the first death-throes of the American Union.[2] Under the double shadows of these tidings we turned our faces westward from the still Orient, to take our share in the struggles and sufferings of our people, for we were of and from South Carolina. It seemed strange to us, however, that sitting, as it were, among the tombstones of one of the oldest recorded empires, upon the fallen shaft of a column from the Temple of Isis, we should first hear the death-knell of the youngest of living nations.

The companion of my life was the companion of that voyage, and when, in the month of December, 1861, I prepared to run the then stringent blockade of the Southern ports, bearing despatches, she claimed the right of accompanying me.

We left Southampton in the West India mail steamer *Atrato*, on the 2nd of January, 1861[2], under an assumed name, to frustrate the espionage of the Vigilance Committee of the North, established at London. It is an act of justice to Mr. Adams, the Minister, to state that he is understood to have indignantly repudiated any knowledge of the proceedings of this institution.[3] Its existence, however, soon became so patent, that Southern men taking the West India route to the Confederate States found it necessary to adopt extraordinary precautions on leaving England to avoid being gazetted in the *New York Herald* or *Tribune*, while taking the circuitous route home which the force of circumstances imposed upon them.

The pen of Anthony Trollope had rendered the *Atrato* and its motley passengers familiar as "household words." It is unnecessary to dwell upon that portion of our

1. Published without author byline by Edwin De Leon in the *Cornhill Magazine* 6 (October 1862), pp. 471–479. This article was substantially used to compose chapter 12 in De Leon's *Thirty Years of My Life on Three Continents* (London, 1890).

2. The dead friend was William Moore, United States vice consul at Alexandria, Egypt. De Leon, *Thirty Years*, vol. 1, p. 294.

3. The Vigilance Committee.

experiences, except to say that "the Bims," whom we encountered on board in considerable numbers, were very agreeable specimens of the colonial population; while the dinner-table reproduced the Tower of Babel in the variety of tongues, and Noah's Ark in the diversity of species and colour, which it exhibited.[4]

On arriving at St. Thomas, we learned that the Southern Commissioners, with their secretaries, had only left that island for England three days before, and, by a curious coincidence, in the very vessel which was originally to have taken them, when intercepted by Captain Wilkes in the *San Jacinto*. Fortunately for us, the blockade of the British and Spanish West Indies was not at that time so very stringent as it now is, and the British flag was respected in our case.

From St. Thomas the *Seine* took us with neatness and despatch to Havana, and in that city of picturesque but unclean environments we were compelled impatiently to attend the uncertain movements of the *indirect line* of steamers for the Southern ports, around and outside of which cruised the miscellaneous cruisers of the "Universal Yankee Nation," as voracious and eager after their prey as the sharks of those latitudes. I term their cruisers miscellaneous, because every old tub of a steamer or schooner that was not too leaky to be kept afloat and carry a couple of guns has been converted into a "blockader," to eke out the very small number of effective vessels in the service.

We reached the city of Havana at a most agreeable season—the end of January; for then perpetual spring seems to smile over that favoured land, and London fogs fade from the memory of the voyager, whose senses are steeped in the soft voluptuous languor of the south. Tennyson should have placed his "lotus-eaters" in this favoured spot, where life seems a masquerade as the *volantes* roll by you on the Paseo, and private life opens its hospitable doors and windows upon the street, through which passing friends converse with the fair or brown occupants of rocking-chairs in the interior, robed in gauzy clouds of gossamer-like muslin.

But Calypso's island could not woo the exile dreaming of home to linger within its enchanted bounds; so we, longing for our Southern home and friends, cast wistful eyes over the horizon for the sail which was to be the herald of our return. At length a long, low, black, rakish-looking steamer, rejoicing in the sovereign name of *Victoria*, sailed into the harbour of Havana, with the Confederate flag flying. She proved to be a well-known craft in western waters, and admirably fitted out for the work in which she was employed, combining the requisites of strength, speed, and small draught of water. She had no masts and consequently no sails; lay very low to the water, her black hull and smoke-stack being the only objects presenting a target for the blockading squadron, should they get within range. As to passenger accommoda-

---

4. Anthony Trollope sailed aboard the *Atrato* in 1858 for the West Indies and Central America. He turned his experiences aboard the ship into his book *The West Indies and the Spanish Main* in 1860. The "Bims" were Barbadians.

tions she had literally none; the only attempt at such a thing comprising two cabins on deck, one for supercargo, the other for captain, with a covered gallery about twelve feet long, serving as dining-place by day and sleeping-place by night. The hold was an open one, with a single trap-door, and no further protection. She was an old wooden boat, and seemed very inflammable when we looked into the engine-room, while the crew were as reckless-looking a lot of dare-devils as could be picked up in New Orleans for a service so full of perils. One of my proposed *compagnons de voyage*, who also had his wife with him, after one preliminary survey flatly refused to make the venture, declaring it was tempting Providence to go in that boat. Another of his party, however—a lady from New Orleans, Mrs. D——, whose husband had left her safe in Paris—insisted on accompanying us, and shared our trials with a coolness and courage worthy of a woman.[5] After my blockading experiences with her and my own wife, I conceive higher praise cannot be accorded, for when men faltered, these women faced the dangers and rose with the necessity for exertion, animating and sustaining us all by their cheerfulness and fortitude. The fortune of our seceding friend was hard. Some months later he embarked on board of a boat with superior accommodations, and of superior size and appearance. The boat was wrecked, and his wife and child saved almost by a miracle; and it was several days before he could rejoin them or know their fate. In this case also the woman acted in the most noble manner; and proud as the Southern men always have been of the virtues and merits of their women, the trials of this revolution have developed in them qualities of heroism such as no one had dreamed to exist under such soft feminine exteriors; for the class of "strong-minded" and strong-bodied women must be sought for in more northern latitudes.

During the stay of the *Victoria* in Havana she passed into the hands of English owners, who determined to run her back at all hazards. She had brought over a cargo of cotton and sugar, on which a very handsome profit was realized, and the proceeds invested in 40,000 lbs. of gunpowder, and a number of rifles and other munitions of war were to be returned in the same vessel. The hold was therefore crammed with these combustibles immediately below the cabin. Bags of coffee were placed above the barrels of gunpowder as a protection—the only precaution taken—and everybody on board pertinaciously smoked cigars and pipes over all parts of the steamer, without special attention to the contingent remainders commonly called "stumps;" so that the chances of capture or blowing up by Federal steamers, or by our own act, were about equal.

The *Victoria*, before the war, had performed the useful but undistinguished duty of a tug-boat on the Mississippi river, but was a good sea-going boat. When we conversed with the captain, he showed a decided disinclination to taking passengers.

5. In *Thirty Years*, vol. 1, pp. 302–303, de Leon identifies this woman as a Mrs. Delpit, mother of the French novelist Albert Delpit.

He pointed out very frankly all the discomforts and dangers of the trip, and so wrought upon the owners as to exact very heavy compensation in gold for allowing us the privilege of participating in them.[6]

There was no Government boat at that time procurable, and this being a private enterprise, my official positions, past and present, availed me nothing, except in being regarded as extra hazardous, like the gunpowder. Having finally overcome all the difficulties, we went on board the *Victoria* on the evening of the 7th of February, and sailed out of the harbour of Havana at 4 o'clock P.M. Our destination was suspected if not known, and many curious eyes watched our departure from the shipping and from the houses on the shore. Among other anxious observers some of our party recognized the United States Consul-General and his Vice inspecting with spy-glass, and doubtless with fraternal fondness, the departure of their Southern brethren. If the last looks cast upon us were not solely of affection, the last words assuredly were of happy augury. As we passed a French man-of-war, the commandant, who knew a lady of our party, came to the stern of his vessel, raised his cap, and called out, "Bon voyage," so that the last words wafted to us by the winds of Havana were those of kindness. The harbour of Havana is probably, next to that of Naples, the most lovely in the world; and serious as our reflections were at the moment of departure, we cast a long lingering look behind, as the Moro Castle rapidly receded from us, and darkness shut us out from it and from the sight of our enemies. We anticipated a chase from the start, for we had reason to believe that the Federal cruisers at Key West and in the Gulf had been notified of our cruise to break the blockade at or near New Orleans. So soon, therefore, as dusk came on, the precautions necessary to baffle those eager inquirers were taken.

Anthracite coal, which makes no smoke and no sparks, was substituted for the soft, which produced both. No lights were allowed on board, on any pretence. We sat in darkness—for moonless nights are always chosen for running the blockade. Our anxieties and the novelty of our position prevented drowsiness, for every sound that came upon the night breezes might mean a pursuer. In addition to our own party, which also comprised a gallant young surgeon, a native of Mobile, who afterwards shared the glory of Beauregard's victory at Corinth, and who, later, fell into the hands of the enemy through over zeal—four or five other Southerners took passage with us, two of whom had been captured, with their schooners, attempting to break the blockade, and sent back to Havana from Key West. The fancy of the reader can picture the noiseless progress of our boat—a black mass moving over the waters, without light or sound of life on board, and the eager look-out kept by the regular and volunteer watch, lest we might be over-hauled or run down by some steamer in the darkness. The first night passed over without incident, though there was not much enjoyment of sleep on board for the reasons assigned. It requires practice to

6. De Leon said later that he paid $100 in gold for the passage. *Thirty Years*, vol. 1, p. 303.

sleep tranquilly over a powder magazine; and Dr. Johnson's graphic description of a ship as "a floating prison, with a chance of being drowned," was illustrated in our case with additional touches undreamed of by the good doctor.[7]

We had heard before our departure that the *Calhoun* (steamer), which preceded us but two weeks, had been chased and captured off the coast of Louisiana, her passengers escaping into the swamps, and undergoing losses and hardships which may easily be imagined. Against all that the wrath of men could devise we were forewarned. We also knew of the other risks incident to the undertaking, but we had scarcely calculated on the presence of another power more dangerous still—

> "For now the storm-fiend came, and he
> Was tyrannous and strong."

On the ensuing morning the lowering aspect of the heavens indicated a coming storm, and by midday the full fury of a "Norther" had to be encountered by our unfortunate bark, which was sorely tried by it. For the whole of that day, the following night, and until the succeeding midday, the storm continued. The ceaseless howling of the wind, and the beating of the rain, made dismal music for us, and crowded us all into the narrow covered space on deck, where we huddled together and cheered each other as best we might. The machinery of the boat, under this strain, suffered severely, and on the second morning I learned from the engineers, who preserved a grim composure, that the steam-pipe was cracked so badly that a continuance of the storm would disable it, and the boat, entirely. The sea was running so high that there was no chance for the life-boats, so that the prospect was not re-assuring.

Determining to ask no further questions, and to conceal the danger from the rest of our company, we resigned ourselves as cheerfully as we could to the course of events, putting our trust in Providence, since human effort was of no avail. And Providence did seem to smile upon us—for the storm subsided; and an after-examination proved that the damage was more serious than we had supposed; the engineer, who took out the steam-pipe after our arrival in Louisiana, declaring it was marvellous that it should have held together to bring us into port.

From this time we came in sight of the Federal cruisers constantly, always giving them a wide berth, seeing them always before they sighted us, in consequence of the peculiarity of our build and the swiftness of our movements. The principle adopted on these excursions is, "Where you see a flag or a ship, avoid it," and, in carrying out this policy, long detours are unavoidable.

The excitement on board in relation to the storm and the cruisers had begun to settle down into a calm, when another incident roused the excitement to fever pitch. While the passengers and almost all the crew were soundly slumbering, worn out by

---

7. De Leon quotes one of the more memorable definitions provided by Samuel Johnson, author of the celebrated *Dictionary*.

fatigue, the cry of fire rose in a frantic shout from the deck, and was caught up and re-echoed by others in every accent of affright, for all thought of the freight we carried in the hold. In their blind panic some of the men rushed madly to throw themselves overboard, to avoid the anticipated explosion, but were restrained by the few who preserved their self-command, though there was no man aboard who did not feel a chill of dread. The women, terrified on first awakening, were soon quieted, and prayed, as women will do when men are forgetful of that Higher Power who holds our destinies in the hollow of His hand. Investigation proved the alarm to have been a false one; but the shock it gave was felt long after the presence of actual danger was removed. The next day dragged its slow length along, and towards midday we suddenly espied upon our right the smoke of several steamers, and their masts. We had unconsciously sailed almost into the jaws of the blockading squadron off the "passes" as they are termed, opening into the mouths of the Mississippi. We immediately put on more steam and sailed in an opposite direction, but too late to escape detection and pursuit; still, when night came on we fondly hoped that we had eluded our pursuers. Another case of anxiety now oppressed us, when so near our destined haven. About sunset, the captain and pilot frankly confessed that our repeated deviations from our course had put them out of their reckoning, and that the part of the coast on which they then found themselves was unfamiliar to them. Fortunately, one of our passengers was a Louisianian, accustomed to hunt and fish in that neighbourhood; and on consulting him, our actual position was made clear to the captain on the chart. A few more hours' sail brought us into Barrataria Bay, once famous as the rendezvous of the buccaneer, Captain Kidd, whose buried treasures still make the staple of many local legends.[8] Then we began to be confident of safety, for Fort Livingston, our destination, was not far distant, and the Federal cruisers seldom were seen in its vicinity.[9] Our over-confidence in the end very nearly proved fatal—for, unknown to us, the enemy was still in pursuit, having divined our object.

Just at midnight we saw a light in the direction of the fort which guards the entrance to the passes leading into the Mississippi river, above New Orleans, the fort itself being about two days' journey from the city; immense bayous, as they are termed—wide wastes of water and of marsh, covered with rushes, intervening, the haunts of innumerable wild fowl and alligators, with a few scattered habitations of men, themselves almost amphibious. The question with us now was whether these lights we saw were in the fort or in some vessel blockading access to it. The darkness of the night, and the distance which we deemed it prudent to keep, rendered this critical matter uncertain.

8. De Leon has confused pirate mythology. Barataria Bay was the haunt of scores of smugglers from about 1808 until 1814, most notably the Laffite brothers. Captain William Kidd was never anywhere near the Gulf Coast of Louisiana.

9. Fort Livingston sat on the western tip of Grand Terre Island, guarding the entrance to the pass into Barataria Bay.

There was nothing for it but to send out an exploring party in one of our boats, which, in the event of danger, was to give us a signal that we might fly; the occupants of the boat taking the risk of capture or of flight to the swamps which surrounded the fort. Two hours of intense anxiety to those left on board elapsed before the boat returned, bringing the glad tidings that it was the fort which, seeing our approach, and mistaking us for an enemy by our having shown some light from the pilot's house, had made the light as a signal, and was preparing to fire upon us when we approached nearer, that signal not having been answered by us. They sent us a pilot, who immediately gave orders to run her in under the guns of the fort; but after repeated trials, lasting until almost daybreak, it was found that the water was too shoal to admit of our approaching nearer than three miles from the fort, whose guns were not of sufficient range to cover us at that distance. Under advice of the pilot we, therefore, anchored there to await the rise of the tide, which he assured us would carry us in the next morning about ten o'clock.

Comforted by this assurance, and confident of safety, almost all went to sleep, myself and a few others keeping watch. All was tranquil for the remainder of the night, and a glorious morning dawned upon us. The tide slowly rose, and at 8 A.M. we were preparing to enjoy our last breakfast on board, when some of us on the lookout with spy-glasses discerned in the distance a moving column of black smoke rapidly approaching. Very soon we could distinguish the masts and spars of what seemed a very large vessel nearing us with frightful velocity, and our premature exultation was changed into bitter mortification: to be trapped at the very last moment, after all our escapes, was almost unbearable. Our council of war was necessarily short: we determined to run in as close under the guns of the fort as practicable, and to beach the steamer if necessary, for we determined that our enemy should never capture her with her important cargo, even if we had to blow her up ourselves.

After repeated efforts to find a channel deep enough, the boat was finally run up to within two miles of the fort, and there she stuck fast. The enemy's boat (which proved to be the steamer *De Voto,* carrying several rifled cannon and other guns) drawing more water, could only get within three-quarters of a mile of our boat.[10] As soon as we saw her stop, our boat ran up the Union Jack, but the Federal cruiser answered this by a shotted gun, which dashed up the water near our stern, and followed it up rapidly with other compliments of a similar character.

The *De Voto* was a very trim-looking steamer, like most of the American war-vessels, and as she gracefully swung round to bring her guns to bear upon us, and the

10. This is a typographical error, the Federal vessel in question being the USS *De Soto,* as De Leon stated in *Thirty Years,* vol. 1, p. 311. *De Soto* was just then arriving for blockading duty in the Gulf of Mexico.

white puff of harmless smoker, followed by the hissing rifle shot or shell, would curl away from her side in light wreaths, the sight was a very pretty one—

"For one who hath no son or brother here,"
as Byron observed, *apropos* to a grander spectacle.[11]

As we on board laboured under that disqualification for enjoying the spectacle, we thought the shore, albeit a swamp, a more eligible position, and hastily packing up a few articles for the use of the ladies and ourselves, we launched the boats and made for the beach.[12] Doubtless supposing the boats were carrying off the despatches which they coveted (which was correct), the enemy seemed to make targets of them, for at that time the Northern warfare was waged against men, and women were treated as they should be by all civilized belligerents. The reign of Butler in New Orleans had not then brutalized the Yankee soldiers, nor had the unutterable horrors perpetrated in Alabama rendered female helplessness and innocence no safe-guard.[13] Be this as it may, we, with our female companions, safely reached the shore, and were welcomed there by the officers who commanded a detachment of 100 men sent out from the fort with two cannon, which covered the steamer, and prevented the Yankees from boarding her in their launches.

Glad as we were to plant our feet in safety on Southern soil, our joy had some al-loy, for we found ourselves on a strip of sandy beach two miles from the fort (an earthwork mounting sixteen guns, and manned by the Louisiana volunteers), while behind us stretched a marshy piece of ground covered with fallen trunks of trees, those still standing draped in the long wavy gray moss which gives so melancholy an aspect to the Southern scenery in such localities.[14] It was my wife's first visit to America, and as she sat on the trunk of one of these fallen trees in the swamp, hold-ing her small dressing-bag in her hand, hungry, muddy, tired, but undismayed, she observed that she now thoroughly understood the feelings of the foreign emigrants whose letters she had so often read to her servants at home. The rest of our company took the mishap with equal philosophy, and as we trudged along towards the fort over the fallen trees, and through the mud and tangled vines, we could hear the sharp whiz of the rifle balls as they sung their sharp song through the air, and the heavy thud as they struck the boat or exploded in falling.

11. George Gordon, Lord Byron.

12. In *Thirty Years*, vol. 1, pp. 312–313, De Leon describes a panic among the captain and crew of the blockade runner that almost left his wife and Mrs. Delpit behind but for his intercession.

13. De Leon refers to General Benjamin F. Butler, Union commander of occupying forces in New Orleans in 1862, whose regime was vilified in the Confederacy due to his orders trying to con-trol insolence among local women toward his soldiers, threatening to treat them as prostitutes. The "unutterable horrors" in Alabama are obscure, but De Leon probably refers to dislocations of civil-ians by advancing Union armies late in the war.

14. This earthwork clearly is not the antiquated masonry Fort Livingston, but is an unnamed Confederate-built defensive work.

Arrived at the fort, every kindness was lavished upon us. The officers gave up their quarters to our ladies, and shared their plain fare with us; for in this remote spot they did not enjoy any luxuries or many comforts. So soon as we had placed the ladies in safety we returned to the sea beach, where our brave compatriots kept the enemy at bay, under a hailstorm of shot levelled at them from the *De Voto*. Standing among them I could mark first the flash, then the report and curling smoke, followed by the dash of the water as the shot first struck, then ricochetted over our heads, often so inconveniently close that we dodged involuntarily. Personal experience convinces me that any human being will and must incline his head under such circumstances. Still the enemy shot very badly, for they did not succeed either in dismounting the guns or wounding any of the groups clustered around them.

All day long this one-sided warfare continued, the *De Voto* carefully keeping out of range of the guns of the fort, which, after one trial to ascertain that fact, wasted no powder, having very little of that valuable article to spare.

During the day the *De Voto* fired 283 times at the steamer and the troops, and, strange to say, short as was the range, but three fair hits were made, doing the *Victoria* no serious damage. One shell passed through the open hold into a coffee bag immediately above the powder, penetrated to within two or three inches, and did not explode. It was taken by us out of the bag afterwards, the coffee having probably extinguished the fuse. Had that shell exploded, the *Victoria* would have been sent up into the air with her perilous freight, to come down in blackened splinters. But Providence, which had protected us throughout the voyage, did not desert us here. At five P.M. the *De Voto* ceased firing, and sailed sullenly away in the direction where we knew the blockading fleet was lying.

Now was our opportunity, for we readily divined her purpose of bringing other vessels of lighter draught to capture the *Victoria*. There was a number of small luggers plying in the bay and through the bayous. These we immediately put into active operation to lighten our ship, and about two hours before daylight we succeeded in getting her in safety under the guns of the fort. When this was accomplished we regaled ourselves with a good supper, and made merry the hearts of our friends, the officers of the fort, who had contributed so greatly to our rescue.

Scarcely had the day dawned when the sentry on the fort proclaimed sails in sight, and the *De Voto* reappeared, accompanied by two others, in one of which we recognized the *Calhoun*, captured but a few weeks before. Drawing even less water than the *Victoria*, escape from her would have been impossible in our previous exposed situation. As it was, we enjoyed acutely the disappointment of our baffled enemies at the escape of their prey. During the day the number of the blockaders was increased to five. They hovered round like birds of prey, anxious to injure, but fearful to attack—just out of range of the guns of the fort; and for two days continued to do so, leading us to suppose they meditated an attack. Had they been aware of the actual condition of affairs, they could not only have cut out the *Victoria*, but also have taken the fort; since shot and shell sufficient for two days' siege those gallant fellows did not have; and, in such cases, valour, without ammunition, avails nothing.

Happily, that danger passed away, and we resumed our march "On to Richmond" by the circuitous route through the bayous, in a little stern-wheel steamer drawing sixteen inches of water, through passages so narrow that in many places we brushed past the trees on either side, and moved over and through the tangled rushes. I have heard before of advertisements of Mississippi steamers to run "wherever it was a little damp," and we appeared to be verifying the promise on this occasion. Two days and nights of this weary way we travelled: on the third morning we reached the Mississippi. We found the father of waters wrapped in an impenetrable yellow fog, as dense as that London product in November, and had to grope our way towards the city; occasional steamers, with their huge house-like upper decks, looming suddenly upon us through the fog, and screaming loudly to warn us of their proximity.

The river is very dangerous for navigation in these fogs, as may be imagined; but just before we reached the city, the sun broke forth, the veil of mist unrolled and drifted away, like the rising of a curtain, and the spires and domes of New Orleans, and its wharves, with the remnants of its great fleet of steamers, broke upon our delighted view.

For we felt we were at home at last—on our own soil, among our own brave brethren battling against tyranny of the most odious kind. For the two days and nights on the bayous we had had no accommodations either for sleeping or eating—foraging on the contents of a hamper, and sleeping on the cabin floor; the luxury, therefore, of a bath, a bed, and the table at St. Charles' Hotel, can be imagined by those who have only "roughed it" in Switzerland or the Highlands.

Of what we saw and heard for the four following months, neither our space, nor the patience of the reader, who has accompanied us through so fatiguing a journey, will permit me here to speak.

APPENDIX 3
THE TRUTH ABOUT THE CONFEDERATE STATES OF AMERICA

———•·•·•———

By Edwin de Leon[1]

For more than a year it has been so difficult to obtain authentic information on the present situation in the Confederate States of America, that those who have a great interest in keeping up to date on the general political situation will read with interest the impressions collected in this part of the new world by a "visual" witness. Readers will be equally curious to learn about the high quality military and civil leadership which have earned Jefferson Davis his title of President, and the unanimous respect of a people who, in combating for its independence and its constitution, has shown itself worthy (as lately in Italy) of being recognized by the European Nations.

I left England last January 2nd, with the goal of visiting the Southern States and to learn of the events that have brought their separation from the Northern States. I arrived in New Orleans in the beginning of February, having eluded the federal war ships from the blockade, and then arrived in Richmond.

After many months of a most interesting stay in the young republic capital, and after a careful and attentive examination of the most important issues of the Confederation, we returned to Europe by way of the port of Wilmington in North Carolina where we again ran the blockade.

For anyone wishing to undertake such a voyage, suffice it to say that we went and returned by an indirect route using steam ships from the South, a route which is quick although uncertain as far as departure times from Southern ports and arrival times in those same ports.[2]

We assured ourselves that the blockade was null in its effectiveness; that is why we do not share the opinion of the *Times* which concluded that whoever succeeded in entering China would not succeed in penetrating into the Confederate States.

We would add that during a one week stay in one of the English colony ports of Antilles, in May, we counted eight steamers and one fleet of small sailing vessels

1. Published in Paris in August 1862 by E. Dentu.

2. "By indirect line of southern steam ships, we mean those ships that ferry to the Antilles where travelers can travel to the Confederate States almost daily." In so saying in this note, De Leon emphasized the ineffectiveness of the Union blockade, a recurring theme in Confederate arguments that it was illegal and therefore the nations of Europe ought to break it.

arriving directly from ports from the South with their Confederate flàgs waving. Since then, all these steamers loaded with arms and munitions returned by forcing the blockade with the exception of two; one captured by Yankees; the other landed against the rocky shore its cargo saved by the Confederates near Charleston.

At our return however, we found that the English ports of Nassau and Bermuda were more effectively blocked than those of Charleston and Wilmington, and that in the neighborhood of these islands, raids of goods were being made which were of much more considerable value than elsewhere.

The warships of the North, for three months, were masters of the sea in these areas. They boarded ships using the British flag, going from one English port to another, firing on them and succeeded, by a great audacity, in seizing them. This was how the *Circassien* was captured. The warships used the same audacity in the waters of Havana and other ports of Cuba, to the great indignation of the captain-general. Spain, it was said, took careful note of these events and facts.

This is however not the point of our story, for one would hope that Lord Russell will have taken appropriate measures to prevent this too liberal interpretation of the clauses of the new treaty agreed upon between Lord Lyons and Mr. Seward, and that one would obtain satisfaction from the offences committed towards the British flag, in the way done by the immortal Wilkes. The recent motion of Mr. Gregory to the Parliament indicates the interest related to this issue and brought to the English government.[3]

Let us return to our subject.

Having arrived in New Orleans just as the Confederates in Donelson suffered defeat, I headed to Richmond via the Western States.[4] The anxiety caused by the successes of the Federalists was equaled only by a profound surprise in the Southern population, who had not appreciated the strength of their enemy, especially the strong naval force that they had, always a very grave error.

The result of this anxiety was to awaken the warlike ardor of the entire population and to stimulate an effective and vigorous action. Never had the inhabitants of the South thought that they would have to test themselves against their adversaries on their own territory. The idea of Yankees occupying the cities of the South never came to mind until the presence of enemy cannon became a reality.

The border was for a long time the only war zone. The occupation of Hatteras and Port Royal, places of minor importance off the Confederate coast, gave the population of the Deep South a good idea of the state of the war.[5] However, the sudden en-

3. De Leon's reference to a Lyons-Seward "treaty" relates to the agreement whereby Mason and Slidell were released. The Gregory motion was covered by De Leon in his memoir above.

4. Fort Donelson, on the Cumberland River in Tennessee, fell to Union forces February 16, 1862, a devastating blow to the Confederate line of defense in the western theater of the war.

5. Fort Hatteras, North Carolina, surrendered to Union vessels on August 28, and Confederate defenses at Port Royal, South Carolina, fell to Union naval bombardment on November 8, 1861.

ergy and the surprising activity deployed by the North in their simultaneous descent on the Mississippi and in the Atlantic ports have, likening to the sound of the trumpet, awakened the plantation owners and the hardy pioneers of the South-West, and all the population ran spontaneously to arms. For the first time, the entire populace of the South transformed itself into an immense camp. The thought that the adversary that they hated, had taken advantage of their unpreparedness to invade their land produced on the public mind an exasperation that could not be expressed.

The dominant emotion that we have observed during our stay in the South was a bitter, mortified sentiment of what the enemy had partially gained following our overconfidence, and that Bull's Run had been followed by Fort Donelson, Fort Pulaski and other losses experienced by the Confederates. The loss of New Orleans could not be blamed on a lack of forethought or of courage by the generals or the people of the South. The river, irritated, swollen by rains, had risen with an irresistible force, sweeping away the barriers that the human genius had vainly tried to oppose its impetuous current. The same flood of this river had elevated the enemy's cannons above the level of the town in such a way that the cannons on the riverside could no longer be pointed against the enemy; capitulation then became a necessity.[6] The capitulation did not profit the enemy, since 3200 bales of cotton, and a large quantity of sugar and molasses were destroyed by water and fire before their arrival, and it was thru the glow of this sinister fire that the hostile fleet presented itself before the town where all the male population, wearing their arms, had joined the different army corps in the interior.

The occupation of New Orleans was, by consequence, an embarrassment for the Federalists who found themselves obliged to maintain a considerable army which imposed on the populace an arbitrary program by General Butler, like the ones he told us of in his celebrated order of the day.[7] Mr. Lincoln's proclamation that opens New Orleans to commerce is not serious; he had forgotten that the neighboring country was still in the hands of the Confederates. In fact the President had restricted doing business to people recognized as "legal citizens," a condition met only by his own soldiers. General Butler does not permit the vessels of France and England coming to New Orleans to communicate with the plantation owners who keep their cotton on their plantations away from their brothers of the North. The lack of cotton in Europe must not then be blamed on the South; it was all available to be sold, but the North snuffs the commerce by its blockade and army and imposes a quarantine of forty days on ships going from the Antilles to New Orleans.

6. This is a highly fanciful description of the loss of New Orleans, to say the least.

7. De Leon refers again to General Benjamin F. Butler's famous "Women Order" of May 15, 1862, in which he warned women of New Orleans that anyone showing disrespect to Union soldiers or enlisted men would be treated as "women of the town," meaning prostitutes. While it outraged Southern sensibilities, the order was designed to avoid incidents of retaliation that might arise from the extreme insults being hurled at Union soldiers.

To briefly summarize the results of our three months observation in the Confederate States, and without going into too much detail, we would like it to be known:

I

With the spirit of the whole population enflamed with hate towards the Yankee invaders, with an army equal in numbers to the one in the North, certainly superior in its morale, commanded by the best generals of the old army and by new ones such as Stonewall Jackson; with equal chances, after 15 months of fighting, to shift to Washington the siege undertaken with so little success in Richmond, the submission of the South must appear as a dream to all men who want to reflect seriously. This was our conviction while we were still in the country and before the recent defeats of the North rendered this opinion popular. This was the firm conviction of the Southern president and the generals from Richmond when MacClellan marched to Manassas.[8] There was never any doubt in the minds of the South as to the outcome of this campaign, and as of April, we heard predictions from well placed people within the government, that the war would change direction and that, instead of invasion of the South, it would become a march to the North.

II

In order to counter balance all the successes obtained by the Confederates, it was rumored everywhere that despite the courageous and desperate defense of the South, which battles for its homes and lands, for its liberty and honor of its women, its resistance could only last for a time; since the North's superior number of soldiers and its considerable resources would assure them sooner or later a complete victory. What exactly are those "resources" after one year of war fought on a grandeur surpassed only by a superb attitude of arrogance? These "resources" are: a Treasury on the point of being bankrupt, supported by a paralyzed credit; banks in open war with the Minister Chase, banks which opposed his efforts to support the State credit by further indebting themselves; gold at 20% prime; a commerce that exists only in name; a new prohibitive tariff which elevated a China wall between the North and the outside; an army composed in large part of foreign mercenaries, commanded by the refuse of the old world and the elite lawyers and politicians of Massachusetts and New York.[9] One must admit that the majority of the soldiers of

8. When General George B. McClellan took control of the Union army in Virginia in the aftermath of the First Battle of Manassas, he occupied Manassas Junction in March 1862, but Confederate forces pulled away without a fight.

9. De Leon used the tools of the propagandist to the full here, presenting in a single sentence almost every exaggeration the Confederates threw at their foes. The accusation that Lincoln's army was mostly composed of foreign "mercenaries" was widely made, and entirely false. Of 2 million

this army were German and Irish emigrants whose mission was to "restore the Union."[10] Add to that the violent recriminations between different leaders; the interests of the North-East against the ones from the North-West; the conflicts of Boston, New York, Philadelphia and Cincinnati; the wasps' nest of corrupt speculators fattening themselves from the war like bloodsuckers, and condemned by the Congress itself and by ministers sent by President Lincoln to an *honourable* exile as overseas ambassadors; a general lack of confidence, the disorganization of the Washington government, the crumbling of this clay colossus may be soon: this is the true picture of the resources so flaunted by the Yankee nation.

There is however an element on which the North is truly strong and where the South cannot fight with equal armed force. The naval officers of the South honorably gave up to Mr. Lincoln all the establishments of the old navy that they had commanded, and the North now had an empire of the sea which they take advantage of to seriously hurt the South. The only true successes of the North were based on its navy and its cannons, and it is only when the South adopted a method of attracting its aggressors far from their support that it obtained a series of advantages. The South has not until now completed its navy fleet, even though we have seen warships in construction in many of its ports, which are probably finished by now, while another part was contracted from elsewhere. A few of the most distinguished and most renowned officers of the old navy (the most part) have followed the South's destiny and are waiting the completion of their ships to challenge the North in its surveillance of the sea. However in spite of these circumstances, it's the South who, when we were in Richmond, was the first to produce a revolution in the way to support a maritime war. We talk of course, of the exploit of the *Marrimac* in Hampton's Roads,

---

men who would wear the blue, about one-fourth were foreign born, and half of those from the British Isles or Canada, whereas Confederates liked to claim that the Lincoln "hirelings" were mostly "Dutch," meaning low-born Germans. None were mercenaries. In fact, the only true mercenaries in the Civil War were in the Confederate service, British seamen paid to crew the commerce raiders fitted out in Britain. The reference to "refuse of the old world and elite lawyers" commanding Union soldiers is to men like Franz Sigel and other veterans of the German wars of unification in 1848 and the "political generals" to whom Lincoln gave commissions because of their influence at home in binding the Union to the war effort. Jefferson Davis did exactly the same thing, though on a lesser scale. The "prohibitive tax" is the Morrill Tariff Act of 1861, a protective tariff that did discourage trade in foreign imports. The "war" between Secretary of the Treasury Salmon P. Chase and the banks refers to Chase's plan for reorganizing the Union's banking system into a unified one based on a uniform currency, rather than the chaotic system then in place in which each bank issued its own notes, requiring a complicated system of exchange rates from one bank to another. The banks resisted the federal intrusion, but in the end Chase won.

10. Again De Leon exaggerates. As stated above, no more than a quarter of Union soldiers were foreign born, and the German and Irish that he specifically cites totaled 16 percent of Union enlistments, hardly "the majority" he claims. He also ignores the fact that the Confederacy encouraged foreign-born enlistments, too.

a conception purely national whose authors are known to us. If New Orleans had not been taken following lucky circumstances that the flood rendered possible, this episode would have ended by three ships whose construction was almost completed but ended with their destruction to prevent them from falling into enemy hands.[11]

III

But it was said the South needs arms and war munitions; it cannot build them lacking tools and workers, nor can it import them because of the efficiency of the blockade. This assertion is similar to the song of the cuckoo clock, so often repeated, that it is becoming a general belief. Well! Our personal observations prove that this is inexact in both cases. The arms and munitions of war are made in the South, where we see on one hand the machines and the intelligent work in full activity, *me ipso teste*; on the other hand, during a week in April, in just one Confederation sea port, we have witnessed the arrival of ships bringing in a complete assortment of arms and artillery and powder by the thousands of pounds. If the Confederates are combating without arms or with inferior arms against the Federalists who, everyone knows, are supplied with the best Enfield rifles and powder of their choice, the losses by the Federal army and the horrible carnage that accompanied them should be considered as miraculous.[12] One has forgotten as well that the customs of the South, where each white person possesses arms and is accustomed to using them, have made this country an immense arsenal; the personal arms are much used, and are generally the best in aim and in battles where the Federalists avoid charging with their bayonets. While we were in the Confederation, the President made a particular appeal to people to produce their arms; the quantity produced was astounding. As well, there

11. De Leon refers, of course, to the CSS *Virginia*, which had been converted from the captured USS *Merrimack* into the war's first successful ironclad. On March 8, 1862, at Hampton Roads, Virginia, it almost destroyed a wooden Union fleet before being stymied the next day by the arrival of the Union's first ironclad, USS *Monitor*. At New Orleans, meanwhile, the Confederates had been building the ironclads *Louisiana* and *Mississippi* and had the lightly armored ram *Manassas* in operation. De Leon's reference to the "lucky circumstances" of a flood helping the Union take New Orleans is unclear, but may refer to high water that repeatedly broke barriers of chains, anchored vessels, and log booms the Confederates stretched across the Mississippi in an effort to impede Yankee vessels. The buildup of debris floating downriver repeatedly broke them, and in any event, they would have been no match for the Union steam warships when they made their advance.

12. "At the moment of printing this, we have received from an official source the following list of conquests made by the Confederates on their adversaries in Richmond. The war material of the South is found to be considerably increased:

80 siege cannons in perfect order, 200 field cannons; 1,700 mules; 2,500 horses; 62,000 arms with accessories. All the munitions and magazines of diverse nature valued at 6,000,000 dollars. The famous balloon, with its equipment.

The prisoners are: 2 major generals, 6 brigadier generals, 13 colonels, 180 officers, 11,000 soldiers."

are continual shipments from abroad, despite the blockade; since the immense spread of the coast cannot be guarded effectively. From the recollection of military history of President Davis, organized from fair experience, regiments of lancers, as visitors from the past, turn the imagination to "regiments armed with imitation weapons" which have nevertheless achieved a certain reputation in Europe. Those that we have seen armed like this did not go to combat, composed of those whom the North humanly designated by the title of "contraband."[13] These brave people would go to their daily work while those who they worked for would harvest far away a harvest of another kind on the bloody fields of Virginia or Tennessee.

IV

Another debatable fact, which is very general, pertains to provisions. It is said that the South may be starving and that it may be lacking provisions. Its immense resources in the productions of grains, farm animals, and other necessities of life prove that this assertion is false. The character of its particular institution which allows all the white male population to go to war, lets it conserve many thousands of workers used to working in fields, which gives a great advantage over the North, where the work is stopped because of army drafts. The state of Texas, the size of France, would supply grains, sheep and other farm animals enough to feed all of the Confederation, while all the States of the South and Southwest would produce corn, rice and other grains in sufficient quantity to indefinitely feed its people without having to recourse to importing. As a precaution and to prepare for unexpected events, the plantation owners of the South have diminished their production of cotton, and increased that of grain. It is true that in the hotels and other businesses in which we were received, the coffee, the tea, the French wines, the English beer and the luxury objects were rare. For clothing for men and women, one is obliged to replace silk, the fine fabrics, for cheaper cloth, coming from local manufacturers. Each person seemed to be proud in making this sacrifice. As for objects of primary necessity, we have not found any lack of them in any part of the country. A great change occurred in the habits of drinking, a vice that is as American as it is British. If the heart of Father Mathew should return to visit this world he would rejoice about what we have seen in the Confederation.[14] Complete abstinence, the most strict and the most

13. De Leon refers to the Louisiana Native Guard, a regiment of free blacks enlisted in New Orleans whom he probably saw at drill when he reached the city after his passage through the blockade. They were purely ceremonial soldiers and the South would not use them in combat. After the fall of New Orleans they were enlisted into the Union army and did see combat service. Early in the war the North designated slaves as "contraband of war," since they were used as labor by the Confederate army, and that allowed them to be confiscated even though lawfully they were private property. The term "contrabands" would thereafter be used as a common sobriquet for blacks, free and slave.

14. The apostle of temperance.

absolute, was ordered by the government to the whole population, the sale and the use of inebriating drinks was outlawed everywhere, under very severe penalty; being sober has become a real institution in the country. Under the empire of this rule, the changes that we have observed in the habits of Southerners has been as sudden as it was perfect; if it can persist, the benefits reaped will be incalculable.[15]

V

But the Negroes! There is the South's weakness, cry out well-intentioned people, whose philanthropy, influenced by Madame Stowe's novel, represents the slave's goal to be to massacre one's master. Our own testimony from our own experiences shows that this is a great error. We have paid special attention to this interesting class while staying in the South. Instead of being a weak source, the slaves have contributed greatly to the South's strength by their resistance to the false "friends of the blacks" (this is how the abolitionists of the North call themselves), and by ignoring their provocations and their desire to renew the horrors of Saint-Domingue.[16] Far from being insubordinate or ready to go to revolt, the slaves have warmly sympathized with their masters (except on rare occasions), and nourish against the Yankee invaders a hate and a fear capable of surprising, especially when they discover their project to give them liberty. Their reasons for that are evident. The Negro's attachment to his locale is very strong; he does not know any other country than the one where he has been raised and where he is living; he does not know any other friends than the family of his master and the blacks and the whites who have grown up with him and lived in the same neighborhood. His life was much more peaceful before the war than now; since the little pleasures they were accustomed to outside of the basic needs of life, were curtailed the day their masters imposed on themselves the same kind of restrictions. He has neither confidence in the Yankees nor affection for them; since they have always mistreated him when they were in contact with him, this Madame Stowe admits, and makes a man from the North in Legree, the brutal manager; that's the only real truth in this book. The negro knows very well by experience that the Yankee has no real sympathy for its race. In the cities of the North, the whites will not permit him to eat, to drink, to marry or to pray with them; the omnibuses in the roads, the wagons on the railroads are closed to him, and the privilege to vote could only be ex-

15. By 1862 several Confederate states had outlawed private distilling, though the motive was necessity, not moral crusade. Distilling used up grain that was vital for feeding soldiers and animals, and drunkenness in the armies was a serious problem at all levels.

16. De Leon refers to the massacres of white residents in the slave uprisings on the island of San Domingue, now Haiti, in the early 1800s. For years Southerners had regarded appeals for abolition and emancipation as thinly veiled attempts to incite a similar uprising among the South's slave population, especially after the Nat Turner rebellion in Virginia in 1831 led to the murder of several whites.

ercised with the danger of losing one's life. His liberty is then a dead letter. During this invasion of the South, the only favor given to the "contraband" was to be placed in the trenches for very hard labor as opposed to the one in the cotton fields, a labor that would endanger their lives each day, which the African race never likes.

Mr. Bright, the debonair representative of the peace party, who now does not want this peace at whatever price, would find in the negro a strong supporter of his first principles. It's only when his affections and the people placed under his protection are in peril that the negroes master their fears. We have seen noble examples of devotion where the slaves have saved property and protected the lives of women and their children who had been placed under their care by the plantation owners. We have never known or heard that this great confidence had ever been betrayed, and while fathers, brothers and sons fight under the flag of their country in many areas of the South, the women and children sleep with as much security under the protection of their "black friends" than if they were guarded by armies. This is why the infernal malevolence that would seek a new Saint-Domingue tragedy in the South will fail in its plan. The desperate expedient of the Yankees to arm the slaves to replace the forces that have been decimated by MacClellan and therefore risk death by the sword or the diseases of the North makes them tremble at having to face its population of 20 million whites, therefore this idea will be in vain and useless despite their best efforts.[17] The black will not become the instrument of such a philanthropy, and will only prefer the state of things he has been used to, and which has permitted him to achieve a patriarchal age in the middle of tranquility and material comfort.

The behaviors of the negro, during this bloody contest, was devoted to such a point that if certain measures to better his life would be taken, their masters would be the first to modify his condition without having to take him away from his land, which had seen him born or to transport him to the exterior as the Northern abolitionists had requested.

We have tried at the risk of being lengthy to transcribe impressions about the South that are based on recent personal observations. The limits that we impose upon ourselves does not permit us to elaborate more on this subject; but we must add that one of the largest successes of the South is the unlimited confidence the masses have in the justice of their cause and in their final triumph, as well as in the statesmen and of the military they represent; Jefferson Davis, Lee, Beauregard, Johnston, Stonewall Jackson, and a plethora of other less well known from the outside, but whose names are familiar in the South.[18]

17. De Leon refers derisively to early Union efforts to arm blacks and create black units. In fact, by war's end some 200,000 Negro men would enlist in the Union armies, and many of them would conduct themselves well in combat. In 1865 even the Confederacy sought to augment its dwindling ranks by enlisting black units, but it was too little, far too late.

18. General P. G. T. Beauregard was still a hero in the Confederacy, thanks to the taking of Fort Sumter and his role in the victory at First Manassas. There were two distinguished generals named

Jefferson Davis is to the second American Revolution, what Washington was the first; the roles of these two illustrious men offer many points of resemblance. As well as Washington, Jefferson Davis has the qualities of a military man and a states- man. A dedicated cabinet worker, administrative tasks and the diplomatic affairs are as familiar to him as those of the war. Destined from his first education to follow a career of arms, he became a distinguished officer during the campaign in Mexico, and an eminent statesman by a long experience acquired in the Union congress.

As with the great Virginia patriot, Jefferson Davis is a Southerner by birth; his as- pirations are entirely for liberty and the glory of his country.[19] The seeds of discord are long standing in the Union, and those between France and England have never been as divided as the North and South have been in the past 20 years as far as their interests, their attitudes, their customs and their aspirations.

Although the state of things was well known by all serious men, and they under- stood its ramifications, they would divulge this with reluctance, and would direct their efforts either toward modifications of the Federal Constitution that united the States between them, or towards a peaceful dissolution of the Union.

The question of slavery was not the issue, although the North adroitly, and for the benefit of Europe, took this as a pretext for war.

The real source of the present difficulties goes back to issues that are purely in- dustrial; the North has manufacturers while the South is agricultural. To these issues are added the differences of race and attitude that existed between the two peoples.

As show the statistics, the North was populated by races of Anglo-Saxon origin; the South was principally populated by a Latin race. The descendant of the Puritans, General Butler, applies himself in making war against women, is now the proconsul of the North in New Orleans where the language and French customs reflect the ori- gin of its inhabitants. The Anglo-Saxon element that we find in the South goes back to the royal nobility which was banned in Cromwell's time, and it is very strange to see today the descendants of these ancient Puritans bringing back in Virginia dis- cord, which a few centuries ago delivered England to the horrors of the civil war.[20]

The North also attracted all the famished revolutionaries and malcontents of

---

Johnston. Albert Sidney Johnston commanded the Southern army at Shiloh, where he was mortally wounded. At the time of his writing, De Leon probably refers to General Joseph E. Johnston, who shared command with Beauregard at First Manassas and was at this time recuperating from a wound in May 1862 in the defense of Richmond. General Thomas J. "Stonewall" Jackson surely needs no explanation.

19. "The portrait included is an accurate reproduction of a copy in our possession, the only au- thentic source that has been published to date."

20. De Leon repeats the popular canard that Northerners were of Anglo-Saxon descent via the Puritans, while Southerners came of more noble Norman blood, a complete myth. In fact, both de- rived overwhelmingly from the same stock.

Germany, all the Red republicans, and almost all the Irish emigrants to sustain its army.[21]

Most of the recent measures of confiscation done by the Northern Congress, condemning twelve million inhabitants to a certain death and having their property seized, show us clearly the spirit that produced this war, and the goal it had: to acquire the properties of the South![22]

This is the ancient Puritan doctrine that was formulated in the following two resolutions:

1. "That all the Earth and all that it contains be the property of Saints;
2. That we ourselves are the Saints."

The North, in draping itself with the flag of the Union, and not having been able to impose its laws on the South which would assure the North the fruits of its labors, resorts to force in order to restrain a people in submission.

It now combats no more for victory but fights with an emotion of hate and vengeance. By looking at policies in the North we can judge up to a point how its affection for the negro directed its actions; it was banned by law to establish oneself in many of those States; in others the they were deprived of all rights and privileges accorded to all other nationalities. Even presently, despite Mr. Lincoln's loud proclamations, Cincinnati experiences outrageous acts against free negroes by white inhabitants.[23]

May those who oppose the cause of the South, reflect carefully on the state of things; let us hope that they will examine anew the opinions that have been formed, by an imperfect knowledge of facts and by a false appreciation of the true character of the struggle, which from the North and from the South, has made two nations now known to the informed public opinion of Europe, although they have not been formally recognized by other foreign governments.

21. Again De Leon repeats the propaganda myth of Union dependence on foreign-born Europeans, with the none-too-subtle hint that these "immigrants" were the refuse of Europe.

22. The Congress in Washington did pass confiscation acts on August 6, 1861, and July 17, 1862. They allowed the seizure of private property of Confederate citizens that was being used to aid the Rebel war effort, including slaves, and further that the confiscated slaves might be employed themselves to aid the Union war effort. De Leon's statement that the acts meant the "certain death" of 12 million whites is pure propagandistic hyperbole, especially since the Confederate white population was only just over 5 million.

23. De Leon does put his finger on a problem for free blacks. While most Northerners did not like the idea of slavery, they also did not want a free black population in their own midst. States like Illinois passed Negro exclusion laws, and in some cities like Cincinnati, and most notably in New York in 1863, the strains between whites and free blacks sometimes erupted into repression or even violence.

INDEX